THE
WAY
OF
FOUR

ABOUT THE AUTHOR

Deborah Lipp (New York) was initiated into a traditional Gardnerian coven in 1981, became a high priestess in 1986, and has taught and lectured on the topic of Neopaganism ever since. She has appeared in the A&E documentary "Ancient Mysteries," on MSNBC, and in the *New York Times*. She is the author of *The Elements of Ritual*.

TO WRITE TO THE AUTHOR

If you wish to contact the author or would like more information about this book, please write to the author in care of Llewellyn Worldwide and we will forward your request. Both the author and publisher appreciate hearing from you and learning of your enjoyment of this book and how it has helped you. Llewellyn Worldwide cannot guarantee that every letter written to the author can be answered, but all will be forwarded. Please write to:

Deborah Lipp
℅ Llewellyn Worldwide
P.O. Box 64383, Dept. 0-7387-0541-1
St. Paul, MN 55164-0383, U.S.A.

Please enclose a self-addressed stamped envelope for reply, or $1.00 to cover costs. If outside U.S.A., enclose international postal reply coupon.

Many of Llewellyn's authors have websites with additional information and resources.
For more information, please visit our website at
http://www.llewellyn.com

THE WAY OF FOUR

DEBORAH LIPP

create

elemental

balance

in your

life

2004
Llewellyn Publications
St. Paul, Minnesota 55164-0383, U.S.A.

First Edition
First Printing, 2004

Cover collage © 2004 by DigitalVision and Eyewire
Cover design by Kevin R. Brown
Edited by Andrea Neff
Interior illustrations by Llewellyn art department

Library of Congress Cataloging-in-Publication Data

Lipp, Deborah, 1961–
    The way of four : create elemental balance in your life / Deborah Lipp.
       p.   cm.
    Includes bibliographical references and index.
    ISBN 0-7387-0541-1
     1. Magic. 2. Four elements (Philosophy)—Miscellanea. I. Title.

    BF1623.N35L57 2004
    133.4′3—dc22
                                    2004048333

Llewellyn Publications
A Division of Llewellyn Worldwide, Ltd.
P.O. Box 64383, Dept. 0-7387-0541-1
St. Paul, MN 55164-0383, U.S.A.
www.llewellyn.com

Printed in the United States of America

OTHER BOOKS BY DEBORAH LIPP

The Elements of Ritual
(Llewellyn Publications, 2003)

In Memory of Scott Cunningham

Throughout the research for, and writing of, this book, I have missed Scott with special poignancy. I have used several of his books as resources and have been writing about topics we discussed often. I have wanted to pick up the phone a dozen times to ask him something, to tweak him about an omission in one of his books, to brainstorm. I hope I am right in believing that he really would have enjoyed this book, and that this is the one he was always nagging me to write. For that reason, I dedicate it to him, with love.

CONTENTS

List of Figures . . . xv

Acknowledgments . . . xvii

Introduction . . . 1

Chapter One: What Are the Elements? . . . 3

The Qualities of the Elements . . . 4

Air . . . 4

Fire . . . 6

Water . . . 7

Earth . . . 9

Air-Fire-Water-Earth . . . 10

The Origins of Elemental Thinking . . . 10

The Three Worlds . . . 10

The Elements in Hinduism . . . 12

We Arrive in Greece . . . 13

Aristotle Adds One . . . 14

Elemental Beings . . . 17

Elementals . . . 17

Guardians . . . 20

Chapter Two: The Elements in Nature . . . 23

Air in Nature: Exercises . . . 24

Exercise One: Sky and Breath . . . 24

Exercise Two: Sky and Cloud . . . 24

Exercise Three: Sky and Bird . . . 25

Exercise Four: Up and Down . . . 25

Exercise Five: Wind and Skin . . . 26

Fire in Nature: Exercises . . . 26

Exercise One: Fire Gazing . . . 27

Exercise Two: The Devouring Fire . . . 27

Exercise Three: In Fire's Wake . . . 28

Water in Nature: Exercises . . . 29
   Exercise One: Walkin' in the Rain . . . 29
   Exercise Two: Water Gazing, in Motion . . . 30
   Exercise Three: Water Gazing, Still . . . 31
Earth in Nature: Exercises . . . 31
   Exercise One: Plant Yourself . . . 32
   Exercise Two: Gathering Stones . . . 33
   Exercise Three: Points of Power . . . 33
   Exercise Four: A Small Cairn . . . 36

Chapter Three: The Elements in Us . . . 39
Your Astrological Elements . . . 39
Elemental Qualities of the Self . . . 41
Your Personal Element Quiz . . . 44
   Determining Your Elemental Makeup . . . 48
   The Four Elemental Personalities . . . 48
   Elemental Pairings . . . 53
The Sixteen Basic Personality Types . . . 55
   The Jung at Heart . . . 55
   Myers-Briggs . . . 56
Your Elemental Life Role Quiz . . . 59
   Determining Your Current Life Role . . . 60
Life Roles in the Tarot . . . 60
   Determining Your Basic Elemental Character Type . . . 61
   The Court Cards as Life Roles . . . 61
   The Sixteen Basic Elemental Character Types . . . 64

Chapter Four: Becoming Balanced . . . 77
Balance: A Pagan Essential . . . 77
Balance Is Addition . . . 78
The Way of Four . . . 79
Positive Elemental Qualities . . . 79
   Things I Like About Myself Quiz . . . 80
Negative Elemental Qualities . . . 85

How to Use the Balance Chart and Balance Worksheet . . . 85

Balance Chart . . . 87

Balance Worksheet . . . 88

Elemental Strength Balancing Exercise . . . 89

Preparation . . . 90

The Meditation . . . 91

General Elemental Meditations . . . 92

How to Do These Meditations . . . 92

The Meditation of Air . . . 94

The Meditation of Fire . . . 95

The Meditation of Water . . . 96

The Meditation of Earth . . . 97

Automatic Writing and Speaking Exercises . . . 98

Automatic Writing and Speaking Pointers . . . 99

Incorporating Automatic Writing/Speaking into the Meditations . . . 100

Chapter Five: The Elements in Daily Life . . . 103

The Elements at Home . . . 103

Air in the Home . . . 105

Fire in the Home . . . 107

Water in the Home . . . 110

Earth in the Home . . . 112

Household Elements Quiz . . . 116

What About Everything Else? . . . 129

Bringing Elements into Your Home on Air . . . 130

Aromatherapy in the Home . . . 130

The Elements and Your Body . . . 131

Elemental Attire: The Air, Fire, Water, and Earth of Clothing and Accessories . . . 132

Who Is Wearing What? Quiz . . . 142

Elemental Attire . . . 144

Elemental Perfumes . . . 145

Elemental Beauty Treatments . . . 159

Beautifying Your Coven or Group . . . 172

Elemental Eating . . . 175

Chapter Six: The Elements at Work and in Love . . . 183

The Elements at Work . . . 183

Your Work Element Quiz . . . 185

Air at Work . . . 191

Fire at Work . . . 194

Water at Work . . . 195

Earth at Work . . . 198

Working Elements in Combination . . . 200

Bringing the Elements to Work . . . 201

Bringing Air to Work . . . 202

Bringing Fire to Work . . . 203

Bringing Water to Work . . . 203

Bringing Earth to Work . . . 205

The Elements in Love . . . 205

Elements in Relationship . . . 206

Air in Relationship . . . 207

Fire in Relationship . . . 207

Water in Relationship . . . 208

Earth in Relationship . . . 209

Why Do You Give Your Ladylove Flowers? . . . 210

Elemental Love Songs . . . 211

Four Dates . . . 211

An Air Date . . . 213

A Fire Date . . . 214

A Water Date . . . 216

An Earth Date . . . 217

Chapter Seven: The Elements in Ritual and Spellcraft . . . 221

The Elements in Ritual . . . 221

The Elements as Building Blocks . . . 221

The Elements as Symbols . . . 222

The Elements on the Altar and as Tools . . . 222

The Elements as Themselves . . . 222

Using the Elements in Ritual . . . 223

Using the Elements as Symbols or Tools . . . 225

The Elements at the Quarters . . . 228

Summoning the Power of the Directions . . . 228

Summoning Elementals at the Quarters . . . 230

Summoning Guardians at the Quarters . . . 232

The Four Elements Working . . . 233

Beginning the Ritual . . . 234

Raising the Power . . . 234

Speaking the Elements . . . 234

Balancing and Centering . . . 235

The Elements in Spells . . . 236

Elemental Purpose and Focus in Spells . . . 236

The Elemental Purpose of a Spell . . . 237

Some Differences Between People and Spells . . . 239

Using the Four Elements in a Spell . . . 240

Using Air in a Spell . . . 240

Using Fire in a Spell . . . 244

Using Water in a Spell . . . 247

Using Earth in a Spell . . . 250

Four Spells . . . 252

The Air Spell: Improving School Performance . . . 252

The Fire Spell: Freedom from Obsession . . . 256

The Water Spell: Finding Love . . . 258

The Earth Spell: Bringing Money . . . 261

Appendix A: Preparation for Meditation or Magic . . . 267

Your Magical Room . . . 267

The Room . . . 268

Meditation Checklist . . . 268

Grounding and Centering . . . 269

Grounding and Centering Meditation . . . 269

Merging . . . 270

Appendix B: Generic Invocations . . . 271

Invocations in Sets of Four . . . 273

Four Formal Invocations . . . 273

Four Informal Invocations . . . 274

Appendix C: Musical Accompaniment for Each Element . . . 277

Air Music . . . 277

Fire Music . . . 278

Water Music . . . 278

Earth Music . . . 278

Appendix D: The Way of Four Balancing Exercises . . . 279

The Way of Four Meditation . . . 279

The Way of Four Ritual . . . 281

Appendix E: Charts . . . 285

Color Groupings . . . 285

Elemental Herbs, Flowers, and Other Plants . . . 286

Herbs of Air . . . 286

Herbs of Fire . . . 286

Herbs of Water . . . 287

Herbs of Earth . . . 287

Elemental Gems and Stones . . . 287

Stones of Air . . . 288

Stones of Fire . . . 288

Stones of Water . . . 288

Stones of Earth . . . 289

Appendix F: Magical Alphabets . . . 291

Runic and Theban . . . 291

Bibliography . . . 293

Index . . . 297

figures

1. Pentagram . . . 15

2. Squared Circle . . . 17

3. Firepit . . . 28

4. Points of Power 1 . . . 34

5. Points of Power 2 . . . 35

6. The Elemental Love Progression . . . 204

7. Magical Text . . . 255

8. Ken (The Torch)—Dispels Ignorance . . . 255

9. Os (The God)—Brings Light, Knowledge, and Speech . . . 255

10. Beorc (The Birch)—Brings Love and Fertility . . . 260

11. Altar Setup . . . 262

12. Magical Alphabets . . . 291

ACKNOWLEDGMENTS

I owe thanks to a bunch of people for the making of this book. My test-takers helped me fine-tune my quizzes. They are: my son, Arthur Lipp-Bonewits, Isaac Bonewits, Vicki Mutino, Linda Crowley, Jacques Ogé, Denise Promuto, and Jennifer Romanowski. I got input on perfumes from Vicki Mutino, Jennifer Romanowski, Cynthia Ellsworth Graham, Denice Cross, and my mom, Paula Gellis. Some terrific people at the Nanuet Mall helped me find the ingredients to perfumes and beauty products, particularly the Estée Lauder and Donna Karan ladies at Macy's, and the really informative guy at the Body Shop, who knew everything there is to know about salt scrubs. Jennifer Monzón, aesthetician, priestess, and friend, was an enormous help as well. Mom also helped me with fabrics, and my sister Roberta Lipp knows all there is to know about wall art. Keath Graham introduced me to the Myers-Briggs scale. The folks at the IMDb Music Discussion Board suggested elemental love songs, and my friend Ken Oerkvitz also came through for that. My dear friend Mickey Adams went above and beyond all possible call by creating a perfume database that allowed me to analyze perfumes by elemental ingredients. Nancy Mostad at Llewellyn suggested this was the best book to write right now and complimented me at opportune moments. When my writing and my confidence were falling apart, I received unexpected and invaluable help in the form of Reiki attunements from Mary Catherine Darling.

As always, I thank every one of my former students, most of whom have impressed me and made me proud, some of whom have infuriated me, and all of whom have challenged me to create better and better teaching materials, which inform all of my writing.

Toward the very end of writing this book, in September 2002, one such infuriating and impressive former student, Kathleen Houlihan, passed into the Summerland. I will never forget her. The questions she asked me and the answers she uncovered for herself appear on many of these pages.

The Way of Four

The Way of Four grew out of my deep conviction that every occult education begins with the four elements, and no occultist worth her salt fails to make use of elemental lore. Everything we do, everything we study, and everything we systematize comes from Air, Fire, Water, and Earth. The Kabbalah is more vastly inclusive, the Tarot more personal, and the Zodiac more universal, but all of them ultimately come down to four.

In my years of teaching Pagan and Wiccan groups, I invariably put a class on the four elements at the beginning of the syllabus. On nights when I was too tired, stressed, or overworked to come up with new class material, I sometimes used a review of the elements as the evening's material. Such reviews were always fresh, lively, and informative.

The Way itself is the way of balance. Wicca and Paganism are all about balance, about moderation, about plurality. We are neither austere nor hedonistic, neither cynical nor credulous, neither irreverent nor somber. When we practice Paganism successfully, we walk in balance. To do so, we must know ourselves well and be brave enough to face the changes we might need to make. The process of self-actualization is vital to a spiritual life. *The Way of Four* comes from my understanding of balancing self within the context of nature and reality.

Exercises in this book run the full gamut. Some are meditations done privately, at home, but others take place by interacting with nature. Many are serious and even involve hard work, but others are fun and playful. The Way of Four is a way that encompasses all of life, including things that seem frivolous. Whether you are meditating in an incense-filled temple or redecorating your living room, the Way of Four can come into play.

This book is also interspersed with quizzes, checklists, and worksheets. It's important that you make the book *yours*, that you participate completely in the processes laid out. Things may turn out differently than the way I've described them. You, as an individual, are the only one who can finally determine how the elements balance in *your* life. That's why the book is designed around your personal self-discovery process. I ask more questions than I answer so that you can find the answers in yourself. I hope you find the process as rich and rewarding as I do.

CHAPTER ONE

What Are the Elements?

In Wicca and much of the occult, the four elements of Fire, Water, Air, and Earth describe the universe and everything in it. Everything can be understood as taking part in one or more elements. Everything that is whole contains all four, and can be understood more deeply by dividing it into four and viewing it through that lens. The elements are the building block of creation; they are the beginning of *things*. The undifferentiated void that preceded creation had no elements, or, to put it another way, all elements were One. But creation—things, reality—consists of the elements.

From a scientific point of view, the periodic table of the elements describes the building blocks of the universe, and the modern magician doesn't reject science. But from a magical point of view, both simplicity and symbolism call for only four elements.

The four elements give us a way of thinking about the world. They give us a structured approach to knowing the unknowable. They provide us with a system of interrelations, and magic is all about interrelations. Have you ever heard of "sympathetic magic"? If you've heard of a Voodoo doll (or poppet), you have. Sympathetic magic means that something that is *like* a thing (has sympathy with a thing) *is* the thing. A doll is like the person it represents; therefore it *is* that person. That's interrelationship—sympathy. A doll is an obvious, direct representation, like drawing a picture. Other sympathetic objects are *parts* of the original. The famous idea of witches using fingernail clippings is an example of sympathetic magic; the part (the clippings) has sympathy with the whole (the person). There are all manner of direct and indirect sympathies that interconnect us. Elemental things have an indirect sympathy with each other. A candle is not the same as a lion, but both represent Fire and therefore have sympathy with each other. These interrelationships add to our understanding of the universe around us.

THE QUALITIES OF THE ELEMENTS

Air

In the natural world, Air is associated most closely with the sky, wind, and clouds. Mountain peaks, which seem to touch the sky, are also Air. Birds of all kinds belong to this element, and hawks and eagles are especially associated with Air because they fly so very high and make their nests at such high altitudes. A stork or duck, by contrast, is a less powerful symbol of Air because, although these birds fly, they live in and near the water.

In a person, Air is associated with thought and with the intellect, corresponding in the Witches' Pyramid to "To Know."[1] Ideas are said to come from Air, as is inspiration, a word that also means "to breathe in." Logic and scholarship are Air functions, which is perhaps why academics are said to live in ivory towers as opposed to ivory basements. People who spend all their time thinking "have their heads in the clouds," and if they're "airheads," they mistake imagination for real life and are impractical (because practicality is an Earth quality, which they lack).

The direction of Air is the East, and since the Sun rises in the east, Air is associated with the morning, with the spring (the beginning of the agricultural and astrological year), and with beginnings of all kinds. Anything that "dawns" is a thing of Air. The things in our lives that dawn, be they projects, creations, or careers, dawn with an idea. Often inspiration feels like the sunrise; a bright beginning full of promise and possibility. Since seeds are beginnings and are associated with the spring, seeds, too, belong to Air.

Air's gender is male. Don't think of this as "men," but rather as yang, or outward-moving, in terms of magical energy. Throughout this book, I will refer to Air creatures and people as male when a singular pronoun is needed, just to use good grammar, although obviously Air people are both male and female.

For Wicca and magic, we need to look at Air's symbolic associations. Its colors are sky colors—white and sky blue. The magical entity of Air is known as a *sylph*. The astrological Air signs are Gemini, Libra, and Aquarius. The Tarot suit of Air is Swords, although there is an interesting story behind this correspondence.

In 1910, Arthur Edward Waite published his book *The Pictorial Key to the Tarot* and his "Rider-Waite" Tarot deck. Waite was a Kabbalist and a member of the Golden Dawn magical lodge. His was the first deck to give all seventy-eight cards unique illustrations, and the first to draw associations between the Tarot and the Kabbalah. The Rider-Waite deck became the most popular and influential Tarot ever created, and its influences are seen in the vast majority of decks available today. (We will discuss the Tarot again when we discuss elemental personalities in chapter 3.)

Waite's membership in the Golden Dawn included an oath of secrecy, so he hesitated to reveal too much in his deck or accompanying book. He decided to switch two of the elemental correspondences in order to preserve his oath. He couldn't very well change the association of Cups to Water, since that's a pretty obvious one, and Pentacles are mostly depicted as coins—again, the association between money and Earth is straightforward and obvious. But Swords and Wands are abstract tools that were not in common usage at the turn of the last century. The Golden Dawn associated Air with Wands and Fire with Swords, so Waite reversed these two and filled his deck with Fiery Wands and Airy Swords.

If you're a Tarot reader who has used Waite's deck or a Waite-derived deck, it's hard to break the mental picture of Air/Sword, Fire/Wand. Every Wand has little flames, salamanders, and orange colors, and every Sword has prominent clouds, sylphs, and a lot of light blue. Perhaps because most Witches read the Tarot, most associate the sword, or athame, with Air.[2]

On the other hand, the original association used by the Golden Dawn and others makes a good deal of sense. The sword is the stronger and more destructive tool, and fire is more destructive than air. The wand is the tool of the intellectual magician, but the sword is the tool of the willful warrior (Fire is associated with will). Once you get to know the tools, it's hard to escape the conclusion that a person wielding a sword means business (has Will), but a person holding a wand might still just be thinking it over.

Other magical tools in a Neopagan ritual that are associated with Air are incense, feathers, and fans.

Fire

In nature, Fire is *itself,* first and foremost. Fire has always been set apart from the other elements, because Fire alone has no natural home on the earth; Air has the sky, Water the sea, and Earth the land, but only Fire stands apart from geography (see the section "The Three Worlds" later in this chapter for more about this). In nature, Fire is the outsider; it is out of control, and it conforms to no known rules.

The place Fire is most connected to is the desert, and Fiery animals such as lions and tigers are distinguished by their fiery color and disposition. Salamanders are also associated with Fire, both because of their bright orange color and because of the way that the licks and curls of a fire can come to resemble salamanders (which is how the magical being of Fire got its name). Other natural things associated with fire either burn, like chilis and cumin, or are red or especially orange-colored, like fire opals. Fire is male and outward-focused.

The personal quality of Fire is *will,* and in the Witches' Pyramid, Fire is "To Will." Willfulness burns hot, and the will to get things done is a spark that ignites. Temper is also associated with Fire; a fiery person is a "hothead," and lust is Fiery—you *burn* with desire. All of these things are closely associated with the life force itself, the spark within that fills us with life. For that reason, healing is a thing of fire; a person who is losing his spark needs Fire magic to reignite him.

Fire resides in the South. It is associated with noon, the hottest and brightest time of day, and with summer, the hottest and brightest time of year. In terms of endeavors, just as beginnings and ideas are Air, things that are "on fire" are Fire. As Air is the seed, Fire is the sprout—emerging. Fire takes the original seed and gets it going; it gives it force. Lots of creativity gets stuck in Air; it needs an application of Fiery will to turn on the power.

Fire can be a transformative force; in fire, the old is burned away and what comes out is utterly different. Transformation by fire is sudden and total: the blacksmith transforms iron ore into steel, raw meat becomes a delicious meal, and logs become embers, all by using fire.

In the occult, Fire is orange, red, and yellow. As mentioned before, its magical entity is the salamander. Fire signs of the Zodiac are Aries, Leo (another lion association), and Sagittarius. As just discussed in the section on Air, the tool and suit of Fire can be either Swords or Wands (I use Swords).

The representative of Fire on a Wiccan altar is one of those little things people like to debate. The obvious choice is a candle, or perhaps an oil lamp. A flame on the altar is a pretty intuitive way to represent Fire—can't argue with that! Others (including me) prefer to use burning incense to represent both Fire and Air.

In a typical Wiccan ritual, the female (yin) elements Earth and Water are combined, and salt water is used to represent them both. So I think it makes sense, and is more balanced, to represent the two male (yang) elements by combining them as well. So, the incense (Air) is put onto the censor (Fire) to make smoke (Air) rising from a burning ember (Fire)—an elegant arrangement.

Water

There are myriad natural forms of water, including not just the sea, but every body of water from a little creek to the Great Lakes. Water is also found in our bodies: in the clichéd "blood, sweat, and tears," in mother's milk, and, perhaps most importantly, in amniotic fluid. Just as life first evolved in the sea, the fetus swims in salt water as it "evolves" and develops. Since all bodies of water have tides, the Moon is also associated with water, and many lunar qualities are also Water qualities.

Sea creatures, both plant and animal, are connected to Water; fish, eels, shells, coral, seaweed, sponges, and driftwood all partake of this element. Dolphins and whales are the creatures most commonly associated with Water, although I suspect this has more to do with our affection for them than with any natural or symbolic imperative.

The personal quality of Water is *feeling*. Emotion flows, following its own path, which may meander. Emotion runs deep, with mysteries not visible on the surface. Emotions can be like sunken treasure, hiding secrets at the bottom of the waters of memory or the subconscious. Emotionality and mood swings are, of course, associated with the Moon, as are secrets—those things that are just barely visible, lit by moonlight and not exposed in the Sun. In the Tarot, the Moon card is full of watery images, like crustaceans crawling up out of the water, and the card's meaning is rooted in secrets, mysteries, and hidden knowledge. Water is female, and looks within.

The Moon and Water are the menstrual cycle, and Water is childbirth as well, making Water perhaps the most feminine of elements. Since Moon phases are cyclic, ending where they begin and beginning where they end, it makes sense that Water is also associated with death, and its not surprising that many people's folklore depicts death as a passage over water. To make the cycle complete, Hindus refer to rebirth as an ocean.

All of these things—the Moon, feeling, depth, birth-death-rebirth, and mystery—combine to associate Water with dreams and the subconscious, and from there to altered states of consciousness in general—trance, vision, and transformation coming from these things. Transformation by water is visionary and may take the quality of a journey, which is probably why the Hero's Journey generally begins with a passage over water.[3] (Note the difference from transformation by Fire: one is sudden and hot, and one is slow and dreamlike.)

Watery people are weepy and overflowing with feeling. They are dramatic, sensual, and otherworldly. They can be draining to be around—wet rags. They can also be the opposite—joyful and full of love; their cup runneth over. The generosity of Water flows forth abundantly; people in love feel love toward everyone, and Water is love.

Water's direction is West. Sunset in the west is also associated with death, with the end of things, and with transformation. Twilight is an in-between and mysterious time, and so is autumn. Neither seed nor sprout, Water is the sap flowing through flora just as blood flows through fauna.

In our creative/becoming process, we used Air to get the inspiration and Fire to provide the get-up-and-go. Now we need to let creativity flow through us. If you've ever written or played music or painted, you know there's a time to let go and let it happen. That's the Water time. Intuition has to play a part in any endeavor, and a "go with the flow" attitude has to allow us to take advantage of opportunities we could never have predicted in advance. Because this is daring in the way that closing your eyes and letting yourself fall is daring, Water corresponds in the Witches' Pyramid to "To Dare."

For magical symbolism, Water has ocean and lunar colors—deep blue, sea green, and silver. The magical *undine* is Water's entity. Water signs of the Zodiac are Cancer, Scorpio, and Pisces (Cancer's crab and Scorpio's scorpion both appear on the Moon card in the Tarot). The magical tool of Water is the cup, which is the Holy Grail. On a Wiccan altar, water is always represented by a simple dish of water—some people add a seashell, generally a conch. A conch can even double as a water dish.

Earth

Finally, we reach Earth. In nature, well, Earth *is* nature. Earth is the substance of the body of our Mother, Gaia, the Earth Herself. Earth is manifest in all things that are solid, or fertile, or both: rocks, green fields, rolling hills, and soil.[4] Caves and other buried places are quintessentially Earthy. Most people consider the bear the animal of Earth, although pigs, boar, and cattle also belong to this element. Bulls are an important Earth symbol both because of their Earthy nature and because they are associated with the astrological sign Taurus. So, astrologically, goats are Earth as well, since they are associated with Capricorn. Also, humans drink milk from both cows and goats. Although all beverages are associated with Water, if one were to choose an Earth beverage, it would surely be milk.

A human being's Earth is her *body*. From Earth comes solidity, stability, and commitment. We call Earth our home, both the home of all life that is Mother Earth, and the house we live in. By extension, Earth is hearth and family and all those qualities that make us feel at home. To be an Earthy person is to be pragmatic, realistic, and tactile. Good Earth qualities in a person make her "the salt of the earth," but an excess of negative Earth qualities make her a "stick-in-the-mud." Earth is that deep, solid, immobile place, both in the negative sense of stubborn and in the positive sense of patient. The Witches' Pyramid describes this quality in the attribute "To Be Silent."

Earth is located in the North and is associated with midnight, because North is opposite the noon of South and because subterranean places are dark. Winter is in the North—the coldness of midnight, the coldness of deep soil, and the stillness and silence of waiting for spring. To be solid is to be patient and to hold still. Contrarily, Earth is also fertility—pregnancy, fruit, the physical manifestation of our labors. In endeavors, Earth is completion, the finished project, the *thing* that results. Earth is female and inward-focused.

The colors of Earth are brown and black for soil, and deep green for fertility. *Gnomes* are the magical creatures said to inhabit the Earth, and the Zodiac signs associated with Earth are Taurus, Virgo, and Capricorn. The Tarot suit of Earth is Pentacles[5] or Disks, which represent money—that most physical of possessions (since it provides all the other physical possessions). Wealth and *buried* treasure are things of Earth. The elemental tool of Earth is also the pentacle, which, in Wicca, is a disk or plate with a pentagram inscribed on it (some traditions inscribe other symbols as well). Since a plate also holds food and since food is also of Earth (the physical product that is the outcome of farming; the sustenance of the body), the pentacle is a doubly good symbol (triply good, really, since the pentagram on it represents wholeness).

The representation of Earth on a magical altar is usually salt. Salt is considered to be an exceptionally magical symbol. It was once used as money and is also used as a food preservative, preserving the body through winter and driving away harm.

Air-Fire-Water-Earth

By now you've noticed how the four elements combine to make cycles, like circling the compass (East-South-West-North), or the seasons, or the time of day. They can make abstract cycles, like the cycle of an endeavor or creation that we described in this chapter: idea, then empowerment, then intuition, then manifestation/outcome. A romance, too, can begin with an idea (Air)—an observation, a crush, a hope. Next comes Fiery lust, then Watery love, and finally Earthy commitment. In Paganism, we know that every cycle ends at the beginning—midnight is followed by dawn, winter is followed by spring, and the manifestation of a creative process gives birth to the inspiration for the next process.

THE ORIGINS OF ELEMENTAL THINKING

The Three Worlds

The four elements of Air, Fire, Water, and Earth are abstractions. But most abstractions are ideas that arise out of something direct and natural. In Bronze Age Europe, life was seen as consisting of Three Worlds: Land, Sea, and Sky. While "Air" is abstract, "Sky" is not. The three worlds were visible everywhere, and the Celts in particular were practically obsessed with the number three. Everything came in threes (or nines, which is three times three), and everything could be divided up into three.

There were three kinds of creatures—land animals, sea creatures, and birds. Social classes were also divided into three. Farmers and other workers who lived off the land were associated with Land. Warriors were associated with the Sea, because they often traveled by sea and because of the blood they shed. Intellectuals, such as druids and priests, bards and poets, astronomers and magicians, were associated with the Sky, whence ideas and inspiration come.

Not just physical beings were associated with the Three Worlds, but supernatural beings as well. The Land was imbued with nature spirits, such as the nymphs of ancient Greece. The Sea was the home of the ancestors—death, and the dead, have long been associated with the sea for a number of reasons, not the least of which is that the warriors have an obvious connection to death. The Sky was where the gods and goddesses resided.

As you can see, the process of dividing people, beings, or things into sympathetic categories begins naturally, but quickly becomes abstract—the association of bloodshed with the sea, for example, is a bit of a leap. But these intellectual and intuitive leaps shouldn't be dismissed, as they are part of a magical and creative process that helps us see the whole of life, of which we are all a part. Nonetheless, Celtic thought in particular was always rooted in the natural world. A philosophical conception, to the Celts, had its basis in a tree, or the weather, or some other observable phenomenon.

It became obvious to the ancients that there was a fourth category, but it wasn't a World. That fourth category consisted of things that were singular and apart. It was the category of Fire.

Fire isn't a World, but neither is it of the Three Worlds. It doesn't exist in the Sky, it is doused by the Sea, and it isn't of the Land. The other Worlds are interconnected; a bird can land on a tree branch, or dive into the sea to catch a fish. No creatures live in Fire, and if one did, it would be alien to us and unable to exist elsewhere. The ancients came to associate Fire with things that were singular, not a part of any World. There was no social *group* associated with Fire—Fire was the King (or Queen), a singular being whose nature set him or her apart from all other people.

Just so, the supernatural quality associated with Fire was singular—Spirit, which imbues all and is apart from all, and which connects all beings but isn't any of them. Here is not only a meaningful correspondence, but one that actually serves to explain Fire's relationship to the Three Worlds. Here, too, is the King's relationship to the people, he is singular and apart, yet he touches them all and rules over them all. (Fire might also correspond to the High God, the first deity who created all the others and rules over them.)

So, prior to the idea of four elements was the idea of *Three Worlds plus one*. The "one" was apart from the three, and also permeated the three.

Three Worlds Plus One

World	*Element*	*Person(s)*	*Spiritual Being(s)*	*Other Ideas*
Land	Earth	Workers	Nature spirits	Fertility, childbirth, food, money, sex
Sea	Water	Warriors	Ancestors	Blood, death, honor, power
Sky	Air	Priests, bards, thinkers, and magicians	Gods and goddesses	Knowledge, thought, wisdom, inspiration, communication
Fire	Fire	The king	Spirit or the High God	Separateness, sacredness, the unknown, madness

The Elements in Hinduism

Meanwhile, in India, a different conception of the elements was developing. The Upanishads (the post-Vedic sacred texts of Hinduism) provide the conception of three elements: Fire (*agni*), Water (*ap*), and Earth (*prithivi*).[6] Earth was thought to be the first element, with Water emerging out of Earth, and Fire emerging out of Water. Just as in the West, Hindu philosophers developed correspondences between the elements, social class (caste), health, and so on. Later, probably influenced by Greek philosophy (see the next section), a fourth element, Air (*vayu*), was added, and later a fifth, *akasha* ("aether"). The new elements were inserted between Water and Fire in terms of emergence into creation. However, even after a fourth and fifth element were added to the Hindu system, the world continued to be divided into threes or three-plus-one in Indian thought.

Hindu Elemental Correspondences

Element	Food	Division of the Body	Desire	Color	Caste
Fire *(Agni)*	Oil, butter, fat	Bone, marrow, speech	Desire for action *(rajas)*	Red	Ksatriya
Water *(Ap)*	None	Urine, blood, breath *(prana)*	Desire for knowledge and goodness *(sattva)*	White	Brahmin
Earth *(Prithivi)*	All others	Feces, flesh, mind	Sloth (desire for inaction) *(tamas)*	Brown or black	Vaishya or Shudra

We Arrive in Greece

Most books ascribe the theory of four elements to a Greek philosopher named Empedocles, who wrote of them in *Tetrasomia, or Doctrine of the Four Elements* around 500 BCE. However, it's pretty clear that Empedocles didn't come up with the elements out of whole cloth. Prior to his work, Greek philosophers had been discussing the nature of the universe for some time, often falling back on theories about the elements. The fact that there *were* four elements was presupposed by most.

A group called the monists got very busy discussing which element was the first element, the one from which all others emanated (not unlike the Hindu philosophers, who settled on Earth). Various philosophers believed that Water was the underlying source of all matter, or that Fire was, or Air (I haven't found a citation for a Greek who thought Earth was the first element). Still others felt that there must be a fifth, unknown element from which all others arose.

This is where Empedocles comes in. He believed that the universe is composed of *all four* elements, that matter exists because four elements combine. In fact, Empedocles had an idea that few occultists even consider anymore, which is that all matter consists of all four elements. The sea, he thought, was mostly Water, but Air, Fire, and Earth were within it, or else it could not exist. Empedocles was quite insistent that the elements were abstracts and *not* real—real water had Earth, Air, and Fire mixed in, so Water was pure only in its abstract and idealized form. This was, of course, consistent with the Greek's idea that matter was "base" and that anything truly fine and good existed "above" matter. Empedocles further thought that the tension that caused the elements to divide into matter existed along an axis of love and strife—what we might look at today as attraction and repulsion.[7]

As the idea of a Universe of Four took hold, other philosophers expanded upon it. Plato, in *Commonwealth,* gave the elements "faculties of the soul." Hippocrates developed a theory of four humors. Galen (*On the Elements According to Hippocrates,* where he cites *On the Nature of Man* by Hippocrates) is the first printed source to include Hippocrates' humors as part of a comprehensive theory of personality types. These types were developed and expanded by Hippocrates, Galen, and others.

Elemental Correspondences in Greek Philosophy

	Empedocles		**Hippocrates/Galen**		**Plato**	**Aristotle**	
	Deity	*Movement*	*Bodily Fluid*	*Personality Type*	*Faculty of the Soul*	*Quality*	*Opposite*
Fire	Hades	Up and out	Blood	Choleric (active, enthusiastic)	Imagination	Dry and hot	Water
Water	Nestis (Persephone)	In and down	Phlegm	Phlegmatic (sad, brooding)	Opinion	Wet and cold	Fire
Air	Zeus	Up and out	Yellow bile	Sanguine (irritable, changeable)	Intelligence	Wet and hot	Earth
Earth	Hera	In and down	Black bile	Melancholic (apathetic and sluggish)	Demonstration	Dry and cold	Air

Aristotle Adds One

Aristotle was very interested in the elements and in their origins. In *Metaphysics*, he explored the idea that the elements arose from four *essences*—heat, cold, dryness, and moistness. (Moistness is fluid, it takes the shape of its surroundings; hence Air and

Water are both moist. Dryness is rigid and retains its own shape.) Aristotle envisioned the essences in constant interplay, and, as shown in the previous chart, this interplay created the elements.

If the essences could combine as wet and hot, dry and cold, and so on, Aristotle wondered if perhaps *all* combinations were possible. What would wet dryness be like? What would cold heat be like? This unworldly "fifth essence" (*quintessence*) he called *aether*, and he believed it was the stuff that composed the heavens.

It is from Aristotle's conception of aether that modern occultists got the idea that Spirit is a fifth element. (Actually, what probably happened was this: The Greeks brought the concept of aether to India around 400–500 CE. The Sanskrit word for aether was *akasha,* which Hindus defined as a fifth element. When Western occultists started importing ideas from Hinduism, *akasha* was translated into "spirit," and so Spirit became the "fifth element.")

Many Wiccans today seem to use five elements: Air, Fire, Water, Earth, and Spirit or Akasha (the term *aether* has fallen into disuse). In fact, the pentagram—the main symbol of Paganism and Witchcraft—is said to represent the five elements (figure 1). Each of the points of the pentagram represents one of the elements, according to this view, with Spirit on top.

You'll often hear that Wiccans place Spirit on top of their pentagram, but Satanists place Spirit on the bottom of theirs. The idea is that Spirit is either above or below matter. Personally, I think a religion focused on the Earth Mother has no

Figure 1: Pentagram

business separating Spirit from matter—to say that either is better than the other implies that they are forever separate. If the Earth is a Goddess, then how can matter be separate from sacred spirit?

"Spirit on top" is all about Spirit being better than the "base" elements. The Greek philosophers were very much concerned with the idea that Spirit was "higher" or "finer" than matter, and of course the goal of the Hindu religion is to be released from the cycle of birth, death, and rebirth in matter. However, in Wicca we *celebrate* the cycle of rebirth, and in the body of the Earth Herself. We *worship* matter.

Aristotle imagined aether as arising from the same stuff as the elements, but the typical Wiccan view of Spirit *separates* it from the elements. I think this is a mistake.

Because Wicca is a religion of the Earth (the *planet* Earth—Gaia—not the element of Earth), I don't feel that separating the sacred (Spirit) from matter (the elements) is a good idea. Instead, it's appropriate to think of the elements in a way that embraces the Earth and matter as sacred. The elements aren't "beneath" us, they *are* us, they are foundational.

A look at a traditional Wiccan ritual can provide us with another way of viewing the relationship between the elements and Spirit.

A traditional Wiccan circle is set up with a candle or torch at each of the cardinal points (East, South, West, and North), representing the elements, around the perimeter. Traditions vary as to where the altar is placed, but I was taught to place it in the center. Over time, I have come to see that a central altar has mystical value. The ritual is a "squared circle," marked at the quarters, and the altar is the meeting place of the elemental points (figure 2).

At the center of the circle is the altar, drawing perfectly balanced energies from each of the four quarters. What's on the altar? The altar is where the representations of the *Gods*, the idols, are placed. Doesn't that make the altar the place of *Spirit*? The squared circle, then, can represent the four elements plus Spirit in a more integrated way than the pentagram (which has mystical significance in its own right).

This is, in fact, similar to what Aristotle had to say (albeit without the temperature/moisture issue): Spirit is what happens when all four elements meet and combine. The *quintessence* is the magical whole that is greater than the sum of its parts. Elemental beings (as we'll learn shortly) have only their own qualities: Earth elementals will only be Earth, and are incapable of acting in any way but Earthy ways; they won't feel or be willful. Fire elementals will only and forever be Fire; we cannot ask

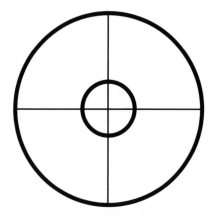

Figure 2: Squared Circle

them to be stable or exercise self-control. But *people*, and other beings with Spirit, have the capacities of all four elements, and the freedom to grow and explore in any direction.

Squaring the circle also represents wholeness; balance. Just as nature is balanced, every person should be balanced in the elements—an idea I call the Way of Four, which we'll spend more time exploring shortly.

ELEMENTAL BEINGS

Elements, as we have seen, are qualities; materials if you will. They aren't sentient and they don't have personalities. There are, however, two kinds of beings, known as *elemental beings,* whose nature is defined by and limited to the elements. They are *elementals* and *Guardians*. Neither elementals nor Guardians are gods, although some people seem to think they are, and treat them as such. Most Witches and magicians, though, don't worship elemental beings so much as acknowledge and work with them.

Elementals

Elementals were identified, named, and described in the sixteenth century by the noted German physician and alchemist Paracelsus. He coined the words *sylph* for an elemental of Air and *undine* for an elemental of Water, and gave the names *gnome* and *salamander* to the elementals of Earth and Fire, respectively. Paracelsus remains an influential force today in medicine (he is considered the father of homeopathy) and the occult. Two of the leading figures of the occult lodge movement of the late nineteenth and early twentieth centuries, Franz Hartmann and Arthur Edward Waite, wrote books about him.[8] (The occult lodge movement, in turn, was one of the most important forces in the eventual birth of modern Wicca.)

Elementals are often called lesser beings. I think this is true, but I don't think this means that they are *inferior* beings. They have fewer components than we do; they are less complex, more basic.

Elementals, unlike elements, are conscious, sentient beings. They have been called the *spirits of the elements*. Each is composed entirely of its own element and partakes only of that element's nature. Each is able to manipulate the forces of its element, i.e., undines can influence both rain and matters of the heart. Although they are *called* spirits, they don't *have* Spirit, in the sense that Spirit is the combination of all four elements, and so they cannot change themselves; they don't have the capacity to become more than the single nature that they are.

It takes an imaginative leap to understand what an elemental is. We are used to seeing the attributes of elements in combination, both in ourselves and all around us, and so it is hard for us to picture beings of just one element.

Sylphs

Sylphs are composed of Air. They think and they float. They are rarified and elusive. They do not respond to feeling, and they do not feel. They cannot be praised, fed, or excited. They are exclusively beings of wind, thought, and flight. You cannot persuade a sylph to care, because caring is emotion—Water. Do not expect deep connections with sylphs, because depth is not in the nature of Air.

Renaissance art depicts sylphs as winged, with human forms, often appearing to be tiny cherubs. It is likely that the modern idea of fairies, such as the Victorian artist Arthur Rackham depicted in his illustrations of fairy tales and Shakespeare, has more to do with sylphs than with the fey folk. Like wind, sylphs move quickly and suddenly, and can travel great distances. Like the element of Air, sylphs are masters of thought and speech. They are intelligent and persuasive. Remember, though, that the gift of gab is a double-edged sword. Sylphs are not known for their honesty or concern. Although no person is made purely of intellect, if you think of people who are mostly intellectual, you'll realize that sylphs can also be superior, disdainful, and dismissive.

Salamanders

Paracelsus viewed salamanders as great, radiant, god-like beings. Woodcuts show them to be dragon-like, some winged, some not, and some with human faces. Some say that the shapes you see when staring into a fire, which sometimes appear to be creatures, actually *are* beings—salamanders, and that is how they should be visualized. Of course, just as a fire is constantly changing its shape, salamanders can be shapeshifters, but they will always look fiery, especially in coloration.

Salamanders are Fire. They burn and explode, they smolder and burst and consume. They are temperamental, impulsive, quick, and willful. They have no caution, no concern, no restraint; none of those are in the nature of Fire. Magicians who invoke Fire elementals must always be careful and cautious, because salamanders are incapable of these qualities. It's very hard to get a salamander to do your will, because salamanders *are* Will. Usually, if they cooperate, they leave their own stamp somehow.

Undines

Undines are Water. They feel and flow. They fulfill themselves in desire, intuition, and love. Do not expect them to be sensible, nor to hold still for very long. Sense is for Air, stillness is for Earth, and undines have none of either. You can't reason with an undine, although you can *attract* her.

Undines can appear to be quite human, as they share many qualities with humans—we can often be irrationally emotional, and often seek love above all other things. Folklore around the world is full of tales of lovely female creatures of the sea who attract men with their infinite sensuality—mermaids, selkies, sirens, etc., are all manifestations of undines. Like the current, they "pull you in," and like the tide, they are quite changeable. Undines are graceful, their movements are fluid, and if they speak, their voices have a liquid, melodic quality.

Gnomes

Gnomes are Earth.[9] Because we live on the Earth and we are solid, we can often relate to gnomes, but we can also be mistaken about their nature. Remember that gnomes are slow, if they move at all, and are both infinitely patient and immensely stubborn.

Trying to talk a gnome into something is like trying to persuade a rock. They cannot be persuaded or enticed, although they do respond to sensory stimulation and to respect.

In appearance, gnomes are solid and squarish of shape, and have craggy brown, gray, or black skin. They blend into their environment, and disappear into shadows. Gnomes live in caves and caverns, and can be sensed in dark, inaccessible crevices whence a compelling stillness can seem almost to be calling you.

Elementals can sometimes be encountered in day-to-day life, for good or ill. The first time I met a salamander was way back in the early 1980s, when my roommate accidentally set fire to the kitchen curtains. I don't think that salamanders caused that fire—I think my roomie's drinking was the problem. But a big fire (it destroyed a corner of the kitchen) can certainly *attract* salamanders, and for months thereafter, small fires burst out all over the apartment—incense dishes fell over, ashtrays got too close to paper, and so on. I was fairly new to Wicca at the time, but eventually it penetrated my thick head that salamanders were living in my apartment. So, I did the nicest, most polite banishing spell I could come up with. The salamanders left—but they took the hot water with them for the next four days!

That encounter probably opened my eyes to the world of elements and elementals more than any magical text or lecture by my High Priestess. I learned that elementals follow their own nature—my salamanders weren't vindictive or evil, they were just fiery. I learned that I could sense and commune with elementals in their own environments—the whisper of a gnome in the back of a cave, the lure of an undine in the deepest part of a pool, and the hypnotic compulsion to watch the match burn down all the way to the end that can mark the presence of a salamander. Elementals should be respected because of their power, but one should be wary because of their lack of balance. If you, the magical practitioner, stay balanced and follow the Way of Four, elementals can open your eyes and empower your work.

Guardians

The *Guardians* are sometimes called the Guardians of the Watchtowers. "Watchtowers" is a term derived from Enochian magic, where the Guardians are also given the names Paralda (Air), Seraph (Fire), Niksa (Water), and Ghob (Earth).[10] The word "Watchtowers" is much used but little understood in Wicca and Paganism; Wiccans and Pagans often learn to repeat the phrase "Guardians of the Watchtowers" without knowing what Watchtowers are. In addition, very few people other than Enochian practitioners use the individual names of the Guardians.

If you're not practicing an Enochian system, it's best not to place the Guardians in towers at all, rather than use terms that don't make sense to the path you're working.

Like elementals, there is one Guardian for each element, and they share the basic nature of the element. The Guardians, however, are considered "higher" than elementals in that their functions are more sophisticated. They have been compared to archangels; some Witches have said that these are different words for the same thing.[11] I don't know if the Guardians *are* archangels—personally, I work a magical system that completely omits any such Judeo-Christian references. However, the comparison is apt in that the Guardians are not gods, but are beings who are otherworldly and who protect and support human beings while serving the Gods. Although I have worked with them in rituals for years, I have little concrete knowledge of them because the nature of the Guardians is elusive. I have come to understand them as beings roughly equal to ourselves, as sophisticated and complex as humans, as spiritually evolved as we, and with a similar relationship to the Gods—sharing in their essence, but still distant from them in practical terms.[12] Their existence is very different from ours, of course, but so is the existence of a dolphin, another creature that many people have begun to view as roughly equal to human beings.

The primary purpose of the Guardians is to serve the Gods; they are involved with humans, protecting and guarding us, only as a sort of byproduct to protecting and guarding rituals devoted to, and sacred to, Them. Outside of ritual, they have little interest in us, and don't seem to watch over people in their day-to-day lives. The Guardians protect a ritual both from danger coming from their direction, and danger coming from their element. So, the Guardian of the South prevents danger from entering a ritual from the South, and also prevents fire from breaking out in the ritual. Their nature is heavily influenced by their element, but the Guardians aren't made up exclusively of their element in the way that elementals are.

Unlike elementals, Guardians are generally found only in ritual space, or on spirit journeys or in visions. They don't flow (or burn, or . . .) through nature the way that elementals do. As such, they are really the provenance of magicians and Witches, but they can be powerful allies and great teachers in that environment.

1. The Witches' Pyramid is the Wiccan name for a magical saying and philosophy that originated with the Golden Dawn. It goes: "To Know, To Will, To Dare, and to Be Silent, these are the four tools of the Magician."

2. An athame is the black-handled, double-edged knife that is the Witch's personal tool.

3. The Hero's Journey, Joseph Campbell's famous "monomyth," is described in full in the classic book *The Hero with a Thousand Faces* by Joseph Campbell (1949; reprint, Princeton, NJ: Princeton University Press, 1972)

4. I have a rock that I found in Lake Ontario. It is very smooth and flat and obviously water-worn. I use it in the West to represent Water because of its appearance and origin. My coveners, bless them, were always getting mixed up and putting it in the North, since rocks are obviously Earth.

5. A pentagram is a five-pointed star. A pentacle is an object with a pentagram on it.

6. The Vedas and Upanishads are the holy books of Hinduism. There are four Vedas, dating from about 1500 to 1000 BCE. The Upanishads are a post-Vedic collection of writings; there are over a dozen principal volumes and many additional ones; volumes range in date from around 800 to 400 BCE.

7. My thanks to Isaac Bonewits for the attraction/repulsion connection.

8. See *The Life of Paracelsus*, by Franz Hartmann, and *The Hermetic and Alchemical Writings of Paracelsus*, by A. E. Waite.

9. Contrary to how they are depicted in Victorian illustrations, gnomes don't have pointy red hats.

10. Thanks to my correspondent James Berry for providing details on the Guardians of the Watchtowers.

11. Stewart Farrar, *What Witches Do: A Modern Coven Revealed* (Custer, WA: Phoenix Publishing Co., 1971 and 1983) 138–139.

12. I don't mean that the Gods are distant from us. I mean that our lives tend to *feel like* and *be lived like* the Gods are distant from us—that there is a chasm between our inner godlike nature and our lived experience.

CHAPTER TWO

The Elements in Nature

Empedocles was right—nothing in nature is all of one element. The sea has plants (Earth) and trapped air bubbles. The soil has moisture and air. Fire burns wood (Earth), and so on. Pure elements live only in the abstract and in the form of supernatural beings (elementals).

Nonetheless, we can best begin to *experience* the elements in nature. Here, we find raw, imposing, striking examples of the elements we wish to know better.

The Elements in Nature

	Locations	Aspects	Animals
Air	The sky, mountain peaks	Wind, clouds	Birds, especially hawks and eagles
Fire	The desert, volcanoes	Heat, bright sunlight	Big cats, salamanders and other dry-land lizards
Water	All bodies of water (sea, rivers, lakes, creeks)	Rain, tides (and therefore the Moon)	Fish, eels, crustaceans, dolphins, whales, and all creatures of the sea
Earth	Rolling hills, fertile fields, caves and other buried places	Soil, stones, earthquakes	Bears, pigs, boar, cattle, goats

The following brief exercises allow you to have direct, visceral, experiential encounters with the elements in nature. To be fair to city dwellers, I provide options in many of the exercises for those whose access to natural settings is limited. Be sure to read all of each element's exercises before doing one, as some of the exercises are best done as a set.

As you venture out to do these exercises, remember that all nature exploration requires some effort at safety. Heights, caves, fires, and waterfalls all present hazards to the incautious. Know where you're going and how to be there wisely before you proceed.

AIR IN NATURE: EXERCISES

Air exercises are best done on an empty stomach. Note that exercises 1 through 3 are done together.

Exercise One: Sky and Breath

If possible, lie on your back where you can see the open sky in the daylight. Try to arrange your view so that you can see only sky—where trees, hills, and buildings don't block your view. If you're in the country, an open field is ideal. In the city, a rooftop is more than adequate.

Allow yourself to see *only* sky. Breathe in deeply, and then, as your breath falls into a more natural rhythm, simply become aware of your inhalations and exhalations. As you watch the sky, become aware that your breath and the sky are part of a single whole. They are both Air, and you are joined to the sky by your breath. Try to confine your awareness of your body to your breathing. As you do so, imagine yourself in the sky you gaze upon.

Exercise Two: Sky and Cloud

Next, find one cloud in the sky to focus upon. This part is easy—all you do is watch the cloud. The cloud moves slowly compared to *your* pace in life, but once you adjust to watching it, your internal rhythm will adapt to it. You'll see it hold still, or speed up, or slow down. You'll see changes in shape. Remind yourself that all of the changes and movement you see are Air changes. The cloud is Air[1] being moved by Air.

Lying on your back following the clouds allows you to move out of your earthbound body into a way of being that is almost sylph-like.

Exercise Three: Sky and Bird

Next, scan the sky until you find a bird. (This is easier to do at some times of year than others.) Your task again is simple—simply track the bird's flight with your eyes. As you do, breathe *with* the flight. *Be* with the flight. This may not come naturally to you the first time, but stay with it. If you let yourself go, you can change your point of view until it seems like you are the bird looking down, rather than the other way around.

Exercise Four: Up and Down

This exercise requires being in a high place. It can be on a cliff, a hilltop, or even the roof of a tall building. I first experienced it at the Grand Canyon, but not everyone is going to be able to use that spot! Although people with full-blown acrophobia won't be able to do this exercise, a little vertigo during the course of it is normal and should not dissuade you. It's best to do this with a partner. That way one of you can experience Air while the other stays safely grounded in Earth and keeps an eye on the "airhead." At a later time, you can switch roles.

From a high spot, there are a lot of ways to go with an Air exercise. Certainly "daring" the edge can give you a sense of *being* without a foundation. On the other hand, it's also a good way to scare yourself, which doesn't do a whole lot for getting to know the element. It has long seemed to me that differences in tolerating heights are as much physical—probably related to the inner ear—as psychological. In any event, you're not going to "cure" yourself by dangling your feet off a cliff.

Okay, so that's what we're *not* going to do. Instead, we're going to work with height *visually*, as we did with the open sky in the previous exercises.

Start by removing yourself and the ground on which you stand from your field of vision. Face not up, but forward. Your straight-ahead vision should show you some open air and whatever is ahead of you. Hold that view and let yourself become aware of both openness and height. The primary quality defining whatever is opposite you is the *openness* between you. You don't touch, there is no *sensation* of connection, yet there is knowing. And you are *above*. Let your gaze move slightly downward, until you are looking twenty feet, forty feet, fifty feet below you. Get a feeling for that distance. Fifty feet is quite a drop—nothing that an earthbound creature like yourself could survive easily. Just hold that view and be with that height, that sense of *up*, for a few moments. Find an object or a point at about that fifty-foot distance below you and define it, in your mind, as *down*. That point is *below*, that point is *down*. Just think about that for a few moments; you are up, your point is down.

Now look again at your *down* point, and move your gaze to about forty to fifty feet below it. Your down point is now *up* and the new point is down. Look at that view, having changed your perspective on the nature of up and down. Now, in your mind, put yourself back in the picture, and know that you are the up above up. (I got really lucky at the Grand Canyon—my first *down* point was a *bird*.)

After allowing yourself to be with that for a bit, the exercise is complete. *Do not* move from your spot until you have grounded yourself—with the help of your partner if necessary—and you feel once again sufficiently earthbound to walk around.

Exercise Five: Wind and Skin

This final Air exercise should be done as close to skyclad (nude) as location allows. Choose a warm (but not too hot or humid) day and a relatively private site so that neither weather nor modesty will inhibit you. You may return to the open area from the first exercise, but that isn't strictly necessary—any outdoor location will do.

Having chosen your spot, strip as much as you choose to, and stand in a comfortable position, with your feet firmly on the ground and facing forward, your legs about sixteen inches apart, knees slightly bent, and arms at, but not touching, your sides. This is a position of openness and reception. Close your eyes.

Become aware of the wind playing over your skin. Maybe it's a windy day, maybe not. Your skin is surrounded by air, and however slightly, the air is moving. Allow yourself to be embraced by the air's touch. As you become more attuned to the air on your skin, you'll become more aware of its variations; sometimes a light touch, sometimes stronger, changes in direction, and so on.

Before going back among people, don't forget to put your clothes on!

FIRE IN NATURE: EXERCISES

Outside of specialized environments (once again, access to Arizona can be really helpful) or manmade environments in natural settings (like a sweat lodge), the only way to encounter Fire naturally is via fire itself.

It is exceptionally important that, when setting a fire for the purpose of elemental study or meditation, you be *twice* as cautious about fire safety as you were taught in the Girl or Boy Scouts. Fire has a hypnotic quality, and when your goal is to commune with Fire, your sense of caution will not be in the fore. It goes without saying that such an exercise will attract salamanders. Remember that salamanders are not evil, but neither are they *good.* The important thing to know is that you and salamanders have different purposes. Salamanders think that forest fires are a good thing—you do not. So bank that fire, have some buckets of sand and water nearby, and don't fall asleep.

You can build your fire in a remote woods or in a public park. The nice thing about gazing into a fire is that everyone does it, so it won't look at all, to an outside observer, as if you are practicing witchcraft.

Exercise One: Fire Gazing

This exercise is deceptively simple because, as I said above, everyone does it. The only difference this time is that you are doing it with *focus* and with *purpose.*

After building a fire and making sure it's safe, assume a relaxed, comfortable position in which you're not at risk of falling asleep. Now, simply gaze into the fire. Forget your body, forget any sounds or sensations that surround you, and just gaze. Look at the *shape* of the fire; notice this shape as the body of fire, its defining boundaries. Imagine yourself having such a changeable, mobile body. Notice the constant movement, the restlessness. Notice the *force.*

Notice that you also *feel* and *hear* the fire; it is hot, dry, and crackling. Feel the way your skin tightens near fire; perhaps your eyes even burn a little.

Either proceed to Exercise Three: In Fire's Wake, or douse your fire thoroughly.

Exercise Two: The Devouring Fire

Set up your firepit and fuel as follows:

As you can see in figure 3, the main fire should be built well within the firepit. This gives the fire the ability to grow past the initial bounds you set up. Place some smaller bits of fuel, such as crumpled bits of paper, tiny twigs, or other small, flammable materials, as illustrated. Don't use dry leaves, uncrumpled paper, or anything else that is likely to fly away.

Figure 3: Firepit

The idea here is that your fire will begin to devour the extra fuel you put out for it. Build the fire as shown, and then light the main fire. Watch it reach its limits and seek beyond. Watch it eat up the extra fuel, changing its shape this time with hunger and purpose. Your focus is on Fire as an active agent, a devourer, and as willful. It is the will of the fire seeking outward, expressing and satisfying hunger, that you are watching.

Either proceed to Exercise Three: In Fire's Wake, or douse your fire thoroughly.

Exercise Three: In Fire's Wake

The final exercise for Fire can follow either the first or second exercise.

Allow your fire to go out. As it fades, look at the what it leaves behind—the ash, the embers, the coals. Allow yourself to see the hunger of fire by seeing what it has eaten. Allow yourself to see the willfulness of fire by its thoroughness and its persistence—notice that even though the fire is out, the embers still burn; fire may be gone, but Fire remains. Find a piece of wood or coal that has a hot center, and watch it crackle—see how full of life it is, even without flames. Perhaps as you gaze a flame will suddenly start up, and you will know the life force that fire contains, and something of its surprises. Finally, with a stick or poker, find a coal that appears to be completely dead. Poke it and find the hot core beneath—this is Fire's deceptiveness and danger, and it is a good thing to remember.

Douse your fire completely before leaving.

WATER IN NATURE: EXERCISES

I've left swimming and other forms of submersion out of these exercises, mostly because swimming in a natural setting (rather than a pool) isn't available to everyone, not to mention that there are an awful lot of people who can't swim. Leaving out such exercises doesn't mean I don't think they're valuable. Probably my favorite watery pastime is to float on my back in a quiet lake in the summer. Another favorite is canoeing. But the simple exercises on the following pages are accessible, beautiful ways of getting in touch with nature's abundant Water.

Exercise One: Walkin' in the Rain[2]

Take a walk in the rain. Don't choose a freezing rain or a heavy downpour; either of these will likely make you so uncomfortable that you won't be able to attend to the Water experience. Likewise, don't go out in a lot of thunder and lightning, as the object is not to see if you would make a good lightning rod.

The trick for making this exercise work is to let go and really allow yourself to walk in the rain. Most walks in the rain are an exercise in resisting the rain. We fight the experience; we protect ourselves in every way possible.

Instead, leave your umbrella and raincoat at home. Weather permitting, dress in only light clothing, nothing waterproof, and definitely no hat. Walk slowly—avoid hurrying. Walk with your head up, and don't shield your eyes. (If you wear glasses, you'll need to take them off.)

If you stop trying to *escape* Water, you can learn a lot *about* Water. The experience here is mostly physical—you'll be letting yourself get really *wet*. They say fish never notice the water, and I think this is true. Just so, I don't think you feel *wet* when you're swimming or bathing, because you're immersed both in the water and in the experience. Rain, on the other hand, lets you experience your body's interaction with the water, its temperature, its movement across your skin, its gradual evaporation. You will be in the *process* of Water.

You will likely be chilled when you get home. Have some towels and a warm change of clothes prepared and waiting for you. Finish your experience with a hot tea. Lemon balm, chamomile, or wintergreen are good, readily accessible teas, and are associated with the element of Water.

Exercise Two: Water Gazing, in Motion

Gazing at moving water is as hypnotic as gazing at fire. The ideal setting for this kind of exercise is at a waterfall; anything from Niagara Falls to a local watering hole can work. (You might be surprised at how nearby such a watering spot might be—often there are natural areas, state or county parks, and nature preserves only a short drive from even very urban areas. A web search might turn up something local to you that you never knew about!) A rapidly moving brook, stream, or river is equally effective. In a pinch, you can gaze into the water of a manmade fountain. The exercise will work by day or by night, but I recommend daylight.

This is a simple gazing exercise, similar to the previous fire gazing exercise. If you've already done the fire gazing exercise, though, you'll notice that it feels different. It will feel the same in some ways—your thoughts will be stilled, you'll have a sense of calm typical of a mild trance, and so on—but the sense of *other* will differ, the sense of the other being or force encountered.

When I gaze at fire, I feel fascinated, compelled. When I gaze at water, I feel almost seduced; I flow. Your experience may not be the same as mine (or else there would be no need for exercises—you could just read the book); however, you should notice a distinct sense of each element's uniqueness.

Allow your gaze to move in and out, from the macrocosm of the water flowing to the microcosm of a few drops. Follow a drop, from one end of your range of vision to the other. Allow yourself to contemplate the individual that is not an individual—the droplet that cannot be separated from its stream, which cannot be separated from the waterfall/river, which flows seamlessly to the ocean. Then do the opposite, contemplating one spot, with an infinite number of drops flowing through it as it stays the same—as if a piece of movement has its own shape.

Note your other body sensations. Perhaps you feel a mist on your face. Notice the music of water, and listen to its rushing, melodic song. At a large waterfall, the sound is deafening, insistent. At a brook, it truly "babbles," playing over its shores like a baby playing in its crib.

When you're finished, don't look away suddenly or all at once. Instead, follow a movement of water to the bank nearest you, and then bring your gaze to the earth, and your awareness back to yourself.

Exercise Three: Water Gazing, Still

This exercise will feel different from the previous one. Gazing into a still pool (or bowl) of water is a traditional form of scrying in Wicca. However, your purpose here is not to see images of the past or future, but to see and experience Water—its depths, its stillness, its silence, and its secrets.

The most magical scrying pool, and an ideal one for our exercise, is a still body of water that catches the moonlight. However, reflected moonlight is optional. A quiet lake, a still pool, or even a small manmade pool such as a fish pond will suffice. As you did the last exercise in daylight, do this one at night or twilight.

Before beginning, you might want to do a calming, centering meditation, especially if you're the kind of person who becomes restless easily; you won't find many distractions in a still pool for a restless mind to latch onto.

Once you're by your body of water, get in a relaxed position, one where you can easily see into the water. As you gaze, notice the darkness and depth. Notice the silence of the water, and notice the occasional sounds. Notice that even the most unmoving of water still has slight movement. Note the tiny ripples that sometimes appear.

This is an exercise to which you should devote some time. You're not going to get much out of it if you sit by the pool for three minutes and then say, "Okay, done!" and go home. That's why you meditated first. The only worthwhile part of this exercise is the experience of water you have over time, as you find yourself connecting to the water's own timing and rhythm.

EARTH IN NATURE: EXERCISES

Is this redundant? Nature *is* the Earth. These exercises will focus not on Gaia, our Earth Mother, but Earth in its elemental form. Just as I left swimming out of the Water exercises, here I omit exploring a cave. Caverns have given me my most profound and moving Earth experiences, and if you have the opportunity to explore them, I highly recommend it. I love finding the dark corners of caves and listening to the gnomes that reside there. However, our focus here is on exercises that just about anyone can do.

Exercise One: Plant Yourself

For this exercise, you need to find a place where you can dig. If you have your own backyard, you're in business. It's *not* a good idea to dig a hole in a public park, but if you have access to even a small patch of woods, there are plenty of private spots, and the soil is likely to be soft. If you went to a stream in the second Water exercise, that's probably a good spot. If the soil is muddy, it adds to the fun!

Sometimes in Pagan and magical practice, your biggest obstacle to overcome is the suspicion that what you're doing is darn silly. This may well be one of those times. This exercise is, well, *earthy*. It can be fun, a bit foolish, and certainly messy, but none of that means it isn't a "real" magical exercise.

Simply put, you're going to bury your feet. Bring a shovel—a full-sized spade is optional, but definitely also bring a hand-held trowel. You'll probably want a towel to wipe up with after the exercise is over.

Dig your hole deep enough so you can stand in it about ankle-deep or a little deeper. That's deep enough to really feel "planted," but not so deep as to have trouble getting unplanted when you're done. Dig the hole, and step in, making sure your trowel is close at hand. Don't stand with your feet too close together; you don't want to lose your balance. Then put the dirt back in the hole. Pack the dirt down so that you're good and buried in there.

Close your eyes for a while and just *feel*. Feel the immobility, the sense of being surrounded by solidness, of being firmly in place. Feel the way that, when you're planted in earth, you're embraced, touched, and enveloped by Earth.

Now open your eyes and take a look around. Spot something—anything—beyond your reach, and decide that you want it. Simply look at whatever it is—your towel, a flower, something glittering on the ground—and think, "I wish I could get closer to that. I wish I could touch that. I wish I could look at that." There you are, Earth, planted firmly in soil, without the freedom the other elements take for granted. You can't reach what you want. You feel frustrated. Be with that frustration.

But to truly know Earth, you must move beyond that frustration. Allow yourself to feel patient. Someday soon, that flower will whither. Someday, that towel will rot away.

But Earth will abide. Earth has no longing because Earth holds still and watches as other things, flimsier things, pass away. Be the Earth; planted, firm, and beyond desire.

When you touch that desireless state, close your eyes again, and be with the still, solid Earth.

When you're ready, unbury yourself, restore the soil to its hole, and clean up with your towel.

Exercise Two: Gathering Stones

For exercises 3 and 4, you'll need a whole bunch of stones. For this exercise, you'll be gathering your stones. These should be small enough to easily lift and hold in your hand—they can range from palm-sized to pebbles. You'll need about enough to fill a small bucket—at least the size of a sand pail such as a child takes to the beach, and as much as twice that size. Most importantly, try to find stones that you *like*. It really doesn't matter what standards you use to decide that you like a stone—perhaps you like how it feels in your hand, or its color or shape, or perhaps you are fond of where or how you found it.

This will be a process that will take place over time; to have this be consistent with the ways of Earth, you shouldn't be in a hurry. It might be that gathering the stones takes place over a period of weeks or months—that's fine. The process of walking around, looking for stones, picking them up, deciding whether or not to keep them, and bringing them to your home or yard is an Earth process and is the whole point of the exercise. Looking at and for stones for weeks or months will add to the experience.

There isn't anything you need to know about what you should be thinking, feeling, or experiencing during the gathering process—if you end up with a bucket full of stones at the end of it, you'll have completed the exercise appropriately and in a way that increases your connection to Earth.

Exercise Three: Points of Power

For this exercise, you may want a partner. Whoever does this Points of Power exercise will need to have first done the previous Gathering Stones exercise. When it's your turn to do this exercise, use your stones; and when it's your partner's turn, use your partner's stones.

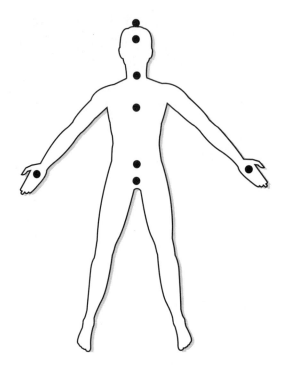

Figure 4: Points of Power 1

You'll want a private, outdoor location. This is an exercise that (a) is best per-formed skyclad, and (b) looks kind of weird to the casual observer. You're going to be lying naked, or as nearly so as comfortable, on the ground—directly on the ground, without a blanket or sheet between you and the Earth. Once you're com-fortably touching the earth, either you or your partner will place seven stones from your collection on your body, and an eighth stone just above your head, as shown above in figure 4. If you're working by yourself, start with one palm, then do the five stones in the center of your body, and finish by resting the hand you've been using on the ground, still holding the last stone. Obviously, it's easier to have a partner place the stones for you, but it's not strictly necessary and you may, in fact, prefer the solitude.

Five of the stones will be on chakra points, as shown above in figure 4:

1. The *root* and *perineal* chakras will both be covered by the stone at the groin level—place it just on the pubic bone.

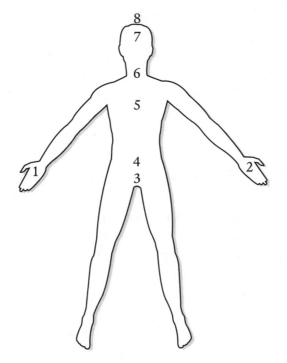

Figure 5: Points of Power 2

2. The next stone will cover the *solar plexus* chakra.

3. The third stone will cover the *heart* chakra.

4. Next will be a (small) stone over your *throat* chakra.

5. You'll have a stone covering your *third eye* chakra.

6. You won't be able to put a stone on your *crown* chakra, because it will fall off when you lie down. Instead, place a stone on the ground just above your head, as illustrated on previous page in figure 4.

7. You'll put the seventh and eighth stones on the palms of your hands. Although not usually considered chakras, the palms are points of power, and are often used to send and receive energy in Wicca and other magical paths.

Now you're just going to stay in that position. Your points of power are covered with Earth (stone) and you lie on top of Earth. Your stillness is enforced (if you move much, the stones will fall off). Allow yourself to absorb and feel the energies of stone and soil. Allow yourself to be filled with the *solid*, the *certain*, and the *concrete*. Know the silence of Earth; know its calm.

Focus on each stone, individually. Begin at your palms, and then go to the root and move upward. (Refer to figure 5 on the previous page, and move in order from 1 to 8.) Often, you'll be able to feel a tingle or a pulse of energy from each stone. You might note that each is slightly different, as though each stone has a personality communicated through touch. After focusing on the third-eye stone, you'll probably even be able to get a sense of the stone at the crown of your head.

After you've given each individual stone its time and attention, start adding back stones; that is, first focus on 1, then the next, in the order 1 to 8, until you reach the crown. Then, maintaining awareness of the crown, bring the third-eye stone back into your consciousness, so that you're focusing on stones 8 and 7. Then focus on 8, 7, and 6. Add each stone, one at a time, as slowly as you need to in order to be able to keep the full group in your awareness.

After you have the full set of stones in your mind, allow the awareness of them to sink into your body, to merge with your awareness of your body and your personhood. Bring your consciousness back to your self. When you're ready, end the exercise by gently removing (or having your partner remove) one stone at a time. When you're finished, wrap yourself in a warm blanket or cloak and eat something hearty and simple—bread is a good choice.

You can add the eight stones back into your collection for the next exercise, or save them for an Earth altar or for a future ritual.

Exercise Four: A Small Cairn

Your final exercise for Earth will take place over a long period of time and, in fact, can be maintained indefinitely.

Take your rock collection to a spot outdoors that you've already selected. This could be anywhere—your backyard, a secluded corner of a public park, a spot deep in the woods—anywhere that is accessible to you on a regular basis, because you'll be visiting this spot again. You're going to build a cairn—a marker made of a pile of stones. For your first layer, set the stones somewhat firmly in the ground; don't dig them in, but press down enough so that they're well in place.

Don't be in a hurry while building your cairn. Place each stone one at a time; don't use handfuls. Each stone was individually picked and should be individually placed.

When you're done, tell the local gnomes that this cairn belongs to them, and go away.

Now your task is simple. Return to your cairn from time to time, at least once for each spoke of the Year Wheel; that is, once for each part of the year marked by a Wiccan holiday.[3] You can visit more often if you like. You don't need to *do* anything when you visit your cairn; just observe it. Note how time and the season affect your stones. Note if some of them are gone or have moved.

This exercise is about the process of experiencing Earth over time. Your observations and feelings about them will come gradually, bit by bit. You'll be learning patience and steadiness in your behavior as you observe Earth in its own environment.

---

1. Don't get scientific on me! Yes, I know clouds are made of water. They are *of* Air, they are *in* the sky, and this *isn't* a technical manual!

2. Inasmuch as people who live in Arizona and New Mexico had an advantage for both the Air and Fire exercises, it is only fair that they have a disadvantage here.

3. The eight spokes on the Wheel of the Year represent the following eight Wiccan holidays: Beltane on May 1, Midsummer on June 21, Lughnasadh on August 1, Harvest Home on September 21, Samhain on October 31, Yule on December 21, Imbolc on February 2, and Ostara on March 21.

CHAPTER THREE

The Elements in Us

As described in chapter 1, elements exist within us as well as outside of us. Each of us has an elemental nature, and while it is true that all of us have all four elements within, it is also true that one or two elements will tend to dominate in each of us. There are people who are "earthy," people who are "airy," people who are "watery," and people who are "fiery." You've probably used one or more of those terms in casual conversation; their relationship with more serious elemental study is not coincidental.

YOUR ASTROLOGICAL ELEMENTS

One of the ways that Pagans and other magical people talk about the elements in personality is astrologically. Every astrological sign has, along with many other characteristics, an element associated with it:

The Elements in Astrology

Air Signs	Gemini, Libra, and Aquarius
Fire Signs	Aries, Leo, and Sagittarius
Water Signs	Cancer, Scorpio, and Pisces
Earth Signs	Taurus, Virgo, and Capricorn

So, an astrologer will say that a Taurus, Virgo, or Capricorn is "an Earth sign." Moreover, if you know a little about astrology, you know that every planet is in a sign. What most people think of as their sign is their Sun sign. You also have a Moon sign, a Rising sign (Ascendant), and so on. (You can find out a Sun sign just by knowing the birthday. For any other astrological information, you need the time and place of birth.[1]) The "big three" of astrology are the Sun, Moon, and Rising sign (the sign that was rising in the east at the time of birth).

In my birth chart, I have a Taurus Sun, a Capricorn Moon, and a Scorpio Ascendant. That means I'm a "double Earth" sign. My ex-husband has his Sun in Libra, and both his Moon and Ascendant are in Aquarius, which makes him a "triple Air" sign. This astrological information is a very handy indicator of how you relate to the elements, as well as what components dominate in your personality and in your perceptions of the world. People with a double, or especially a triple, influence of one element will show that element's qualities with particular intensity. Usually they will also show a distinct weakness in the other elements.

You can round out your astrological knowledge of the elements in your life if you know the placement of your remaining *inner planets:* Venus, Mars, and Mercury. Venus tells us who we are in romance, friendship, and in relationship to beauty and femininity. Mars tells us who we are in terms of aggression and drive, and in relation to masculinity. Mercury is how we communicate.

Don't think, though, that you have to become an astrologer in order to understand your elemental makeup! Later on in this chapter, we'll work with quizzes and checklists that will help you determine how much of each element is present in your personality, and where your strengths and weaknesses are. These quizzes and lists will also pinpoint the location of elemental weaknesses and strengths in various aspects of life, such as romance, work, and home. Instead of using a tool (astrology) that tells you where the elements are, and therefore what you are like, we'll use tools (quizzes and lists) that will ask you what you are like, and therefore where the elements dominate or are under-utilized.

For now, though, let's chart out the basic ways in which elements define who we are.

ELEMENTAL QUALITIES OF THE SELF

To begin with, let's look at the basic human qualities associated with each element.

Basic Human Qualities

	Part of Body	*Part of Self*
Air	Lungs, breath	Thought, intellect
Fire	Fever, body temperature, nervous system, immune system	Will, life force
Water	Bodily fluids: blood, sweat, tears, amniotic fluid, menstrual blood, mother's milk, sexual fluids (male and female), urine	Emotions, the subconscious
Earth	All solid parts of the body: flesh, muscle, bones, organs, tissue	Physical body

Note that there is some overlap. As a *part of the self*, the entire body is Earth, but as *parts of the body*, some solid parts (such as the lungs) are associated with another element.

Our main focus is on the *parts of the self* section of the chart. The *parts of the body* can also be useful in a number of ways. For example, if you were healing a blood disorder, you might focus more on Water, whereas if you were healing a nervous disorder, you might focus on Fire. However, for the purposes of this book, we are primarily interested in the aspects of *being a person*, of self-improvement and self-actualization, and of magic. For these, the parts of the self are more important.

These elemental parts of the self relate quite clearly to things like the Witches' Pyramid and the time- and process-related elemental attributions. Look at the following chart:

Connected Concepts of Elemental Attributions

	Air	*Fire*	*Water*	*Earth*
Part of Self	Thought, intellect	Will, life force	Emotions, the subconscious	Physical body
Witches' Pyramid	To Know	To Will	To Dare	To Remain Silent
Part of Process	Beginning, originating idea	Empowerment, growth, taking action, transformation	Becoming, intuition, "evolution," risk taking	Completion, result, "having"
Time of Day	Dawn	Noon	Sunset	Midnight
Season	Spring	Summer	Fall	Winter
Direction	East	South	West	North
Part of Plant	Seed	Sprout	Sap	Harvested plant (food)

The concepts connecting Air are *thought* and *beginnings*. Things begin with ideas. When you first get an idea, you say, "Something just *dawned* on me." That's the beginning, the time of day, and the thought, all in one common saying. Dawn happens in the east, spring is the dawn of the year (and the original New Year—this is the reason that Aries is the first sign of the Zodiac), and a seed is the beginning of a plant's life cycle. For that matter, a *seed* is another common metaphor for a beginning or an idea.

The concepts that connect Fire are *heat, transformation,* and *will.* The life force is the *will* to live. The phrase "a burning will to live" is a common cliché that associates will with fire. Fire transforms and anneals. This force, this *spark,* gets things going. Ideas can remain simply fantasies; they go nowhere without the application of will. So it is Fire that causes growth. Summer and noon are both hot, and summer is also the time of lush, green growth. In the Northern Hemisphere, south is the hottest direction, and the direction that sunrise has moved toward by midsummer.

The concepts connecting the Water attributions are *flow* and *the subconscious*. In fact, Water, which has arguably the largest, widest-ranging list of attributions, also has the simplest, most unifying explanation. Water is the subconscious. The subconscious has often been described as a "pool" or as the "depths"; subconscious thoughts are those that occur "beneath the surface." These are all Water images. From the deep, dark pool of the subconscious, we get a long list of associations, including feelings, mysteries, intuition, dreams, and anything that has flowing movement or liquid at its core.

The connecting concepts for Earth are *physicality* and *silence*. Earth is the physical manifestation of whatever it is a part of. In a person, it is the body. In a plant, it is the harvest. In a process, it is the completion. In creation, it is the product. Earth is also silent, I think, because that which is solid is still, and rooted. The Earth exercises from the previous chapter are all about patience and stillness—they don't lend themselves to noise or conversation. Midnight and the winter are silent times, times requiring patience while waiting for warmth and light to return.

Now that we've seen how the element of Earth is connected to the earthy qualities in a person (and so on for each of the other three elements), let's take a quiz to get some more information about how the elements manifest themselves in our psyches.

Your Personal Element Quiz

Follow the instructions in each section. Choose the answer that seems best for you. Sometimes more than one answer may seem true, and sometimes none of them may seem quite right, but choose the one that fits you best.

Section One: Multiple Choice

For each question, choose just one answer:

1. If I could choose only one of the following, I'd take . . .

____ a. Power
____ b. Love
____ c. Wealth
____ d. Genius

2. When I am confused, my preferred decision-making method is to . . .

____ a. Make a list of the pros and cons and do what scores best.
____ b. Do whatever has worked in the past.
____ c. Go with my first instinct, whatever it is.
____ d. Examine how I feel about the situation and do what feels right.

3. If that doesn't work, I might . . .

____ a. Do some research on the issue.
____ b. Meditate or do a Tarot reading.
____ c. Ask the advice of someone who has been in a similar situation.
____ d. What do you mean? Of course it will work!

4. After a hard day at work, I usually prefer to . . .

____ a. Read a good book.
____ b. Cuddle up under a fuzzy blanket.
____ c. Talk to a friend about everything that happened.
____ d. Take a soothing, soaking bath.
____ e. Go out and have some fun.

___ g. Make love.

___ h. Have a nice glass of wine.

___ i. Eat some "comfort food."

5. The people I respect the most are . . .

___ a. Intelligent.

___ b. Charismatic.

___ c. Compassionate.

___ d. Sensible.

6. The people who baffle me are the ones who . . .

___ a. Prefer to be alone almost all of the time.

___ b. Don't care to educate themselves.

___ c. Have no mementos, souvenirs, or other precious keepsakes.

___ d. Don't play games to win.

7. I could never be . . .

___ a. A vagabond (wandering about with no home and few possessions).

___ b. A hermit (entirely alone).

___ c. A monk under a vow of silence.

___ d. Celibate.

8. I admit I have a hard time with . . .

___ a. Humility.

___ b. Discretion.

___ c. Possessiveness.

___ d. Moodiness.

9. When I'm upset, I . . .

___ a. Cry.

___ b. Yell.

___ c. Distract myself—think about something else, watch TV, or read a book.

___ d. Eat or sleep.

Section Two: Choose All that Apply

Check as many answers as are true for you.

10. People like me because . . .

____ a. I'm nurturing.

_X_ b. I'm witty.

_X_ c. I'm a good listener.

_X_ d. I'm the life of the party.

_X_ e. I'm smart.

____ f. My door is always open.

____ g. I'm caring.

____ h. I'm brave.

11. But behind my back, I bet they say . . .

____ a. I'm an airhead.

_X_ b. I'm a stick-in-the-mud.

_X_ c. I'm a hothead.

____ d. I'm a crybaby.

_X_ e. I'm bull-headed.

____ f. I have my head in the clouds.

_X_ g. I'm bossy.

_X_ h. I'm moody.

Section Three: True or False

_F_ 12. If it doesn't make sense but it feels right, I'll do it.

_F_ 13. I would never go somewhere if I didn't know how I was getting home.

_F_ 14. Taking action without some kind of plan is crazy.

_T_ 15. Privacy is very important to me.

_T_ 16. You can never have too many facts at your disposal.

_T_ 17. If you know you're right, you don't need others to agree with you.

_T_ 18. I believe in embracing opportunities; you shouldn't wait to see what the consequences will be.

_F_ 19. It's important to me to be a part of a family, even if I have to put up with difficult people.

___T___ 20. Choosing to love and be loved is always worthwhile, even though sometimes you or someone else gets hurt.

___T___ 21. I have to speak my mind—honesty is more important than hurting someone's feelings.

Answers

1. a = Fire ✗
   b = Water
   c = Earth
   d = Air

2. a = Air ✗
   b = Earth
   c = Fire
   d = Water

3. a = Air ✗
   b = Water
   c = Earth
   d = Fire

4. a = Air
   b = Earth ✗
   c = Air
   d = Water
   e = Fire
   f = Fire ✗
   g = Water ✗
   h = Earth

5. a = Air ✗
   b = Fire
   c = Water
   d = Earth

6. a = Water
   b = Air ✗
   c = Earth
   d = Fire

7. a = Earth
   b = Water
   c = Air
   d = Fire ✗

8. a = Fire ✗
   b = Air
   c = Earth
   d = Water

9. a = Water
   b = Fire ✓
   c = Air
   d = Earth

10. a = Earth
    b = Air ✗
    c = Water ✗
    d = Fire ✗
    e = Air ✗
    f = Earth
    g = Water
    h = Fire

11. a = Air
    b = Earth ✗
    c = Fire ✗
    d = Water
    e = Earth ✗
    f = Air
    g = Fire ✗
    h = Water ✗

Score for True answers only:

12. One each for Water & Fire
13. Earth
14. One each for Earth & Air
15. Water ✗
16. Air ✗
17. Fire ✗
18. Fire ✗
19. Earth
20. Water
21. Air

A = 7
E = 3
F = 10
W = 4

A = 8
E = 4
F 2
w = 8

Determining Your Elemental Makeup

Count up your answers and see how many points you scored in each element. Most people will notice a strength in one or two elements, and a distinct weakness in one or two. Each of us is a unique blend, and no one is all of one element to the exclusion of the others. However, even very balanced people will notice a slight tilt toward or away from an element.

My score is: Fire, 8; Water, 7; Earth, 6; and Air, 5. Overall that's pretty darned balanced, and I have to say, I like my Fire. However, I can see that I need to strengthen my Air, and maybe even build up my Earth.

My son, Arthur, scored Air, 8; Water, 5; Earth, 4; and Fire, 1. It looks like Arthur is very Airy but might need to build up the other elements, especially Fire.

In chapter 4, we'll talk about making changes that can shift your elemental balance. For now, just make a note of your score. Look at both your primary and secondary element. My primary element is Fire, with Water secondary. Arthur has a primary element of Air, with Water secondary. Also make a note of your weakest element: mine is Air, and Arthur's is definitely Fire.

The Four Elemental Personalities

On the following pages, you'll learn what it means to be an Earth or Air or Fire or Water person. Since you aren't *just* your dominant element, none of the character sketches will describe you perfectly; however, they ought to give you some insight and understanding that will carry over into chapter 4 and beyond.

Elemental Personal Traits

	Positive Qualities	Negative Qualities	Experiences	Roles, Jobs
Air	Thoughtful, studious, witty, free, animated, lighthearted, open, open-minded, rational	"Airhead," "spaced-out," impractical, "flaky," unreliable	Inspiration, ideas, imagination, language, speech, multi-tasking	Scholars, educators, students, communicators, writers

	Positive Qualities	*Negative Qualities*	*Experiences*	*Roles, Jobs*
Fire	Willful, passionate, intense, spontaneous, exciting, dominant	Impulsive, hot-tempered, "hotheaded," obsessive, violent	Lust, desire, transformation, passion, intense focus, outbursts	Leaders, warriors, salespeople, healers, smiths, artists
Water	Sensitive, fluid, mysterious, dramatic, sensual, generous, empathic, compassionate	Inconsistent, over-sensitive, tearful, a "wet rag," depressed, psychotic, addictive	Dreams, visions, secrecy, emotion, falling in love, menstruation, childbirth, lactation	Therapists and counselors, clergy, midwives, doulas, morticians, theater
Earth	Stable, patient, enduring, realistic, tactile, rooted, practical	stubborn, "stick-in-the-mud," dull, resistant to change	commitment, pragmatism, home, family, pregnancy	Farmers, builders, engineers, artisans, homemakers, nannies, manufacturers, parents

The Air Person

The Air person thinks before he feels, and sometimes thinks *instead* of feeling. He is rational and often quite clever. Some Air people are quiet, studious, and bookish, but Air is the element of speech, so Air people can also be entertaining, spinning colorful stories and being great wits who delight in wordplay. Their gift with words may lead them to writing or communications as a career, and particularly glib Air people are excellent marketers. The Air person is often proud of his ability to think things through, and may even have disdain for those who rely on feeling or intuition.

Air people can be quite abstract, seeing things in broad strokes, seeing "the big picture." As such, they are excellent theorists, philosophers, economists, and politicians—people who must see life in its systems and structures, rather than in individuals and details. Sometimes they can be radical thinkers, because they don't necessarily value experience over theory, nor do they worry about how things have always been done. Tradition means little to the free-thinking Air individual.

Air people also excel at doing several things at once, or keeping several ideas in their head at once—"keeping many balls in the air." There is an exception: some Air folks are too easily distracted. Multiple tasks scatter them, like seeds in the wind. Attention-Deficit/Hyperactivity Disorder (AD/HD) is an Air problem. Such Air people are at their best when using their powers of thought to concentrate intensely on just one task at a time.

The stereotype of the absent-minded professor is pure Air. He is brilliant, even dazzling, but utterly impractical. He is the genius with untied shoes who misses appointments. He is the "science geek" whose brilliance doesn't seem to apply to the real world. The Air person has charm, but often lacks social graces (which are based on following rules to which he pays little attention).

Since commitment doesn't come naturally to Air (picture tying down the wind), and since they aren't generally in touch with their feelings, Air people can have difficulty in relationships.

They are generally poor housekeepers, having a sort of scattered style, "as if a windstorm hit the place," as some Air person's mother once said. If they *do* keep a tidy home, they do so in a systematized way. They can become very disconnected from people and the normal concerns of day-to-day life, and be poorer for it.

However, the Air person can choose to balance his airy nature with relatedness and practicality and enrich his life.

The Fire Person

Fire people are impassioned, they are "on fire," whether with ideas, goals, or causes. They are natural leaders, as they convey their passions with an intensity that compels others to pay attention. Fire people can be as fascinating, as hypnotic, as watching a campfire. In politics, a Fire candidate might have an Air strategist working beside him, but it's Fire's face that will appear in the TV spots.

Rather than thinking, like an Air person, or feeling, like a Water person, the Fire person "just knows." He goes by his gut and once he is sure of something, he doesn't waver. He commits fully to whatever his passion is.

The Fire person "lights up a room." He has a "burning" presence. Of the four elemental characters, Fire is the most interesting and exciting to be around. Arguably, he is also the most dynamic sexually, as his nature is to be lustful and desirous. He's an impassioned and devoted lover, and may tend toward flamboyant romantic gestures.

His heat and passion can become negative. He can be hot-tempered, prone to rage, and even violent. His combination of lust and impulsiveness might make him unfaithful, and his utter faith in his gut instinct might make him self-righteous, barreling past the considerations and concerns of others. With his knack for passionate focus, he runs the risk of becoming obsessive. Fire is also impulsive, which is neither good nor bad; it depends on the situation, and it depends on the Fire individual and how he expresses it.

Fire people also have the gift of transformation. They can turn their negativity into a new, more positive way of being. They can choose to take in other elements, thereby assuring they won't burn out.

The Water Person

The Water person feels first and foremost. "Thinking never solved anything—only our hearts should be our guides!" She has a great facility with feeling; she is compassionate, caring, and a great listener. Water people can be wonderful therapists. They "go with the flow," but don't flit about like Air people. Their movements have a definite path, albeit an often unexpected one.

The Water person's open heart makes her generous, and her empathy can make her quite social, although not all Water people are "bubbly." She is often very dreamy, and can be mystical. Water people are strikingly magical, even among other magical folk—they meditate, light incense, take steamy baths, wear consecrated herb bags, and so on (not that others don't do these things, but Water people, in my experience, do them *more*). Water people are often artistic as well, and are especially found among painters and musicians.

Water people often move with a sensual grace that reminds one of their element, and often have wide, open eyes, the kind that look deep and liquid. Very Watery people often dress in flowing clothes or have flowing accessories. They can have a mysterious quality that is compelling to those around them. Some Water people are dark, brooding, and perhaps even silent, an inward rather than outward Water manifestation.

Romance comes naturally to Water people; they give and receive love easily. Some share themselves effusively, and some are very secretive, withholding information while being open with emotion. Perhaps surprisingly, not all romantic Water types are particularly sexual; many find the physicality of sex to be a distraction from love's emotional and spiritual nature.

All that feeling can lead to its share of problems. Depression and addiction are Watery illnesses, and flowing with dark, negative feelings can make some Water people irrational, or even psychotic. More likely, the Water person will simply be prone to tears, often needing to "get serious" at moments when others would prefer to be lighthearted. They can be as inconsistent as the tides, changing their minds the way Earth people change their socks. Their wonderful sensitivity can go overboard, making them perceive every offhand remark as a major emotional statement.

The Water person can choose to balance herself. Water needs to be offset by rationality, decisiveness, and groundedness. With some balance, the Water person can follow her flowing nature, and be happier for it.

The Earth Person

The Earth person cares about what is real, physical, and experiential. She learns by doing. She doesn't care for "pie in the sky," and she isn't a dreamer. Her goals are achievable, and she is patient and methodical in working toward them. She likes things that are real, things that she can touch; which will show even in her aesthetics. If she is an artist, she will be drawn toward things like sculpture, or toward handcrafts, which have a "product" as an end result.

She loves her home, and although it may or may not be tidy, it is a welcoming place, with comfortable chairs, plenty to eat, and pictures on the walls. The Earth person has a highly developed nesting instinct; her home is always a touchstone, she always wants to return to it, and being "settled" is her favorite state. She may very well live near where she grew up, as her sense of rootedness is quite meaningful to her.

The Earth person commits readily—she doesn't experience much conflict when choosing to commit, and may not see it as having negative aspects. Her friendships, romances, and jobs will all tend to be long-lasting. She doesn't mind tedium, and is patient and tolerant of the "rough spots" in a relationship. Romantically, Earth people are marriage-minded; they think in the long term and are generally faithful. They are unabashedly physical and enjoy their sexuality.

Earth people are at home in their bodies, not just sexually. They touch readily; a hand on the arm, a pat on the back, or a sympathetic hug are the natural communication media of Earth. They enjoy the physical, even the vulgar, and they love to laugh.

Earth people can be stubborn and bull-headed. They can refuse to change their minds or their ways, even when they're obviously stuck and *need* to change. They can be difficult to argue with, sticking to their position tenaciously for no other reason than it's *their position*. Likewise, an Earth person can be difficult to get out of the house. Earth people are the ones whose friends drag them to parties because otherwise they'd just stay in every night. Their lives can become an endless rut.

Earth people also have an unfortunate tendency toward obesity. Although some love to exercise, and recognize it as a basically *physical* activity, many don't—there's a lot of Fire in exercise. Probably the unhealthiest Earth people are the ones who stay in terrible, even abusive, situations because they fear change. Agoraphobia—literally a fear of open spaces, but really closer to a fear of leaving the house—is a debilitating Earth disorder.

An Earth person can choose to become balanced, adding Fire, Water, and Air to her makeup for a happier and healthier life.

Elemental Pairings

When looking at personality traits in relation to the elements, it often happens that elements pair up, and the four elements look like two sets of opposite. For example, Water and Earth are the humanistic pair—they are connected, they relate to others. For Water, one can view this as empathy and emotion, and for Earth, one might see a more physical connection—warmth, touch, family. The opposite pair is abstract: Fire and Air. With Air, it is the abstraction of ideas, and with Fire, of *ideals*, but both look past the human to the "big picture."

Here are some elemental pairings:

Rational	*Irrational*
Air and Water	Fire and Earth

This is in the Jungian sense, and doesn't mean that Fire and Earth are irrational in the conventional sense. (See the next section.)

Unconventional	*Conventional*
Air and Water	Fire and Earth

Fire and Earth have more interest in rules, laws, and traditions. Air and Water march to their own drumbeat and might not even be aware of the expected way of doing things.

High libido   **Average or low libido**

Fire and Earth   Air and Water

Fire is lustful and Earth is physical. Both value sexual contact for their own reasons. Water can see sex as a distraction from real or spiritual love, and Air can become disconnected from the body entirely.

Creative   **Methodical**

Fire and Water   Earth and Air

Fire's burst and Water's flow can be seen as creative; Earth's structure and Air's logic can be seen as methodical. Projects "just happen" with Fire and Water, whereas Earth and Air tend to follow a systematic approach.

Impulsive   **Planned**

Fire and Water   Earth and Air

This pairing is similar to creative/methodical, except that it relates to behavior rather than projects.

Verbal   **Silent**

Air and Fire   Water and Earth

Air is naturally verbal, and Fire likes to make bold statements. Both Water and Earth are more comfortable with silence.

Social   **Solitary**

Fire and Water   Earth and Air

Fire and Water gain energy from being around people. Earth and Air need solitary time for rejuvenation.

Abstract   **Humanistic**

Air and Fire   Water and Earth

Air's ideas and Fire's ideals are abstract; looking past the human to the "big picture." Water and Earth relate and connect. For Water, it's empathy and emotion, and for Earth, it's touch and family.

THE SIXTEEN BASIC PERSONALITY TYPES

By combining two elemental characteristics—your personality type, revealed in the Personal Element Quiz that you took in the previous section, and your current life role, which you will determine in the Elemental Life Role Quiz in the next section—sixteen elemental character types can be described. In studying this, I've found it interesting that the famous Myers-Briggs test also has an elemental basis and also has sixteen basic personality types.

The Jung at Heart

The seminal psychologist Carl Jung (1875–1961) identified four functions of the personality, which correspond to the four elements. This wasn't a coincidence; Jung studied alchemy, astrology, Tarot, and other spiritual disciplines, and was well versed in Greek philosophy, alchemical humors, and so on. He added the insight he gained studying these topics to his psychological theories, and his understanding of psychology influenced his interpretation of the occult material he studied.

Here are the four Jungian functions:

- **Thinking** corresponds to Air. Thinking is one of the "rational" types, meaning that thinkers *judge* rather than simply *perceive*. (To judge is to decide with finality; to perceive is to stay in the moment, and retain an open mind.) Thinkers make their evaluations through intellectual input and have a tendency to be out of touch with feeling (their opposite).

- **Feeling** corresponds to Water. Feelers are also rational, and judge based upon emotional reactions. Feelers are sensitive to moods in people or situations, but have a tendency to get muddled in an intellectual situation.

- **Sensing** corresponds to Earth. Sensation is considered "irrational" because those who primarily sense are more interested in perceiving than deciding. They experience through sensation and pragmatism. They have a tendency to be weak in the intuitive function (their opposite).

- **Intuiting** corresponds to Fire. Intuiters are irrational, perceiving based on gut instinct and possibility. They look more toward the future than the present. Sensation—that is, reality—is their weakness.

Jung also determined that each individual had a basic orientation inward or out-ward, which he called **introversion** or **extraversion** (the spelling was later changed to extroversion). Although all people are sometimes social and sometimes in need of alone time, Jung saw the difference as being how your energy flows. Extroverts are energized by being among people, and introverts are drained by it. Introverts renew their energy by being alone, and extroverts become enervated by solitude. It's inter-esting that Jung saw energy moving in two directions, inward and outward, in per-sonalities that parallel the elements, while Empedocles saw energy moving in two di-rections, love and strife, and he applied this to *all* elemental interactions.

Like Empedocles, Jung saw that combining his polarity with his elements created life as we know it. By multiplying each function by each orientation, Jung came up with eight basic personality types:

- Introverted Thinking
- Introverted Feeling
- Introverted Sensing
- Introverted Intuiting
- Extraverted Thinking
- Extraverted Feeling
- Extraverted Sensing
- Extraverted Intuiting

Myers-Briggs

In the 1950s, the mother-daughter team of Katharine Cook Briggs and Isabel Briggs Myers reshaped Jung's four functions and polarity and came up with sixteen, rather than eight, personality types. The result, the Myers-Briggs Personality Type Indica-tor, differs from Jung's original theory in some interesting ways.[2]

First, they turned each function into its own polarity, so that not only is Intro-version/Extraversion a polarity, but so is Thinking/Feeling and Intuition/Sensation (recall that these latter pairs were considered opposites by Jung; the first pair, ratio-nal opposites, and the second pair, irrational opposites). Then they separated the ra-tional/irrational polarity, which Jung had considered an inherent part of the four functions, into its own polarity: Judging/Perceiving (with judging being the rational mode and perceiving the irrational mode, as described in the previous section). With four pairs of opposites, it was now possible to come up with sixteen distinct types.

The Myers-Briggs survey asks questions that place your position in each polarity, determining if you're more introverted than extraverted, more sensing than intuitive, and so on. The basic questions are as follows:

- **E/I—Extraversion/Introversion:** Is your *energy* mostly directed outward (extraversion) or inward (introversion)? Do you feel rejuvenated by speaking, acting, and interacting (extraversion) or by solitary thinking and/or feeling (introversion)?

- **S/N—Sensing/iNtuiting:** Do you *process information* based on known facts and tangible reality (sensation) or based on potential and the possible future (intuition)?

- **T/F—Thinking/Feeling:** Do you *make decisions* based on objective data and logic (thinking) or based on personal values (feeling)?

- **J/P—Judging/Perceiving:** Do you *organize your life* based on decisions you have made, preferring to know where you stand (judgment) or based on taking what comes, preferring to be flexible (perception)?

Based on your answers to these questions, you find yourself on the following chart of the sixteen Myers-Briggs personality types:

ENFJ	ENTJ	ESTJ	ESTP
ENFP	ENTP	ESFJ	ESFP
INFJ	INTJ	ISTJ	ISTP
INFP	INTP	ISFJ	ISFP

Followers of Jung are often not as occult-oriented as Jung himself was. We can see that the Myers-Briggs types do not conform as closely to elemental characteristics as Jung's original work. The Myers-Briggs test is a valuable one; many people find the description of their personality type to be startlingly accurate. (I'm an ESFJ, and I do find that descriptions of that type suit me to a T, or perhaps to an F.[3])

As intriguing as these personality types are, though, our concern here is to find ourselves in the elements. Since Myers-Briggs doesn't strictly adhere to elemental knowledge, it is less useful for our current work. However, it could be quite interesting to take the tests in this book as well as the Myers-Briggs test, and compare your answers for overlap and divergence.

For now, though, let's stick with a more mystical approach. The following quiz will show you the elemental role in life you're currently playing.

Your Elemental Life Role Quiz

Check each statement that is true for you right now. Check as many as you like.

____   1. I am currently changing my career or learning a new career.

____   2. I like to be in charge.

____   3. I am currently pregnant or lactating.

____   4. I am constantly trying to learn new things.

____   5. People always come to me for a shoulder to cry on or an ear to listen.

____   6. I am frequently in a hurry.

____   7. I am established in life and my role is secure.

____   8. I consider myself a grown-up.

____   9. I often act as a messenger between other people.

____   10. My career is really moving.

____   11. My main task is nurturing or helping others.

____   12. I am focused on action.

____   13. I know who I am and that's not going to change.

____   14. I am still in school.

____   15. I'd describe myself as "up and coming."

____   16. I like to be there for people as much as possible.

____   17. At this stage in my life, I really need things to happen.

____   18. I am just starting out in life.

____   19. I function mostly in the background or in a supportive role.

____   20. People look to me for answers or leadership.

Answers

1 = Air	11 = Water
2 = Earth	12 = Fire
3 = Water	13 = Earth
4 = Air	14 = Air
5 = Water	15 = Fire
6 = Fire	16 = Water
7 = Earth	17 = Fire
8 = Earth	18 = Air
9 = Air	19 = Water
10 = Fire	20 = Earth

Determining Your Current Life Role

Count the number of checked responses for each element. Whichever element shows up the most in your answers determines your role in life as it is today. If you happen to have a tie, use the descriptions in the next section to make your tie-breaking decision.

· If Air dominates, your role is **Page.**

· If Fire dominates, your role is **Knight.**

· If Water dominates, your role is **Queen.**

· If Earth dominates, your role is **King.**

LIFE ROLES IN THE TAROT

If you know a bit about Tarot cards, you know that every traditional Tarot deck contains sixteen "Court Cards."[4] There are four "characters" in each of four suits: Pages, Knights, Queens, and Kings (modern playing cards dropped Knights, and Pages became Jacks):

· Pages represent beginnings, messages, children and teens, students, and education.

· Knights represent young men in their twenties or early thirties, rapid movement, change, and "the coming or going of a matter."

- Queens represent women, motherhood, nurturance, support systems, and "home and hearth."
- Kings represent men in their late thirties or older, authority and establishment.

Determining Your Basic Elemental Character Type

It was my dear friend and former student Barbara Giacalone who first pointed out to me that the Court Cards correspond to the elements. Since the suits of the Tarot also correspond to the elements, each Court Card shows an element in the aspect of an element, as shown in the following chart:

Elemental Character Types

	Swords[5]	Wands	Cups	Pentacles
Pages	Air of Air	Fire of Air	Water of Air	Earth of Air
Knights	Air of Fire	Fire of Fire	Water of Fire	Earth of Fire
Queens	Air of Water	Fire of Water	Water of Water	Earth of Water
Kings	Air of Earth	Fire of Earth	Water of Earth	Earth of Earth

This chart shows the sixteen basic elemental character types. By combining the result of your Personal Element Quiz with the result of your Elemental Life Role Quiz, you'll find yourself on this chart. For example, on my Personal Element Quiz, my dominant element was Fire; on my Elemental Life Role Quiz, I scored highest for Earth/King. Therefore, I'm *Fire of Earth* (the King of Wands).

Keep in mind that the Court Cards are a jumping-off point. This is about your elements, this isn't a Tarot reading. In the Tarot, I tend to be the Queen of Swords, but a reading is its own thing. Remember what we said about correspondences in chapter 1; just because Earth *corresponds* to King doesn't mean Earth *is* King.

The Court Cards as Life Roles

I use the phrase "Life Roles" rather than "Life Stages" because not everyone will experience all four roles, whereas a stage is something we expect everyone to pass through. In particular, many people settle into a Queen role without experiencing much King, and vice versa.

Pages: The Role of Air

People who are living the Page role are often children or teens. They are either formally students or they are, in one way or another, in a learning, rather than doing, process. Although every one of us learns throughout life, the Page is learning things he *isn't yet doing*—the Page has not yet had a lot of direct experience in the area he is studying. Sometimes an older person will choose to restart life—ditching a career and going back to school, for example—and that person is a Page because, even though she has a lot of life experience, she isn't applying it at the moment.

In the Tarot, Pages are sometimes read as messages. I think this is not just because Page is the "Air" role and Air communicates, but also because the "in-between" part of life is a natural time to act and be perceived as a messenger. It's sometimes the case that people who are "always in the middle" are a little naive, and subject to manipulation by others. Sometimes it's not negative at all; the messenger simply has no agenda of her own, and is able to act as a go-between without adding any baggage.

A Page usually doesn't have a relationship of any significance. (If someone reverts to a Page role, he may have built a relationship during a non-Page part of life.) In a Wiccan or magical context, a Page is a seeker or a Dedicant.

Knights: The Role of Fire

The Knight role is when we are making our lives happen. People who are in the role of Fire are active, sometimes aggressive, in creating their lives, their relationships, and their careers. At work, they are "up and coming," doing whatever needs to be done to steer their career in the right direction. They probably don't see what they're doing as "the" job, but as a stepping stone to a better one. In relationships, they are seeking the right partner, or have a partner and are exploring if this will become permanent. They may want children, but do not yet have them. This is the time of life when some women hear their "biological clock" ticking with distressing volume!

In a Tarot reading, Knights sometimes represent movement, "the coming or going of a matter." In life, Knights are moving; they're not settled in any one spot. A Knight is far more likely than a King or Queen to relocate for a job or to conduct a long-distance relationship.

In the magical or Pagan part of life, a Knight is someone who has found her path and is pursuing it. Perhaps she is a first degree initiate and is working toward elevation. Perhaps she has decided to run her own grove and is seeking to build that. Or, she may have chosen a solitary path and is working magic regularly to increase her skill and experience, perhaps also networking with other solitaries.

Queens: The Role of Water

The person in a role of Water is functioning to emotionally, spiritually, and physically support and nurture someone(s) or something(s) in life. She is more focused on giving love or support than she is on any particular activity. That love may be quite *active*—there is nothing passive about being an at-home mom or someone else's second-in-command—but the idea behind it is nurturing and caring. (The language of the Tarot may be sexist, but I don't intend to be. Either men or women can be either Kings or Queens, although pregnancy, lactation, and being at home with a baby are Queen activities, making it more likely for women to be Queens at some point in their lives.)

The Queen's career may not be where she expresses her Watery role. Many people's jobs are just jobs after all, and if the Queen is absorbed by her social and emotional priorities, she may have decided that work is just the thing that pays the bills. Lots of Wiccan Priestesses do this, for example, putting so much focus on their creative and supportive work in Wicca that their 9-to-5 lives just can't compete for their interest and passion.

The important thing to know about the Water role is that it can be expressive, creative, impassioned, or thoughtful, but it is always *giving*. The Queen simply doesn't put herself first; she has a partner, children, students, a boss, or a cause that she puts ahead of herself. Because of this, when a Queen *does* focus entirely on her own needs, it is sometimes not in her own best interests.

In Wicca, a Queen is often a Priestess. As a solitary, she may be devoted to the Goddess or to one particular deity and focus her rituals on devotional worship.

Kings: The Role of Earth

Both Kings and Queens are "grown-ups," but only the King is really in charge. The King is the life role that is established, secure, solid, and authoritative. Some people never get there, but many do. They may not be captains of industry, but they are in charge of their own lives, unlikely to change, not *desirous* of change, and at peace with the way their lives have turned out. It is unlikely for you to be a King under the age of forty.

If a King has children, either he is not the primary caretaker, or his children are old enough that nurturing is not his main concern. A King is usually married, in a long-term relationship, or just not interested in being in a relationship. He is probably satisfied with his career, but if not, he's settled—he's not looking to move or change it much; he's not on the fast track. In the Craft, he takes an "elder" role, and he probably gives valuable advice.

Even Kings don't have everything they want. When a King lacks something, he tends to seek it methodically, as if with a shopping list. The focus is not on the seeking, but on the having.

In the Tarot, the King is often your path to something—he's the boss, the judge, the loan officer; the person you have to get through or around in order to get what you want. He is also the mentor, the guide, the sage. All of these roles are Earth roles, bespeaking a presence that is real, meaningful, and functional in a day-to-day, earthy way.

A King in Paganism might be a Priest (or Priestess) or a respected elder. He has stepped back from the active guidance of beginners, and works in a more advisory capacity.

The Sixteen Basic Elemental Character Types

Now let's sketch the sixteen basic elemental character types, and find ourselves in them. These types are a combination of who we are at the core (our Personal Element) and who we are in life right now (our Elemental Life Role). Since few if any of us will have quiz results that are entirely one element with no colorations of the other three, none of us are perfectly pigeonholed in the sixteen types. However, they're useful (and fun) to look at.

Air of Air: The Thoughtful Scholar

The Air person with an Air place in life is a thinker who is utterly involved with his thinking. Because he is in his natural milieu, there is a great deal of satisfaction in his life. He has little in the way of connections or relationships, but he is at a period in his life where he doesn't need them. Perhaps he imagines that he will acquire these things later on, or perhaps he doesn't notice the lack.

The Thoughtful Scholar analyzes each piece of life, of knowledge, that he comes across as if he were the very first one to ponder its meaning. His extreme Airiness makes him "above it all," perhaps even a bit of an intellectual snob. His nose might always be in a book, or he might be involved with grander plans, formulating theories and systems that books cannot contain.

Lacking in Earth, he is unkempt. His clothing and eating habits are haphazard at best. Lacking in Water, he is happily alone, but lacks an emotional outlet. His moods may be sudden and intense in order to compensate for how rarely they are given reign.

Because his Air is untempered, our Air of Air person can be glib, or even dishonest. His only priorities are his thoughts, words, and knowledge, and his sense of morality can easily get lost. On the other hand, his brilliance can be a gift, freely given.

Fire of Air: Let's Get Going

The combination of a Fire type with an Air role is a real go-getter! He brings boundless energies to new projects of all kinds. He may lack follow-through, but he sure knows how to get things started. He focuses on learning and on beginnings with an effective intensity and power. He may love to build things and may have little projects and hobbies throughout his home. Most might be unfinished, and many will never be finished, but some will benefit from his unwavering focus.

He can tend to exhaust those around him. Although a great organizer, he is the type who draws others to him and persuades them to participate in whatever it is he has his sights on, and his friends and associates may have trouble keeping up. He'll drag you to a party, or out to the woods to cut cordwood, or to some out-of-the-way, very spicy Mexican restaurant. At a Pagan festival, he's the one who can organize six guys to build a sweat lodge in no time flat.

Fire of Air is usually a very good-looking character. He has a youthful face full of brightness and, yes, fire. His eyes are bright and his skin has a ruddy look. His laugh is infectious. His flaws are Fire flaws—a hot temper, an excess of impulsiveness. This can be particularly difficult in the Fire of Air person, because Fire's flaws are often childish ones—tantrums, rash actions—and the Air role of life is usually a role of youth. Fire of Air's task is to mature past the Air stage in one piece.

Water of Air: The Dreamy Student

In the Air stage of life, the focus is on ideas, on learning, and often, on abstracts. The Water person is, among other things, a dreamer; someone conversant in and comfortable with the world of dreams. This combination creates a person lost in a dreamy, abstract world of ideas, imagination, and fantasy. "Castles in the air" are built by the Water of Air person—built, furnished, and populated.

Water of Air is the kind of person who stops mid-bite, fork in air, to stare off into space at the beautiful dream/idea she has just conceived. She can appear to be completely distracted, but it is her own conceptions, creativity, and inspirations that distract her. The Dreamy Student's comfort in a dream state makes her unaware that she is divorced from reality (at least the reality of which Earth people are so fond).

Depending on the individual, Dreamy Student can be immensely productive, creating constantly, or she can live in a world so fantastic that she fails to notice that her lovely ideas have not come to fruition. The danger for Water of Air is that she won't be able to distinguish between the inspiration and the end result. If you are in the Page part of life and the Personal Element Quiz earlier in this chapter showed you to be a Watery person, a lot depends on what element "came in second" on the quiz. If you have a good portion of Fire, you're more likely to get that creativity *out* (Fire is outward-directed, Water is inward-directed). If you have a good portion of Earth, you'll be able to distinguish fantasy from result. But if your secondary element is Air, your balance may be an issue. You may find yourself unable to produce, always having great ideas that never go anywhere, and you may be prone to sadness and disorientation.

In her explorations, Water of Air might choose to explore her own inner depths. This can be spiritually fulfilling or it can be very dark. A lot of youthful Goths and vampire fans are Water of Air people.

Earth of Air: Making It Add Up

Earth of Air has a pencil behind her ear and a notepad in her pocket. She is convinced that she is making the world work, and she has a formula for that. It all adds up, it's all worked out. Education has a purpose, and learning is an act of building—building up a knowledge base by which to achieve clear, established goals. She's well organized and moves forward in a methodical fashion.

Earth of Air rarely majors in liberal arts; she studies accounting or law, or goes to a trade school. She likes to do things with her hands, and even if her field is abstract, she'll enjoy holding the books and turning the matter into a real-world scenario. Law isn't "justice," it's problem-solving. Accounting isn't "numbers," it's my money and yours. The future is as real as the money.

The Earthy Page may have a hard time appreciating beauty and knowledge for its own sake, as she is far too busy implementing her plan for the rest of her life, which will be starting just as soon as she's finished getting it ready—and she will. Like all elemental combinations, Earth of Air has her flaws, but failure isn't one of them. She may never lead, but she will always manage. Without Fire, her successes will be merely ordinary successes, but they will satisfy her for at least the near future. Without Water, her life may lack beauty, and she may dress plainly and be uninteresting to her friends and acquaintances, but her Earth-Air combination will give shape and pragmatism to her ideas and beginnings.

Air of Fire: I Meant What I Said and I Said What I Meant!

The Air of Fire individual lives a life of movement ("like the wind") and words. He talks rapidly and often. He opines, negotiates, cajoles, and teases. He has the gift of gab—patter, spiel, pitch—and he uses it to get his way, to open doors, and to silence objection.

He can be argumentative and insistent, pushing himself forward with his Airy gifts. In the Fire life role, the Air person can be prone to shouting and arrogance, but he need not be negative. He can be funny, a sparkling wit, and full of play.

Air of Fire has thought his life through, and is moving, probably swiftly, through a series of logical steps. He has a plan. He is discerning and careful when making decisions, tempering the Fire of his life role with the thoughtfulness that is Air's boon. He can be judgmental in the cool, distant manner of Air, sitting back, letting you play out your hand, and giving you enough rope to hang yourself.

Air of Fire may have an almost James Bond approach to matters of taste, sampling the best of everything, analyzing, and deciding what he likes. For example, he may sample a wide variety of cuisines, but he is probably in the process of picking his favorites, and once picked, his taste may not vary much afterward. His decisions are final.

Fire of Fire: The Man of Action

Fire of Fire is a dynamo. He aggressively pursues several courses of action at once, at any given moment—he has lots of "irons in the fire." He is passionately interested in the things he does. The drive of his inner Fire combined with his Fiery role in life doubles the intensity of the most intense element. He burns.

Fire of Fire has many involvements. He may be very involved in community or political causes, and is attracted to activism. Fire people tend to believe in the power of the individual to effect great change, and this is especially apparent in the Fire Knight. He is a rescuer.

Like all Fire people, the Fire Knight is willful. In business matters, he is likely to be an entrepreneur, as he chafes under another's authority. He is convinced he knows best, and he is perfectly prepared to pay the consequences if he's wrong.

Romantically, Fire of Fire tends to be promiscuous. Knighthood is a lustful part of life, and Fire people are highly libidinous. The combination of youth, energy, and a taste for conquest combines with Fire's natural sexuality, passion, and desire for experimentation. The Fire of Fire person is the least likely Knight to settle into a monogamous, long-term relationship. Fire of Fire is unlikely to experience any shame or discomfort about his romantic choices, however. He is who he is.

Water of Fire: Prince Charming[6]

Water of Fire is a lover, not a fighter. His actions, his drives, and his aggression are focused around emotional, heart-based goals. He is Prince Charming, offering a loving cup. He has stars in his eyes as he seeks his perfect mate; he knows she's out there,[7] and if he thinks he has found her, he will pursue her with all the trappings of cinematic romance. Water of Fire brings flowers, leaves secret messages, and writes poetry.

Water of Fire's entire outlook is romantic, not merely in terms of relationships, but in terms of his way of looking at the world. Prince Charming has romantic values, is honorable, and is often spiritual as well. Water of Fire is idealistic—young enough not to have been hurt too badly by his ideals, which are still shiny and untarnished. He is loyal and compassionate, and he values his principles, his feelings, and, yes, his nobility above material gain or common sense.

His impracticality can get him into trouble, and his openness makes him easy to hurt. The ongoing drama of his loves and losses can sometimes become too much for those less Watery souls who know him. In general, though, if you can handle the ups and downs, Prince Charming is a good friend, always willing to commiserate and to take on your cause as his own.

Earth of Fire: One Step at a Time

By the time that Earth of Fire has gotten out of school, she's taken the pencil out from behind her ear and placed it firmly in her pocket. Of all the Knights, Earth is the only one who isn't in a hurry, who isn't antsy or rarin' to go. The Earth person handles the anxieties in the Fire life role by being *more* methodical, more cautious. In another role, the Earth person can lighten up, but for now, while in the process of building her life, Earth is a firm believer in being the tortoise of Aesop's fable: slow and steady is the Earth race.

Earth of Fire is reliable, steady, and comfortable. Romantically, she is the type who is often seen as a friend and overlooked as a lover. However, once she finds someone, she will start viewing the relationship—in her cautious way—as at least potentially permanent. By the time Earth of Fire marries, she is unlikely to have had many partners.

The Earth Knight might not seem too smart, but that's not because she lacks brains. She just lacks an inclination to be flashy, or to display knowledge she isn't sure of. It is a rare Earth Knight who is talkative or demonstrative. She might seem plodding and might even walk with her eyes downcast, staying close to the ground physically as well as metaphorically.

Air of Water: Tough Love

The Air of Water person is loving and generous, but not in the way you'd *want* him to be. He expresses his caring by rationally explaining the right thing to do, by communicating honestly and by being straightforward. Sometimes the Tough Love person is sharp-tongued, and people who don't know him well may think him unkind. In reality, he is sharing his honest perceptions and analysis because he knows those are the best things to give, or at least the best he has to offer. He can go overboard—at a moment when you want a hug, he can look you in the eye and tell you the hard truth instead. But his insight can be startlingly accurate.

He can be a fine friend (if you can take it) because he won't hold himself back. He has brought his analysis to his friendship with you, and has no illusions about who you are—so you can trust him with the real you. As a parent, he can be distant in the early months; he is more at home with verbal relationships, so the first year of life may be taxing.

Air of Water doesn't shy away from an argument, and brings considerable verbal resources to bear. Beware his sharp tongue! He can also be a cynic or even bitter. In general, Air of Water isn't a simple person; there's more to him than meets the eye. In the Tarot, the Queen of Swords is often "someone with a past," and this applies here—Air of Water has been gathering experiences and allowing those experiences to change him.

Fire of Water: Stoking the Hearth Fire

Perhaps surprisingly, the Fire person usually thrives in the Water role. Fire in this role becomes the warmth of the hearth, the passion in the bedroom, and the focus of the attentive parent.

Some Fire people chafe at the Watery role; they feel trapped and struggle to free themselves. But most of the time this is not the case. Water tempers Fire in a way that is often quite healthy. Fire's passionate focus falls on to the object of nurturance—the home, the child, the spouse, the job, or the cause. In this context, his heat warms but doesn't burn; there is a great deal of fulfillment within Fire of Water, and those around him will share in that fulfillment. Fire of Water can be a superb cook, an excellent healer, and a good friend. He has tempered his lust with the desire to give, and so is a superb lover.

Fire of Water can become *too* focused on nurturing and giving, in which case he is obsessively controlling, micromanaging every inch of the lives of the people he wishes to support. He is the parent who refuses to let a teenager choose any of her own clothing, the spouse who wants a detailed account of every moment of his partner's day, or the office assistant who is tyrannical in his need for perfectly filled-out forms. Fire of Water can start to believe that "there is a right way and a wrong way," and that he is the final authority on the right way. A household run by such a Fire Queen can be incredibly neat and well organized, but the people living under him may be full of fear.

Water of Water: My Cup Runneth Over

The Water Queen is overflowing with feeling. She loves without constraint. Her unconditional love is wonderful for her babies and her pets, but can sometimes be demanding or clinging with older children and adult friends and relatives.

She perceives her giving role with an almost mystical eye, perhaps seeing it as a higher purpose or a spiritual path. She imbues the role with creativity: birthdays are occasions for elaborately decorated cakes, Halloween is a time for exquisite hand-made costumes, and so on. Her home displays samples of her lavish creativity, if only in hand-sewn curtains. She is a delightful companion, appreciating "the little things," listening when you pour out your heart, and taking in stride sudden changes in plans. However, when she is ignored or unappreciated, she can be prone to sulking or silence.

Her open heart makes her a bit gullible, a "soft touch." She probably has more pets than she ever planned to have, as at some point she no doubt adopted the stereotypical "three-legged dog."

Water's secretive nature suits her role—her attention is on others, and she has no need to share her own feelings. However, her feelings are deep, and her unwillingness to express them can become dark, depressive, or paranoid.

She may or may not be a practical person. She might be the type who decorates her child's lunch bag with stars and glitter, but leaves out the milk money.

Water of Water inspires great affection. She is kind, compassionate, and attractive. She is cuddly with even casual acquaintances, stroking the hand of a friend while listening to his problems, patting the shoulder of a troubled co-worker, and, of course, kissing her spouse and children. Her partner finds her alluring and magical, but perhaps also baffling; he may be frustrated by her moods.

Earth of Water: Comfort Food

Earth of Water is a comfortable combination, and the Earth Queen is likely to be a comfortable person. She nurtures and loves in a way that is real and tactile. She may not be a gourmet cook, but she is a generous one—no one leaves Earth of Water's home hungry! Of the four Queens, it is the Earth Queen who is happiest in the at-home mom role, and she usually enjoys pregnancy as well. Earth people are at home in their own bodies, and don't shrink away from bodily processes—she doesn't mind diapers and messy children. As such, she is a natural in any job that is both nurturing and physical—she'd make a fine doctor, nurse, midwife, veterinarian, grade school teacher, chef, or massage therapist.

In a relationship, Earth of Water is deeply committed and sees the individual's flaws and the relationship's problems as less important than the commitment itself.

She can be tolerant and patient to a fault, meaning that while she's an ideal partner in a good marriage, she'll also stick with a bad relationship far too long. She is sometimes the wife who becomes more interested in her children than in her husband, but generally Earth of Water retains a healthy libido that is undiminished by familiarity. She may not be experimental, but she's always enthusiastic.

The Earth Queen is likely to be "everyone's mom," the Ann Landers of her group of friends. She might not be as compassionate a listener as Water of Water, but she's ready with a loving hug and some down-to-earth advice. Ever resourceful, she can help you figure out how to mount a cabinet, file for government aid, or find a qualified specialist.

The Earth Queen has a bad habit of letting her comfort express itself in overeating and a reluctance to exercise. The couch looks just fine, thanks. She can easily neglect her own health while caring for that of everyone else.

Air of Earth: The Judge/The Professor

Air of Earth is the authoritative reasoner. He is the judge, the systems analyst, the sober-voiced political commentator. He lets reason, fairness, and rationality be his guide in all things, and he uses those guides to make his decisions.

Another version of the Air of Earth type is the absent-minded professor. Here we see Air as less a force of decision and more a force of pure thought. Albert Einstein is the classic Air of Earth type—scatterbrained, disheveled, disconnected from emotional and earthly reality, and yet brilliantly authoritative in his highly intellectual field.

These two Air of Earth types *look* very different—the buttoned-down businessman type with his conservative white shirt and club tie, or the tweedy professor type with wild hair and elbow patches. But Air types never care all that much about their appearance, and both types merely throw on clothes appropriate to their position. Both are concerned with reason—one for what it produces and one for its own sake.

As a spouse or parent, Air of Earth can be distant or even cold. He functions by reason and he has little patience with those who expect something more or different. He is assiduously fair, and he considers his fairness an expression of goodness and decency. He tries hard to pay attention to the needs of home and family, but, by gosh, there's a lot on his mind. The concerns of people and their feelings rarely reach the top of his priority list.

Fire of Earth: The Tyrant/The Advocate

When Fire takes the leadership Earth role, he lets his instinct and his passions determine right and wrong. Once decided, he follows the right firmly and often rigidly. He can be small-minded in his myopic focus on the Right Way of doing, being, and behaving.

Most of us know this kind of Fire King, the stern, strict enforcer of rules who shows no mercy. We've all experienced bosses, teachers, parents, or partners who seemed to value obedience more than kindness.

But just because we remember such people with displeasure doesn't mean that's the only way that Fire of Earth manifests! The thing about this character is that he has the self-assurance, strength, and authority of Earth, and he brings to it the passion, the intuitive sense of rightness (or self-righteousness), and the burning focus of Fire. To paraphrase the nursery rhyme, when it's good, it's very, very good, but when it's bad, it's horrid. I'm sure that many historical tyrants have been Fire of Earth. On the other hand, the great men and women who have given their all to a cause, even to a hopeless cause, have also, often enough, been Fire of Earth. When Fire of Earth takes you on as a protege, as a friend, or as worthy in some way, you have all his power behind you. I like to think of the great advocates like Clarence Darrow as Fire of Earth, taking on lost or even crazy causes in order to make a point, in order to be on the side of right.

If Fire of Earth spends his Fire on important things, he'll have a softer warmth to bring to his family and friends. He is only harsh and difficult when his Fire isn't channeled into a really meaningful purpose. When he finds his purpose, he can accomplish great things.

Water of Earth: The Sage/The Creep

As with the two previous Kings, Water of Earth falls into two distinct personality types. In this case, one is decidedly good, and one is if not evil, then at least really creepy.

Most people who take on the Water of Earth persona embody the Sage, the wise advisor, the person of great insight. Their Earth role is like an island on their Watery nature, a stability that gives perspective and balance over the sometimes bumpy waves of Water's ocean. The Sage has a stable, even reserved exterior. Her face and manner are warm, and her smile is kind and sincere, but she keeps her own counsel—her role is to listen, not to reveal. In the process of reaching the Earth stage, she has mastered her inner waters, but not forgotten them. Her power is in the realms of feeling, mystery, and dreams. She is a sage, a therapist, a guide, or a Priestess. She has lived her life fully. Her distance is not coldness, but the nonjudgmental mirror that the wise present to those who need guidance, so that they see themselves and not their guide.

But Water of Earth doesn't always find firm balance above the water—sometimes she dives in. One hesitates to say that this dark figure is truly in the Earth life role, because she is hardly mature or a leader. Instead, this is a person of an Earth age who has thrown away the Earth influence. Diving deeply into the waters of her own fantasies, she is isolated and obsessed. Predators, stalkers, and dark figures in alleyways are this perversion of Water of Earth.

Thankfully, few Water people become so dark and unpleasant, and the majority of Water Kings have a great deal of goodness and warmth to share with the world.

Earth of Earth: The Banker/The Benefactor

Earth of Earth has achieved mastery over the material realm. Life has brought, and continues to bring, material satisfactions of the sort that can be fulfilling at a spiritual level. One may view Earth of Earth as superficial, and she may be, but she may also be deeply in touch with the abundance of Mother Nature and Her manifestations.

Earth of Earth is comfortable. She surrounds herself with good things; if she is not wealthy, her environment will still reflect a sense of luxury. She is not spare—no Japanese-style decorating for her. Her chairs have soft cushions, her kitchen is stocked, there are curtains on the windows, and there's money in the bank. Earth of Earth is concerned with security; she probably had a savings account, IRA, or 401K when her peers thought they were too young to bother with such things. Security is never a "bother" for Earth people, and she has her nest egg in order by the time she is old enough to be in the King role.

In authority, Earth of Earth is either the Benefactor or the Banker. As a Benefactor, she is generous and helpful. She is a mentor, a guide through a maze of rules or insider information, a help into the Old Boy's Network, and especially, a provider of financial assistance. She does all of this out of Earth's natural generosity.

As a Banker, she is a penny-pincher, a loan officer, a demander of exact accounting. She is Scrooge McDuck, and she never wants to let go of a dime that is hers. If she helps, she does so stingily and at a high rate of interest. This aspect is in the nature of Earth, too—possessive, greedy, and materialistic.

1. There are several computer programs and websites where you can plug in your time and place of birth and get your astrological chart. My favorite website is Astrodienst: http://www.astro.com.

2. For the full, official Myers-Briggs test, contact its publisher: Consulting Psychologists Press, Inc., 3803 East Bayshore Road, Palo Alto, CA 94303, (800) 624-1765 or (650) 969-8901, www.cpp-db.com.

3. An excellent write-up of the sixteen Myers-Briggs types can be found from Team Technology, Inc., at www.teamtechnology.co.uk/tt/t-articl/mb-simpl.htm.

4. There are hundreds of Tarot decks out there, some of which are very different from the traditional Tarot. I can't speak about *every* deck, so I'll use the Rider-Waite Tarot, designed by Arthur Edward Waite and illustrated by Pamela Colman-Smith, as my standard. Since it's the most popular deck in the world, that's a safe bet.

5. Since we're using the Rider-Waite deck, we're assigning Air to Swords and Fire to Wands.

6. Throughout the text, I've been referring to Air and Fire as male, and Water and Earth as female. However, calling the Knight of Cups "Prince Charming" is such common parlance among Tarot readers that I've chosen to keep him a Prince for this section.

7. Or she knows he's out there. Or he knows he's out there. Or she knows she's out there.

chapter four

Becoming Balanced

After reading the basic elemental profiles and reviewing the sixteen elemental character types in chapter 3, you know for sure that each element has good and bad qualities. We have already talked a bit about people who are "too Fiery" or who have "an excess of Water" or what have you. The obvious implication is that it's not the element itself that is the problem, but the *quantity* of that element. In other words, the element is *imbalanced*.

BALANCE: A PAGAN ESSENTIAL

In Paganism generally, and especially in Wicca, balance is emphasized. We are neither ascetics nor hedonists. As a religious group, we are not teetotalers, but we recognize the dangers of alcohol abuse. We are a sex-positive religion, but most Pagans choose to be monogamous (eventually) and to practice safe sex. *Balance*. Neither extreme is right, either magically or psychologically.

In "The Charge,"[1] it is said: "Let there be beauty and strength, power and compassion, honor and humility, mirth and reverence within you." As instructions from the Goddess, as a spiritual compass, and as good advice, this is the very essence of balance. Mirth is good, but reverence is also good. Too much mirth should be offset by a proper amount of reverence, and excess reverence should be tempered with a healthy dose of mirth.

Balance is nature's way. Day balances night, and if, at the summer solstice, there is much more day than night, it is balanced by its opposite, the winter solstice, when the scales of dark and light are reversed. In nature, growth is balanced by decay, youth is balanced by age, and planting is balanced by harvest. As we learn balance, and learn to live our lives in Nature's path, we learn to take the bad with the good, and become happier as a result.

In Wiccan ceremony, balance is always sought, and the elements in a well-put-together ceremony are always balanced. If the quarters are marked, all four are marked. If an element is represented on the altar, all four are represented. An object may be presented at the center of the circle, or it may be presented to all four quarters, but I've never seen an object presented to one, two, or three quarters!

BALANCE IS ADDITION

In ceremony, as just described, we balance our presentation or invocation by going to all four quarters, or putting all four elements on the altar. If at first we thought of invoking one quarter, it's unlikely that we'd say, "Oh, it has to be balanced—never mind then." In other words, we wouldn't subtract what we have (the invocation); we'd add what we don't have.

The same is true in your personal elemental makeup. If you're hot-tempered and have a tendency toward frequent, impulsive rage, you don't have "too much" Fire, you have Fire *unbalanced* by Water, Earth, or Air. The solution for you would be to increase the elements you're weak in, rather than trying to decrease your strengths.

All four elements are a natural part of your makeup. Trying to make one of them go away won't work, and isn't wise. It's like an amputation of a spiritual limb. In Paganism, we work *with* Nature, and the elements are Nature's building blocks. We don't want to push them away. We are more empowered when we choose to strengthen something rather than weaken something. Look again at the results of the Personal Element Quiz from chapter 3. It's unlikely that you scored a zero even in your weakest element. Even if you did, that element is within you and can be brought out, nurtured, and placed into better balance with the rest of you.

THE WAY OF FOUR

Ultimately, you'll want to do elemental work in all four elements, including those elements in which you are already strong. Again, this is part of being balanced, and it is also part of *knowing* the elements. As we know the elements, we know ourselves. The Way of Four is a way of combining outer and inner knowledge. We know the elements in nature, we know them in mysticism, we know them in our daily lives, and we know them in ourselves. The results are spiritual, intellectual, psychological, and pragmatic.

You can approach your elemental work in a number of ways. We have already looked at the elements in nature and in our personalities. In later chapters, we'll look at the elements in our day-to-day lives and in a ritual setting.

You can do the exercises in this book grouped by topic, which is how the chapters are laid out. That is, you can do all four groups of nature exercises, then all four personality-balancing exercises, and so on. Or, you can choose one element, and work it thoroughly for a while before moving on to the next. For example, you can do the Air in Nature exercises (chapter 2), followed by the Air Balancing exercise, the Meditation of Air, and finally the automatic writing exercise for Air, all of which are described later in this chapter. You might devote a full cycle of the Moon to each element in this way.

Remember, though, to take breaks between periods of intensive meditation. The Way of Four is a way of moderation, of balance. Don't spend more than a month fully absorbed in one element, or else that element will begin to extract a cost! (See the "Negative Elemental Qualities" section later in this chapter.) Restore yourself to a more balanced state periodically, between workings—use the Way of Four Meditation in appendix D whenever you need to restore your inner equilibrium.

POSITIVE ELEMENTAL QUALITIES

As you know, elemental qualities can be positive or negative. The following checklists will determine in which elements you have positive traits. (This will not necessarily match your personality traits from the Personal Element Quiz in the previous chapter.) This one isn't exactly a quiz—you know which item goes with which element in advance. You'll be referring back to these results later, and it would be hard to find what you're looking for if the answers were scrambled, as in a regular quiz. So, make an extra effort to be honest with yourself—don't assume you already know what the answers are.

Things I Like About Myself Quiz

AIR Things

____ I have a great library.

____ I am lighthearted.

____ I am able to detach when I need to.

____ I have good verbal skills.

____ I am precise.

____ I am unconventional.

____ I am well-read.

____ I am witty.

____ I think things through.

____ I am persuasive.

____ I am good at finding information; I do research well.

____ I am comfortable being alone.

____ I am a free thinker.

____ I am a good communicator.

____ I don't lose my head in an emergency.

____ I am a good teacher (not necessarily professionally).

____ I am skilled at visualization.

____ I can love without being possessive.

____ I am smart.

____ I am good at fixing things.

____ I don't miss details.

____ I am able to analyze pros and cons clearly.

____ I am open to new ideas.

____ I have a way with words.

____ I am good at planning things.

   My Air Total: __*III*__

FIRE Things

____ I am talented at magic.

__X__ I have a deep sense of freedom.

__X__ I have a distinctive personal style.

____ I am brave.

____ I am focused.

__X__ I am goal-oriented.

____ I am sexy.

____ I am healthy.

____ I am passionate.

__X__ I am creative.

____ I have a great social life.

____ I make things happen.

__X__ Sometimes I just know things.

____ I have lots of energy.

____ I am aware of what's going on in the world.

____ I am enthusiastic.

____ I am able to get my way.

____ I have leadership skills.

____ I have inner strength.

____ I don't have to get too bogged down in details in order to make up my mind.

____ I am true to myself.

____ People are drawn to me.

____ I am willing to fight for myself if needed.

____ You never know what I am going to do next.

____ I am comfortable with sudden changes of plan.

My Fire Total: __5__

WATER Things

_X_ I can keep a secret.

_X_ I am undemanding.

_X_ I am compassionate.

_X_ I don't hold back my feelings; I am free with my tears or my joy.

_X_ I am a good listener.

____ I'd bend over backwards to help someone who needed me.

_X_ My friendships are very deep and special.

____ I am a very loving person.

_X_ I give to charity.

____ I am graceful.

_X_ I am imaginative.

___ I am trustworthy.

_X_ I am musical.

_X_ I am a good diviner (Tarot, runes, scrying).

___ I have a healing talent (of some kind).

___ I take care of my appearance.

_X_ I am romantic.

_X_ I am not tied down to the clock.

_X_ I am forgiving.

___ I am kind to strangers.

_X_ I am generous.

___ I am empathic.

___ I am good with animals.

_X_ I am easygoing.

___ I am sensual.

   My Water Total: _15_

EARTH Things

___ My home is a place people enjoy coming to.

_X_ I am not afraid of hard work.

___ I feel good about my body.

___ I am not afraid of commitments and I keep the commitments I make.

___ I am handy around the house.

____ I love to dance.

____ I am cuddly.

____ I am family-oriented.

____ I am nurturing.

_X_ I am patient.

____ I am not easily fooled—I know B.S. when I hear it.

____ I am practical.

_X_ My friendships last for many years.

_Y_ I am grounded.

____ I am a good parent, or I am good with kids.

_X_ I am loyal.

____ I give great hugs.

____ I finish what I start.

____ I don't waste money.

____ I make people laugh.

____ I have a green thumb.

____ I keep my promises.

____ I can take the bad with the good; I have the strength to handle hard times.

____ I am a good cook.

____ I am sexually uninhibited.

My Earth Total: __5__

What did you find out? I bet you discovered you have positive qualities in all four elements![2] This is great news for you, because it means you have strengths in all four areas, which you can use to balance your weaknesses. If you have a weakness in Earth, for example, you can look again at your answers here to find your Earth strengths. In fact, a little later in this chapter, we'll use the positive qualities you discovered in yourself here as part of an elemental strengthening exercise.

NEGATIVE ELEMENTAL QUALITIES

Your connection to each of the four elements is a valuable thing in and of itself. That connection is not something that's just there to fix your personal flaws; it's part of knowing yourself and becoming closer to Nature and the Gods. That's why you should do *all* the exercises in chapter 2 and *all* the general elemental meditations later in this chapter, so that you get to know *all* the elements, not just the ones that these quizzes show could use bolstering.

All that being said, many of the things we don't like about ourselves *can* be connected to our relationship to the elements, and can be modified through balancing exercises.

How to Use the Balance Chart and Balance Worksheet

The following Balance Chart lists qualities that you might not like about yourself. You might call them "elemental flaws." For each negative trait, the element that dominates that trait is listed, as well as one or more elements that might soften or balance that trait.

Here's how to use the chart, using the first trait as an example. Stubbornness is an Earth trait. The chart shows that it can be balanced by Air (stubbornness is sometimes a refusal to listen to reason, and Air is reasonable) or by Water (Water is adaptable to change, so if your stubbornness is a resistance to change, Water diminishes it).

Only you will know exactly what your stubbornness is like, and therefore what it is best balanced by. Look at your totals for Air things and Water things on the Things I Like About Myself survey that you just took. You might find that you checked one or more traits that are a good balance to stubbornness, like "I am able to detach" (Air) or "I am easygoing" (Water). In that case, you've found a natural, positive counterpoint to your negative trait that is already there, that you're already aware of.

Even without a natural match, you'll find positive traits in Air and/or Water that feel intuitively, experientially, or logically as if they might work to balance stubbornness. Maybe "I am graceful" (Water) has no obvious connection to stubbornness, but it might be that when you feel stubborn, you also feel physically ill at ease, and so grace would be an effective way of changing the feeling.

Use the Balance Worksheet to make a note of what you discover. Write down the traits in yourself that you'd like to change or modify, and then write down the balancers among your positive traits. Don't feel trapped by what has been presented here. If you think of additional positive elemental qualities that you possess other than those listed, and you think they might bring balance, write them down as well. Remember that not all the balancers will be obvious matches/opposites—they'll just be the right ones for you.

Please note that some of the problems listed here are medical problems or are problems that require outside help. These exercises *cannot* and *should not* be considered a substitute for the assistance of a competent professional! There is no reason to believe that you can't seek medication for relief of, say, depression, and still do these exercises. Pagan practice works *with* science, not against it, and not usually instead of it.

Balance Chart

Negative Trait	Element of the Trait	Could Be Balanced by . . .
Addiction[3]	Water	Fire
Anger	Fire	Water or Air
Arrogance	Fire	Water
Attention deficit	Air	Earth or Fire
Boredom/In a rut	Earth	Fire
Depression	Water	Fire
Difficulty making decisions	Air	Fire or Earth
Gossip	Air	Water
Impractical	Air	Earth
Impulse control problems	Fire	Earth
Inability to finish things	Air	Fire or Earth
Inconsistent	Water	Earth
Laziness	Earth	Fire
Low self-esteem; self-hatred	Water	Fire or Earth
Moodiness	Water	Air or Earth
Obesity	Earth	Fire
Obsessiveness	Fire	Air
Procrastination	Air	Fire or Earth
Stubbornness	Earth	Air or Water
Unable to leave a bad situation	Earth	Fire or Air
Unreliability	Air	Earth
Violence	Fire	Water or Air

Now add your own:

Balance Worksheet

Negative Trait: _Attention Deficit_

Balanced by: _Earth- my friendships last for years/loyal_

_____

Negative Trait: _Depression_

Balanced by: _creative- goal oriented_

_____

Negative Trait: _gossip_

Balanced by: _, can keep secrets (sometimes)_

_____

Negative Trait: _Impractical_

Balanced by: _patient_

_____

Negative Trait: _Inability to finish things_

Balanced by: _God oriented / patient_

_____

Negative Trait: _low self esteem_

Balanced by: _creative, distinct personality style_

_____

Negative Trait: _procrastination_

Balanced by: _hard work / goal oriented_

_____

N – unreliability

P – long friendships

ELEMENTAL STRENGTH BALANCING EXERCISE

For this exercise, you'll choose one element at a time to work on. You can do the exercise as many times as you wish. A good schedule might be to do one element every night for a week, then take a break for a few days, and then do the next element. In our example from before, if you were working on stubbornness, you'd do Air the first week and Water the second week.

During the meditation part of the exercise, you'll be holding an appropriate elemental token. The token should fit comfortably in your hands or lap (although if you use a lit candle for Fire, you should have it on a stable surface, and just *look* at it). If you normally light candles as part of your meditations, then a candle as a Fire token might not be separate or different enough for this exercise. The same may be true for burning incense for Air.

Some Ideas for Elemental Tokens

Air   Feather
Fan (or a feathered fan)
Egg
Incense

Fire   Lit candle or oil lamp
Amber
Tiger's-eye

Water   Seashell
Coral
Driftwood
Bowl or cup of water

Earth   Stone (an ordinary stone such as granite, not a gemstone)
Bowl of potting soil
Dish of salt

If you have an idea for a token that isn't on this list, go ahead and use it. Some unusual elemental tokens I've used are: a small figurine of a whale for Water, a stone for Water (I found it at Lake Ontario; it is flattened and shaped by water), and a piece of petrified wood for Earth (stonelike strength and great age are both Earth things). You can also use one of the elemental magical tools (wand, athame, cup, and pentacle). However, you may want to keep a small altar just for your elemental workings, in which case using separate, permanent elemental items is a better idea than "borrowing" from your main ritual altar.

Preparation

- Decide which problem or trait most urgently needs work.
- Refer to your Balance Worksheet for positive qualities that address that problem. Select only qualities for one element; if your worksheet has more than one element represented for a single problem, work with the one that you're weakest in. Use the other one at a later time.
- If you'd like, write down the balancing positive statement(s) that you'll be using on a separate piece of paper or index card. An ideal number of statements is between one and three.
- Have your elemental token at hand.
- Set up a space for meditation in your usual method. If you normally light candles and burn incense, do that. If you play sitar music and sit on a special cushion, do that. (See appendix A for more on preparing to meditate.)

Example: Stubbornness

I'm in my meditation room. The phone is unplugged and my favorite frankincense-and-myrrh blend is burning. I'm working to balance this Earth problem with Air, and my eagle feather is in my right hand.[4] In my left hand is an index card that looks like this:

I am unconventional.
I think things through.

The Meditation

After whatever preliminary grounding, centering, or relaxation you normally do, you'll be chanting, intoning, reciting, or reading from the card. If you can memorize the statements, then you have the option of closing your eyes, but it isn't necessary. In this example, you would say the following:

Chant or speak the first statement: *I am unconventional.*

Chant or speak: *I am (Element).*

Chant or speak the second statement: *I think things through.*

Chant or speak: *I am (Element).*

Continue chanting or intoning as long as you'd like. It shouldn't take more than a couple of times through before you know it by heart and can close your eyes. Visualize the element filling you, being a part of you. Visualize the element coming to your aid when you need it (in this example, you'd visualize thinking something through instead of being stubborn about it).

Some people use meditation timers of some kind. For example, joss sticks burn out in about fifteen minutes; you can light one or a few when you begin.

When you're ready, say *So mote it be!* and end your meditation.

Example: Anti-Stubbornness Chant

I am unconventional.

I am Air.

I think things through.

I am Air.

I am unconventional.

I am Air.

I think things through.

I am Air.

I am unconventional.

I am Air.

I think things through.

I am Air.

GENERAL ELEMENTAL MEDITATIONS

These meditations aren't "corrective" like the elemental balancing exercise in the previous section. Instead, they're *deepening;* their purpose is to deepen your knowledge and experience of each element. The meditations in this section are sensory and experiential. You'll be going deep within and reaching out with your senses, exploring the inner realms.

You can work through all four meditations in order, or start at your weakest element and work toward your strongest; but over time, you should definitely do all four. Don't do more than one meditation in any given session—allow each to sink in. Put at least a day or two between each.

You'll find that these meditations, although brief, are more intense than the previous work. These will tend to fully immerse you in one element, and for most people, it can be a bit rattling, a bit *weird,* to be totally absorbed in Air, Fire, Water, or Earth. Coming out of the meditation can also be disconcerting. For that reason, consider doing this work with others, if you can. Having a guide, who isn't a part of the meditative trance, can be helpful in easing the transition back to normal reality. For that same purpose, each meditation is built with instructions at the end that reestablish you as a being of all four elements. Even if everyone is meditating together (see below), it can be supportive and grounding to do this work in a group.

Another precaution that you haven't needed before, but that is wise here, is to end your elemental meditation with something that counters the effect of the particular element. For Air, Fire, and Water, eating something works very well. Food, especially starchy food, is of Earth, and helps "shake off" the grip of the other elements. For an Earth meditation, try drinking ice water after it's all over to shock you out of Earth and into the balanced world of four elements.

How to Do These Meditations

These meditations can be done as part of a ritual or on their own. If the latter, they are done in a meditation space as described in appendix A. All of the meditations should be preceded by a grounding and centering, such as the one in appendix A.

Group: Reading

One person reads from this book while the others meditate.[5] Before doing this as a meditation, the person who will read should have reviewed the meditation a few times, reading it out loud at least once. This helps you find any words you might stumble over. If you need to, make a note to replace any phrases that are really problematic. For example, if you find yourself stumbling over the letter *f*, replace the alliterative phrase "Feel air fill you" from the beginning of the Air meditation with something easier for you to say, like "Allow air to imbue you" (a thesaurus can be useful for this).

Group: Recording

One person records the meditation from this book, and the tape is played for all. If you are using this method, record the grounding and centering from appendix A at the beginning of the same tape, so that they flow one into the other. When the grounding and centering ends and the elemental meditation begins, just keep talking as though they were part of the same thing. You can get really fancy with tape recordings, using music for cues and pauses (some suggestions are in appendix C). Of course, this requires rehearsal, but it's worth it.

When ending a recorded meditation, be sure to leave some blank lead time at the beginning and (especially) at the end (which can also have some instrumentation) so that the "click" of starting and stopping isn't jarring. A long lead time at the beginning also gives the person who starts the tape the opportunity to get back into a meditation posture.

Record one meditation and try it out before recording the other three. This will give you a feel for the rate of speaking and length of pauses used.

Solitary: Recording

This is essentially the same as a group recording. Once you've decided to record the meditation, it makes little difference if one or many are listening to it.

Solitary: Memorization

If you're not comfortable with any of the other options, you can simply work to memorize (more or less) one meditation, and then meditate on the images. Definitely only attempt to memorize one at a time.

With this method, you'll be memorizing a sequence of events and a series of images. Don't try to memorize a word-for-word script, as this will only make it more difficult to relax into the experience. In fact, the letting-go of meditation is not terribly compatible with the concentration of memorizing a script, which is why this method is not recommended. The meditations are written with repetition and rhythm, designed to aid in achieving a mild trance. You won't be able to take full advantage of this when working from memory, so be sure to repeat key images to yourself several times before proceeding.

These meditations start within your own body, with pure physical experience.

The Meditation of Air

Start with the grounding and centering in appendix A.

Begin to notice the air in your lungs. Notice that you are breathing. As you inhale and exhale, focus on the air moving in and out of your body. Feel air fill you and depart from you. *(Short pause . . . 15 seconds.)* Feel the air moving in, moving out. Air entering you, air coming out of you. *(Short pause . . . 15 seconds.)*

Now allow your consciousness to follow the air as it awakens and nourishes your entire body. Let yourself know the nourishment of air throughout your body. Feel the air that oxygenates your blood. Feel the air that awakens your flesh. Feel the air that enlivens your very molecules. Feel the air that is everywhere within you. *(Short pause . . . 15 seconds.)*

Now move your consciousness outward. Allow your mind to follow the air as it flows from your lungs and joins a world of air. Be with the air that leaves your lungs as it mingles with the air in this room. Float with the air that circulates to the outside. Move with the air through the sky, through the wind and clouds. Envision yourself floating there, with the air, with the clouds. Travel in the realm of Air, and see everything around you from Air's point of view. *(Pause . . . 60 seconds.)*

As you move through Air, as you partake of Air, allow yourself to *become* Air, and picture every part of you, inner and outer, as Airy. Picture this now. *Know* that you are Air. *(Short pause . . . 15 seconds.)* As you float in the clouds, allow yourself to become one with the clouds. Allow yourself to be made of that Air that makes up the clouds. You are made of Air, your body is an Air body, your spirit is an Air spirit. Enjoy this now. Float and fly as Air for a while, before my voice brings you back. *(Long pause . . . 3–5 minutes.)*

It is time to start coming back. Come to know that you are no longer made entirely of Air. Realize that you are still *in* Air, but you are separate from Air. Pull back from Air. Allow yourself to be surrounded and touched by Air, but not in flight. Gently land upon the Earth.

Now notice that the ground beneath you is solid, is Earth. Feel the solidness. You are aware of Earth.

Now realize that there is Water in you. Feel the flow of blood through your veins, and picture the Water around you. Picture moisture in the air, or a nearby body of water, or running water indoors. You are aware of Water.

Now become aware of Fire. Feel energy and warmth. Feel the heat in your own body. You are aware of Fire.

Feel enlivened, refreshed, and strong. As you do so, know that you have returned from Air and are fully balanced in the four elements.

Knowing that you are balanced, become aware of your surroundings—the room, the floor. You know who you are and where you are.

You are back—open your eyes.

Touch or slap the floor or a wall. This will give you an immediate feeling of Earth. Follow up with a piece of bread and a drink of water.

The Meditation of Fire

Fire is the hardest of the meditations; it is not a world that creatures live in—there are birds and fish, but no fire-dwellers. Your Fire meditation, then, will be the most imaginative of the four, the least reliant on day-to-day scenes.

Start with the grounding and centering in appendix A.

Become aware of the heat in your body. Begin by feeling physical heat—the simple fire of your body temperature. Now feel the pulsing fire of your center, of your Will. Feel how you are made alive by fire. *(Short pause . . . 15 seconds.)* Picture that same fire, the Fire of Will, all around you, as if everyone near you, or everyone you know, were glowing.

Allow yourself to know that you have a glowing, fiery center. Feel how hot, yet comfortable, it is. Now allow the temperature to rise. Let it be hotter and hotter, and know that you are comfortable with that heat, that the heat is safe and natural for you. Let it become quite hot, while you remain comfortable. *(Short pause . . . 15 seconds.)* Now picture yourself surrounded by flames. The flames come closer and closer, but you remain at ease. Become aware that the flames have the very same nature that you do. You have the nature of flame. *(Short pause . . . 15 seconds.)* The flames surround you, burning their way closer and closer, until you are *in* the fire and *of* the fire. Know that you are in the fire, a creature of Fire, in your natural element. *(Pause . . . 60 seconds.)*

Now allow yourself to *become* Fire, and picture every part of you, inner and outer, as Fiery. Know that your form is a form of Fire. Know that your spirit is a spirit of Fire. Look out from your Fiery self, and see the world as Fire sees it. Embrace this experience now. Be a burning, fierce Fire for a while, before my voice brings you back. *(Long pause . . . 3–5 minutes.)*

It is time to start coming back. Come to know that you are not made entirely of Fire. Picture flames receding, so that you're surrounded by, but not actually *in*, Fire. You're sitting in a circle of flames, which is backing further away, further away, until it's gone. Now move your mind away from thoughts of heat. Allow your perception of temperature to decrease. You no longer feel Fiery. You no longer feel hot. You are a comfortable, natural, human temperature.

Now notice that the ground beneath you is solid, is Earth. Feel the solidness. You are aware of Earth.

Breathe in deeply and become aware of Air. Know that there is Air within you.

Now realize that there is Water in you. Feel the flow of blood through your veins, and picture the Water around you. Picture moisture in the air, or a nearby body of water, or running water indoors. You are aware of Water.

Feel enlivened, refreshed, and strong. As you do so, know that you have returned from Fire and are fully balanced in the four elements.

Knowing that you are balanced, become aware of your surroundings—the room, the floor. You know who you are and where you are.

You are back—open your eyes.

Touch or slap the floor or a wall. This will give you an immediate feeling of Earth. Follow up with a piece of bread and a drink of water.

The Meditation of Water

Start with the grounding and centering in appendix A.

Become aware of the moisture in your body. Feel the saliva in your mouth, feel your sweat. Notice the moisture behind your closed eyelids. Now move deeper. Focus your mind within your body and become aware of the moisture coursing throughout your entire system. Notice that water makes up much of your body; feel its flow. Feel water everywhere in you. *(Short pause . . . 15 seconds.)* Now, allow your mind to reach out to the water that surrounds you every day. Recall the water you drink, the water you cook with, the water you wash with. Recall the last time you were rained on. Remember that feeling—of rain touching your skin.

See yourself now as being *in* and *of* that water. Allow yourself to *become* Water, and picture every part of you, inner and outer, as Watery. *(Pause . . . 60 seconds.)* You are droplets, not held together as a single unit. You are not one distinct thing, instead you are a flow. You are flowing in and around everything that is Water, with no clear boundaries between. The body of water that you are is rained upon, and that rain, added to you, also *is* you. That rain that you are dissipates into the lake or river you land in, yet you are still *you*, still Water. You evaporate and disappear, and yet you are still there. Everything is flow, and nothing is still. *(Long pause . . . 3–5 minutes.)*

It is time to start coming back. Come to know that you are not Water. You are *in* Water, but not entirely *of* it. Know yourself as a being connected to Water. Notice that the water in your life and in your body is just a part of who you are. Notice that you're also Earth, and feel your solid body.

Notice that you're also Air. Feel your breathing, and recognize that you are a thinking being.

Notice that you are also Fire. Feel energy and warmth. Feel the heat of life.

Feel enlivened, refreshed, and strong, and see yourself fully balanced in the four elements.

Knowing that you are balanced, become aware of your surroundings—the room, the floor. You know who you are and where you are.

You are back—open your eyes.

Touch or slap the floor or a wall. This will give you an immediate feeling of Earth. Follow up with a piece of bread. If you can, SHOUT!

The Meditation of Earth

Start with the grounding and centering in appendix A.

Become aware of how solid you are. Your body is solid. Your flesh, your muscles, your bones, they all have the weight of Earth. Notice how much of you is made up of solid mass, how still it is, how rooted. *(Short pause . . . 15 seconds.)* You are surrounded everywhere by things that are solid: the floor is solid, the earth beneath you is solid. The rocks and concrete around you are of Earth. *(Short pause . . . 15 seconds.)* As you picture more and more of the world as solid, you start to feel more and more rock-like. You start to feel the connection between the Earth within and the Earth without. You feel massive, heavy, immobile. *(Pause . . . 60 seconds.)*

You are becoming Earth. *(Short pause . . . 15 seconds.)* Notice that Earth is timeless, notice its longevity. You are the minerals and the soil, lasting a long, long time, watching as briefer forms of being come and go. You are a mountain, looking down upon the generations of animal and plant that pass in your shadow. You are geology itself, unmoved by the passage of time except in its furthest reaches. Know yourself now as Earth, and be with the experience of Earth. *(Long pause . . . 3–5 minutes.)*

Begin to come back now. You are no longer Earth, although still solid. Shift your weight a little. Notice that you can move, that you are no longer as immobile as a rock.

Wiggle your fingers and notice that they're touched by Air.

Lick your lips and feel the Water in your body.

Feel the warmth of your body that is Fire, and feel, too, the *Will* that is Fire. Notice your *desire* to move, to feel, to touch.

Discover now that you are Fire *and* Air *and* Water *and* Earth. Know that you are fully balanced in the four elements.

Knowing that you are balanced, become aware of your surroundings—the room, the floor. You know who you are and where you are.

You are back—open your eyes.

Get up and move your whole body—wiggle, shake, dance. Shake off the immobility of Earth to regain the balance of four elements. Drink some ice water.

AUTOMATIC WRITING AND SPEAKING EXERCISES

Automatic writing is a psychic art in which the practitioner writes without conscious control of the words that come out on the page. Generally, the writer will first achieve a mild or deep trance state, usually with a specific purpose or question in mind, and will then begin writing. The writing comes from a deity, from a disembodied spirit, or from the deep subconscious or superconscious mind of the practitioner. An old art, done at one time with quill pens, it can be done today on the computer if the writer prefers.

Automatic speaking is more often called *channeling*. In this case, the practitioner, having achieved the trance and asked the question or focused on the purpose, simply speaks, letting the deity, spirit, entity, or layer of consciousness use her voice for its communication. The practitioner is the channel through which the entity speaks.

It is possible, and fascinating, to speak or write while "under the influence" of each element, channeling Air, Fire, Water, or Earth.

People are often surprised to find that success in automatic writing or speaking is not all that difficult to attain. Of course, you have to have realistic goals, which is to say, a realistic definition of "success." If you imagine that you will disappear into a trance like a movie character, your eyes rolled back in your head, with strange, otherworldly voices coming from you, you are likely to be disappointed. If, on the other hand, you give yourself permission to have conscious awareness of, and thoughts about, the experience you are having, if you understand that a trance can happen to you while you remain recognizable yourself, you will probably find meaningful results within your reach.

Automatic Writing and Speaking Pointers

When Writing

Have your writing materials ready in advance, easily and comfortably accessible, before the trance begins. Some people use special, even consecrated, paper and pens for this purpose. If you're using paper and pen, have more paper than you think you'll need and an extra pen—even a consecrated pen can run out of ink. If you're using a typewriter or computer, be comfortably seated at the keyboard before you start, with paper in the typewriter or with the word processor booted up. Lighting should be dim; you need to see, but you don't need to see too much detail—remember that you'll be writing, not editing, and you won't need to attend to spelling or other mistakes. When you write automatically, *keep going*.

When Speaking

Speaking a trance is something that should be done in a group or with a partner. Speech is a form of communication, and your subconscious mind knows that. The words that will form will be most meaningful when they are addressed *to* someone. When alone, you'll have a tendency to fall silent, to *think* the words. It isn't the same—the processes of writing and speaking engage more of the brain than just thinking to yourself does. So, reserve the spoken channel for when you have some-one to whom to speak.

You might want to have a tape recorder available to record what you say, or to have your partner or a member of the group take some notes. If you remember it all, you might wish to write it down after the experience is over. It's useful to have a glass of water handy—speaking with a parched throat is likely to disrupt the trance!

How to Write/Speak the Elements

When speaking/writing the elements, you are exploring what the element is. You are allowing yourself to speak/write as if you are that element. So, use "I" statements and see where they lead. Begin by saying, "I am . . ." and see what comes out. Don't plan and don't edit.

Incorporating Automatic Writing/Speaking into the Meditations

You can do this in a ritual, bringing paper and pens into the circle if you're going to write. Or you can modify your meditation space to accommodate your writing in-struments. Or you can do the entire meditation seated at your desk.

Since, in this method, you're working from the tape or script, you'll need to ad-just it slightly. At the point in each meditation where it calls for a 3–5 minute pause, add language as follows, to allow for the automatic writing/speaking to happen:

- **Air:** Replace the sentence "Float and fly as Air for a while, before my voice brings you back" with the following: "As you are Air, floating and flying, allow yourself to speak/write[6] your experience. Begin with 'I am Air.' Speak freely in your Air voice/Write freely your Air words, letting the words move out of you like wind."

- **Fire:** Replace the sentence "Be a burning, fierce Fire for a while, before my voice brings you back" with the following: "As you burn with the Fire you are, allow yourself to speak/write this fierce experience. Begin with 'I am Fire.' Allow your Fire voice/words to come forth like flames."

- **Water:** There is no need to replace any language. After the sentence "Everything is flow, and nothing is still," add the following: "As you are Water, speak/write as Water, beginning with 'I am Water' and allowing speech/words to flow freely."

- **Earth:** There is no need to replace any language. After the sentence "Know yourself now as Earth, and be with the experience of Earth," add the following:

"From the silence of Earth, allow words to come forth. Write/Speak as Earth. Begin with 'I am Earth' and communicate from your Earth self."

Automatic Writing as a Follow-Up to Meditation

You may not wish to interrupt your meditation by opening your eyes and writing, or by opening your mouth and speaking. Instead, you can use automatic writing as a follow-up to the meditation experience. (You will probably find that the follow-up techniques work better with writing than with speech.) At your writing desk, typewriter, or keyboard, replay the audiotape you used in your meditation. At the long pause, begin to write.

Alternately, simply close your eyes for a moment, and run through the meditation experience in your memory. When you reach the point where you are the element, begin writing.

---

1. "The Charge" (a.k.a. "The Charge of the Star Goddess"), written by Doreen Valiente, is probably the single most important and ubiquitous Wiccan document. An authoritative version can be found in *The Witches' Way: Principles, Rituals and Beliefs of Modern Witchcraft,* by Janet and Stewart Farrar (London: Robert Hale, 1984) 296–297.

2. You have other positive qualities, too—I left out anything I thought was ambiguous as to element, and anything of mixed elements.

3. In addition to seeking help, as already recommended, remember that no recovery process—magical, medical, psychological, or any other—works unless you *stop partaking of the addiction*.

4. Since the token serves as a kind of magical tool, hold it in whichever hand you normally hold your tools.

5. Pauses are suggested throughout the meditations so that the person reading aloud will give enough time for people to establish images and to "travel." Of course, every person needs a slightly different amount of time, but these pauses provide a rule of thumb. In a ritual space, in which clocks and timers aren't used, measure your pauses by counting to yourself, by the amount of an incense stick or candle that has burned, or by the timing of recorded music.

6. Obviously, you will have decided in advance which you are doing (speaking or writing), and will have chosen the right word accordingly.

CHAPTER FIVE

The Elements in Daily Life

So far, we've learned what the elements are, and where the concept of the elements came from. We've explored the elements in nature, and we've gone within, looking at how they affect our personalities for good and ill. We've done some inner work, getting to know the elements better, and learning to balance ourselves in the Way of Four.

Just as the elements aren't only in nature, they aren't only *anywhere*. In fact, as you have probably figured out by now, the elements are *everywhere*. Their qualities and effects permeate every part of our lives. There is an Air, Fire, Water, and Earth of your job, of your love life, and even of your clothing.

THE ELEMENTS AT HOME

If I just said the word "home," you already know enough about the elements to assign it (correctly) to Earth. Home is your Earth place, your hearth, your foundation, your stability. But people of every elemental nature have homes, and all four elements exist in the home, just as they exist everywhere.

Since we all tend to compartmentalize our lives to some extent, our home elements might not reflect our personality elements. That is, you can be a basically Airy person and have a Fiery home. You approach different aspects of your life with different resources, and for different reasons. Perhaps, although Airy, you grew up in a

Fiery home, and so Fire means home to you. Or perhaps your Fire nature is not something you're comfortable with in public, so you express it in the privacy of your home. Or perhaps, being Airy, you're not that home-oriented, and you've let your spouse, partner, or housemate dominate your home environment. The reasons don't matter right now. What matters is simply to know that your home has an elemental quality, and just as you can balance your personal elements, you can balance your home elements.

Why do we bother with elements in the home? The previous exercises, focusing as they do on nature and the self, seem a lot deeper and, perhaps, more important than what we're doing in this chapter. However, our home elements have a daily, regular impact on us. They are the elements we see, feel, and experience when we get up in the morning and when we go to sleep at night. Home represents a lot of things to us: safety, privacy, peace, relaxation, comfort, and more. If these important parts of life are unbalanced, it will surely have an effect on us.

Balancing the elements in your home can also be used in conjunction with the work from the previous chapters. For instance, while doing the Elemental Strength Balancing exercises from chapter 4, you might set up corresponding elemental areas in your home. You might "re-dress" your meditation area for an element, or you might simply arrange to have corners of elemental energy—an Earth alcove, a Water area by your night table, etc.

You might use your home (among other things) to bolster weak areas found in chapter 3. If, for example, you look at the Things I Like About Myself quiz, you'll find there are several positive qualities that are (or can be) reflected in the home:

Air
I have a great library.
I am unconventional.

Fire
I have a distinctive personal style.
I am sexy.

Water
I am imaginative.
I am musical.

I am very romantic.

I am good with animals.

Earth

My home is a place people enjoy coming to.

I am cuddly.

I am practical.

I have a green thumb.

I am a good cook.

From this list we can easily see that, for example, you could work on improving your relationship with Earth by having cuddly things in your home.

Air in the Home

The Air home is, above all, airy. Is that too obvious? A home that is stuffy, dark, or windowless suffers from a lack of Air, both physically and metaphysically. The Air home has open windows and is well ventilated. The curtains are lightweight—a soft flutter in the breeze is much airier than a heavy drape against the chill. The Air home relishes natural light, and may take advantage of it with sun-catchers, window prisms, or stained glass.

The colors around the Air house are white, pale to bright blue, pale to bright yellow, and perhaps gray. Fabrics are light and smooth, but not slippery—cotton, linen, light blends, and denim are probably favorites.

Wall art reflects the concerns of Air. Skyscapes, of course, are a must, as well as art depicting flight. The work of Maxfield Parish is airy on a number of levels. Alphonse Mucha had an Airy feel, with his thoughtful, well-planned designs and his curling, elaborate wisps of smoke. Artists who approach their work with a mathematical or scientific eye are very Airy: M. C. Escher and Georges Seurat are good examples. Air homes might also have framed sayings, documents, or calligraphy on the walls. Mechanical drawings and depictions of architecture, towers, or any transportation, especially airplanes, are Airy. Model airplanes or a kite hanging on the ceiling are dead giveaways of an Air home.

Air can also be reflected in the home in austerity. Japanese-style decorating, with stark simplicity, is often an Air approach. In such a home, the simple brushwork of traditional Japanese art might be seen. So is the kind of "I just hang my hat here" careless austerity that characterizes some Air people. Open spaces fill a room with Air.

In nature, the element of Air is sky, wind, and light, as reflected in the colors, fabrics, and art just mentioned. In a human being, though, Air is primarily thought; your logical, studious, intellectual side is Air. So, in the home, Air is seen in books—lots and lots of books. A well-stocked library indicates a home that welcomes the Air side of oneself.

Air in the Kitchen

In the next section, we'll talk about taking the elements into our bodies, so that's a good place to talk about food. For now, let's look at the kitchen just as a room, and at cooking just as a process (rather than a product).

The Air kitchen emphasizes light and openness. The kitchen is a great place to have clear, clean, white countertops, as well as highly polished chromes and metals that reflect light and increase the sense of space. Formica, light tile, and highly bleached wood are Airy kitchen accents. Air people are often very high-tech; their logical minds love mechanical gadgetry, and the kitchen is a great place to express that.

The act of cooking has Air in it when the method of cooking actually uses air. Both steamers and double boilers require air—a *space* between the food and the water. A wire whisk aerates food, and sifting flour adds air to baking.

Air in the Bedroom

Some Air bedrooms will have simple tables as nightstands, if they have nightstands at all. These are the austere, open-space kind of Air rooms. But Air people are *readers*, so a bulkier nightstand might be in evidence, with small shelves or cubbies for the books that tend to pile up.

The bed will reflect the colors and textures of Air, favoring crisp cotton sheets in white or pale blue. Airy beds don't have too many blankets or pillows, although they may have bolster pillows designed for those who read in bed. The bed itself is not all that elaborate; if it has headboards and footboards, they are of an open design. Air bedrooms (along with Fire) might have some visual stimulation on the ceiling above the bed—in Air's case, a skylight or a sky or space motif.

How to Bring Air into Your Home

Here are some ideas, some simple, some requiring more effort, for bringing the influence of Air into your home decor:

· Wash your windows. This isn't the easiest exercise in the book, nor the most fun, but it's a sure-fire way to create an airier atmosphere in your home.

· "Air out" your rooms. Leave the windows open for several hours on a cool day. The cool air will linger even after the windows are closed and the house warms up. (I hate this exercise—I'm always cold and am usually found in thick socks and an extra sweater. But Air people don't seem to mind the cold, and even I will admit that the cool air feels great in the house. I bundle up and tolerate the cold to achieve the result.)

· Create a vase of feathers. Use found feathers, natural feathers, or brightly dyed feathers bought in a craft store. Create a "flower arrangement" out of the feathers and place them in a clear or frosted glass vase. Use the vase as a centerpiece or place it on a knickknack shelf.

· Create a "sky door." Paint the molding around a doorway sky blue. After it dries, sponge-paint over it in white to create a dappled, cloudy effect.

· Put up sun-catchers. The reflective decals are available for sale all over and dapple a room with colored light. Another Sun-catching option is to hang crystals or prisms in windows—they send rainbow reflections all over the room.

· Burn sage or cedar, or use cedar balls to scent an area.

· Hang wind chimes by the door, or a mobile inside.

Fire in the Home

The Fire home is warm, dramatic, and eccentric. It reflects the passions of those who reside in it. Fire is present in any home that has *flair*. A typical feature of a Fire home is an unusual or one-of-a-kind object, set apart in a singular display. Contrarily, a collection can reflect Fire's intense focus, and so a shelf with two dozen Betty Boop dolls or a display case full of rare stamps might be part of a Fiery home.

Fiery decorating has reds, oranges, and bright yellows in evidence. Fabrics might have a shiny surface or a bold pattern. Wood is highly polished and reddish in tone, such as mahogany or cherry. A fireplace or wood-burning stove is a straightforward way of bringing Fire into the home, although Earth people love fireplaces as well, because you can cuddle in front of them.

If the Japanese section of the decorating catalogue appeals to Airy folks, then Fire gravitates toward the Southwestern. The colors, shapes, and styles of Southwestern decorating are all related to a hot environment. The softer Southwestern shades—sand, cactus green, coyote brown—make good accent colors for the hotter Fire hues.

Accessories and art in a Fire home will have a bright, passionate effect. Not every Fire home looks like an art museum, of course, but even a conservative beige living room is likely to feature a bright red throw pillow or a brightly glazed ceramic bowl. Masks might be used as decor, as they are symbols of both drama and transformation, and butterflies (transformation again) might be depicted. Artists such as Mondrian, Kandinsky, or Keith Haring, with their bold sense of color and movement, are Fiery. Van Gogh was always Fiery—whether he painted fields, flowers, or sky, it always seemed to be in flames. Cubism is usually Fiery, with its intense, disorienting view of reality. Because *fame* is Fiery, posters showing movie stars or rock stars might be seen. Because Fire is energetic, posters of athletes are another possibility—LeRoy Neiman's sports paintings are Fiery. Ornamental swords hung on the wall can be quite Fiery as well.

Fire in the Kitchen

Given a choice, the owner of a Fire kitchen prefers a gas stove over an electric one. A highly visible spice rack is a must. A really Fiery kitchen might even have red chili peppers or garlic hanging in bunches. Fiery kitchens have a good set of cooking knives that are well sharpened. Kitchen decor might favor painted tiles or red exposed brick; the kitchen is a room where the color red is right at home. From brick to flooring to cookware, it fits naturally into this room and doesn't seem as loud as it might elsewhere in the house, and so the Fiery homeowner can cut loose.

A Fiery cooking experience involves open flame. Grilling, wok-cooking, "blackened" dishes, and, of course, flambée are processes based in Fire.

Fire in the Bedroom

Let's not forget that Fire is the most overtly sexual of the elements—love may be Water, but lust is Fire. If your bedroom is an erotic wonderland, it's a Fire bedroom. Erotic art on the walls, "toys" in the bedside drawers, and mirrors on the ceiling are all Fiery. Not everyone with a Fiery bedroom has the freedom or inclination to have such a bedroom, but a Fire bedroom will always have a hint of the erotic, even if it's discreetly hidden. Of course, the Fire bedroom has plenty of candles, and probably incense as well.

Fire favors mirrors, not just on the ceiling, as Fire tends to be the element of vanity. A typical bit of Fire flair in the bedroom is to display something personal as decor. For instance, I have my earrings hung up on the wall and draped about with a boa. Not only is it a practical way of keeping the earrings from getting tangled up (that's my Earth pragmatism), but it has Fire's artsy quality, as well as a bit of Fiery ego—showing off something that others might tuck away.

How to Bring Fire into Your Home

Here are some Fiery decorating ideas:

- Set up a candle tray. Get a metallic or mirrored tray or platter, and put on it a dozen or so candles of different sizes, shapes, and colors. Add a small dish to keep the matches in, and use it as a dining room centerpiece.

- Hang an African or Balinese mask. These tend to be particularly Fiery in both color and appearance; their startling, almost gruesome expressions create a "hotspot" in a room. Many discount stores such as T. J. Maxx have started carrying such items quite inexpensively.

- Leave a bottle of hot chili oil out on the kitchen counter in an attractive cruet.

- Acquire some throw pillows in fiery colors (red or orange). Both the color and a scattered placement will create a sense of flame.

- Hang a mirror someplace where you can primp. Sure, you probably already have one or more mirrors, but get an extra one and make a "vanity spot." Get some cheap beads in wild colors—the kind that everyone seems to want to unload at garage sales—and hang them around the outside of the mirror.

- Put some erotic art in a discreet location. Many people will balk at having their home appear less than "wholesome," but if a picture is small and attractively framed, and placed so that it escapes most notice, it can heat up the house without shocking the neighbors. My late stepfather had some high-quality erotic sketches framed in his bathroom. It was an unusual location, but an amusing one, and it allowed visitors to look at them privately. Something very artistic or exotic, such as Indian Kama Sutra illustrations, might be a good choice.

Water in the Home

A Water home is a dreamworld. Romantic and fluid, it is reminiscent of a fantasy painting of a mermaid's realm, or of Atlantis. Water colors are oceanic, primarily deep to pale blue and deep to pale sea green. Accents are the pale off-white and pink of seashells and coral. Fabrics are soft, silky or gauzy, and plentiful. The Water home has draped, flowing features—double curtains with valances, pleated fabric lampshades, tablecloths, and so on. Lighting in a Water home is indirect, and cushions are soft and plentiful. There may be cushions on the floor instead of armchairs, as Water tends toward the freeform.

The general decor may be haphazard, even careless. The flow of Water can create a decor that "just happens," without planning or design. On the other hand, a Water home may express artistry, and be as beautiful as a painting. Although many Water homes have a relaxed appearance, the romanticism of Water may be present in ornate, lacy design. Victorian furniture and objects may be favored, and the curling woodwork of various antiques may be present.

Water artwork is romantic and impressionistic. In fact, the great Impressionists, such as Monet and Renoir, may have a place of honor on the walls. Themes in art will be bodies of water (oceans, waterfalls, lakes), rain, marine life, and romance. The photographs of Robert Doisneau have a Watery look, including some depicting rain and kisses. Other photographers working in his style are popular, and one often sees photographs now of couples kissing in the rain—the epitome of Water photography. The lover's embrace as a theme in art, whether the painting *The Kiss* by Gustav Klimt, a black-and-white photograph by Doisneau, or a still from *Gone with the Wind,* are favorites in the Water home. The Pre-Raphaelites, especially Waterhouse (apt name!), have the rich romanticism of Water.

The objects found in a Water home will almost certainly include seashells collected on the beaches that Water people love. There may even be an aquarium. Water containers (goblets, vases, ewers, and basins) may be used as knickknacks. Since sentiment and nostalgia tend to be Watery—Water tends to have a flowing attitude toward time, and to see the past in the present—sentimental keepsakes will be found in a Water home. Music is usually an important part of the Water home, and one or more musical instruments and/or a good stereo system will be in evidence.

Water in the Kitchen

The kitchen can be very expressive of Water, starting with a good water purifier, or perhaps a cooler (the kind where they deliver five-gallon jugs and you have to hoist them onto the cooler base). Other water-processing equipment is of the highest quality the purchaser could afford—the coffee maker is a fancy model and the teapot is very special.

If the budget has allowed for it, the refrigerator/freezer has an icemaker, or a water dispenser, or both. The designer of a Water kitchen also prefers a double sink, but, perhaps oddly, a Water kitchen doesn't necessarily have a dishwasher. Since Watery people don't mind being wet up to the elbows, washing dishes in the sink may be fine with them.

Cooking with water is probably the kind everyone learns first—boiling.

Water in the Bedroom

The bedroom is where Water's romanticism will really let itself loose. Although one's first thought is "waterbed," and although that may well be the case, a Water bedroom is far more elaborate than one piece of furniture would suggest.

A bedroom can be the center of one's romantic self-expression. A Water bedroom might have a four-poster canopy bed, hung about with silk or lace curtains. The bed might have a frilly dust ruffle, perhaps with matching pillow shams. Once again, indirect lighting is important; lamps are small and discreet.

A less feminine approach that is still Watery is one replete with dark colors in moody, moonlit strokes—blues and greens, satin bedcovers, and perhaps one striking print of a nighttime scene, in midnight hues, on the wall.

Opaque curtains are a must in any Water bedroom, as privacy is vital. Fabrics reflect the sensuality of water; they are silky-soft; one slides into bed like slipping underwater.

How to Bring Water into Your Home

Here are some Watery decorating ideas:

· Get a fish tank. If this seems too elaborate, how about a betta? This Siamese fighting fish is kept in a very small container and is kept alone, because he attacks tankmates. Like goldfish, bettas are nontropical and don't require special heaters or filters, but they tend to be hardier than goldfish. So, this kind of fish is a fairly small investment in terms of money, time, and space.

· Find all those seashells you've been picking up on beaches and put them in a bowl, preferably a clear or blue one. You could also put them in a vase, in which case it would need to be clear. This is easier than a fish in that the shells don't need to be fed.

· Get one of those little Japanese-style fountains. They're available for sale in sizes ranging from about that of a jewelry box to that of a chair, with a similar price range. The smaller ones are quite affordable. The steady sound of running water is soothing and creates a Water atmosphere that goes far beyond the physical.

· Make an ocean shelf. If you know how to knock together wood, that's great. Since I don't have that skill, what I've done is buy a pre-made knickknack shelf of unfinished wood, which is available at any crafts store. Paint it a deep oceanic blue (two coats). After it dries, try decorating it with oceanic designs. You don't have to be a skilled painter to do it; some pink or white "twigs" with knobby ends for coral, and some squiggly vertical green lines for seaweed will do the trick. You can use decals, or glue on cheap imitation pearls, to create a shelf that looks a bit like an oceanic oasis. You might use this shelf to display your bowl or vase of seashells.

· Get some water-themed accessories for your bathroom, such as a fish-shaped soap dish. The bathroom is a watery place anyway, so spending some extra time there, decorating, cleaning up, and rearranging, will help you focus on Water. Adding fish or seashells or other watery items to the room will be fun and meditative at the same time. Plus, if you need a frequent Water reminder in your life, you'll see them whenever you brush your teeth.

· Make a display or centerpiece out of a pitcher, goblets, a pitcher-and-goblets set, or a very special cup. Place your cup(s) on a silver or blue tray.

· Get a wine rack for your kitchen. Decorate it with blue, sea green, and/or silver ribbon.

Earth in the Home

Earth homes are welcoming, comfortable, and easy places in which to relax. Some express Earthiness by having all the amenities of earthly comfort, while others are simply "lived in," undecorated and practical. An Earth home isn't spare (that's Air), but it might not be pretty either. An Earth homemaker may have paid more attention to items that were available, sensible, economical, and cozy than to whether or not they match the color scheme. Secondhand is just fine for Earth.

Earth colors tend toward brown, beige, forest green, and rust, as well as undyed fabrics and unfinished woods. Textures tend to be soft and comfortable, but also highly tactile, with bumps or ridges to stimulate the fingers. Likely fabrics found in the home are chenille, boucle, or corduroy. An open weave, eyelet, a fringe, or quilting might also add texture. The homemade look also finds its way into the Earth abode. Natural weaving may be found in place of commercial throws and blankets, or as wall art. Baskets, particularly of a coarse weave, are likely objects. Unglazed ceramics may be the material for favorite bowls, dishes, or other accessories.

Earth homes are likely to have art *objects,* such as sculpture or statuettes, and *crafts,* such as ornamental bowls, boxes, planters, or other items both useful and artistic. The physical quality of a three-dimensional object appeals to Earth, as does the practicality of a beautiful craft rather than something that's just there to look at. Nonetheless, there's plenty of two-dimensional art that might be found on the walls of an Earth home.

Earth art might depict nature or fertility themes. Folk art and illustrations are also Earthy in their direct method of self-expression. Frida Kahlo's art is visceral and physical—very Earthy.

The lush, frank sexuality of Georgia O'Keefe's flowers is Earthy. Norman Rockwell is an Earthy illustrator, and Anne Geddes, with her fertile, natural themes, her fat, happy babies, and her fun-loving approach, is very Earthy. A number of Renaissance painters had an Earthy feeling to them, such as Rembrandt and Vermeer.

Because Earth is possessive and tends to collect things, and also because Earth is family-oriented, the Earth home will have souvenirs, family memorabilia, and photos on display. This may remind you of Water, because the Water home displays sentimentality. It is true that the *reasons* for the collection may be more elemental than the collection itself. However, Earth's mementos are more likely to involve family, family history, or childhood, while Water's are more likely to be random keepsakes, snapshots (literally or metaphorically) of meaningful moments, or romantic remembrances.

Earth in the Kitchen

The Earth kitchen can be fairly low-tech. Not only does frugal Earth tend to refrain from making luxury purchases like food processors, cappuccino makers, and electric juicers, but the Earth cook doesn't mind getting his hands dirty. Earth is happy to chop and prepare manually.

The Earth kitchen relishes its ingredients. Cannister sets are on the counter, so that the supply of flour, rice, and beans is visible and part of the room's look. They might even be of clear glass or plastic, so that the ingredients themselves can be seen. Pots and pans may have a storage system that doesn't hide them away in cabinets. These features create an organic, lived-in feeling; the kitchen feels active and purposeful, and decor and function form a seamless whole. In an Earth home, the kitchen is generally the social center, where conversation and relaxation, as well as meals, take place.

Earth cooking is a slow, steady process. The oven is an Earth appliance—prehistoric ovens were holes dug in the ground and heated with rocks. Unlike stovetop cooking, which is generally Fiery, baking is an Earth activity. Other long-cooking processes, like crockpot cooking, are also Earthy. Any cooking or preparation procedure that involves putting your hands in the ingredients and getting messy has an Earthy quality. This includes kneading bread, mixing up the ingredients of a meatloaf, forming cookies or rolls with your hands, and so on.

Earth in the Bedroom

You can spot an Earth bed right away by the huge pile of pillows and blankets. Earth beds are nests in which the Earth person burrows. On my own Earth bed there are five pillows (counting the double-sized "body pillow") and three blankets (counting the electric one). And we still haven't gotten to the stuffed animals! There are several reasons that Earth favors stuffed animals in the bedroom: Earth is cuddly and enjoys the pillow-like quality of a teddy bear in bed. Earth is frank and unembarrassed, so an Earthy adult's room displays its owner's childish fancies openly. And Earth is a natural collector, acquiring toys and dolls for reasons of nostalgia or possessiveness.

The Earth bedroom has a natural, warm appearance. Blankets are knitted or quilted, perhaps homemade. A blanket chest or trunk is a distinct possibility, combining warmth (blankets), a natural look (wood), and a passion for storing one's possessions. Because of the strong emphasis on comfort, there is likely to be a cozy chair, a rocker, and/or a footrest.

How to Bring Earth into Your Home
Here are some Earthy decorating ideas:

- Get one or two mohair throw pillows to add texture and a natural hue to your living room.

- If you don't have a blanket throw on your couch or easy chair, get one. A fleece throw is Earthy both in texture and color, or get one with an open weave. It will not only look Earthy, but will give you a cuddly spot.

- Get a sturdy basket, about seven inches in diameter. The kind made of sticks of natural, unstripped wood is especially nice for our purposes. Fill it with medium-sized stones—about fist-sized or a little smaller. Use it as a centerpiece or keep it on a shelf or stand by the front door. In that position, it will act as a reminder to be grounded as you enter and leave the house.

- Use a dowel or rack with S-hooks to hang utensils in the kitchen. Mount the rack or dowel on the wall, hang the S-hooks from it, and hang the spatulas, whisks, serving spoons, etc., from the hooks. This is a very handy way of keeping your utensils organized (especially the tall ones that don't fit conveniently in a drawer), and it looks great. Earth loves to use something practical as a decorative display.

- Add one more pillow or blanket to your bed than you think you really need.

- Get a bed tray. A cozy breakfast or midnight snack in bed is a wonderful way to enjoy Earth in the home.

- Get a few houseplants.

Household Elements Quiz

This quiz is organized into elemental sections. Finding a hidden answer wasn't going to work this time, because you've already read the preceding sections and have a pretty good idea of what's what—the "element" of surprise is lost.[1] Instead, what you'll be doing is walking around your house and taking an inventory of the elemental items, colors, themes, and qualities you find. The quiz is broken into sections to make it easier, and there's room for subtotals and totals for each element.

The results of this quiz will allow you to discover how you are manifesting the elements in your domestic life. It will uncover elemental strengths and weaknesses that may surprise you (remember what we said earlier—the household elements don't necessarily match the personality elements). If you find that certain elements are strongest in certain areas (i.e., Fire is strongest artistically, Water is strongest in the bedroom), then that, too, is educational. Remember that your goal here is self-discovery. Allow yourself to enjoy the process.

Overall Style
Look for general impressions, decorating schemes, repeated themes, or large household items.

Air

____ Lots of windows, sunlight

____ Open space, bare walls, bare floors

____ Lightweight curtains or no curtains

____ Stained glass

____ Lots of books, a real library

____ Cool, airy home

____ Japanese decor

   Subtotal for Air ____

Fire

___ Artistic display settings (i.e., pedestals, lighted curio cabinets)

___ Art in progress (i.e., a painting on an easel)

___ Fireplace or wood-burning stove

___ Warm home, good heating

___ Southwestern decor

Subtotal for Fire ___

Water

___ Plentiful fabrics (drapes, tablecloths)

___ Cushions instead of chairs

___ Indirect lighting

___ Aquarium

___ Musical instruments

___ Good stereo

___ Highly ornate furnishings

___ Victorian decor

___ Marine-theme decor (fish- or shell-shaped objects)

Subtotal for Water ___

Earth

___ Comfortable, relaxed home

___ Undecorated (no theme), but not spare

___ Secondhand furniture

___ Heavy, sturdy furniture

___ Large easy chairs

___ Unfinished wood

___ Sculpture

___ Lots of plants

Subtotal for Earth ___

Colors

Look at large areas of color—walls, upholstery, carpeting, flooring, curtains. Don't ignore something like paint just because you didn't select it—if you really couldn't stand it, you would have changed it. Disregard small spots of color—a green couch with tiny flecks of beige counts as green, not beige. Do look at small but striking spots of color, like a bright red knickknack shelf.

Air

___ Light to bright blue (sky tones)

___ White

___ Pale yellow

___ Light gray

Subtotal for Air ___

Fire

___ Red

___ Orange

___ Bright yellow

___ Sand

Subtotal for Fire ___

Water

____ Deep to pale blue (water tones)

____ Sea to pale green (sea tones)

____ Coral shades (peach, pink, off-white)

    Subtotal for Water ____

Earth

____ Brown

____ Beige

____ Rust

____ Grass to forest green (plant tones)

    Subtotal for Earth ____

Objects

These are three-dimensional objects found on the walls, on shelves, on tables, in curio cabinets or other display pieces, and incidentally around the house. They are knickknacks (or, in Yiddish, *chotchkes*). Some may have specific uses, such as storage, but most are primarily decorative.

Air

____ Sun-catchers

____ Wind chimes

____ Mobiles

____ Feathers used in decor

____ Few or no incidental objects at all

    Subtotal for Air ____

Fire

____ One-of-a-kind art objects

____ A collection on display

____ Highly glazed ceramics

____ A grouping or tray of candles

____ Masks, especially African or Balinese

____ Ornamental weapons

Subtotal for Fire ____

Water

____ Seashells

____ Water containers (goblets, ewers, basins) as knickknacks

____ Sentimental keepsakes

____ Fountain

____ Multiple vases[2]

Subtotal for Water ____

Earth

____ Artistic handcrafts (boxes, planters)

____ Souvenirs

____ Stones or rocks

____ Baskets

____ Unglazed ceramics

Subtotal for Earth ____

Fabrics

Look at upholstery, curtains, bedding, throws, and slipcovers. If you have fabric wall-hangings, include them.

Air

____ Light cotton or cotton blends

____ Denim

____ Linen

Subtotal for Air ____

Fire

____ Satins or shiny fabrics

____ Jacquard

____ Decoratively textured or painted fabrics

Subtotal for Fire ____

Water

____ Silk or very soft fabrics

____ Gauze

____ Lace

Subtotal for Water ____

Earth

____ Undyed wool, linen, or raw cotton

____ Fleece

____ Chenille, boucle, or corduroy

____ Open weave

____ Eyelet

____ Fringed

____ Quilted

  Subtotal for Earth ____

Art
This section addresses the *themes* of two-dimensional art, or wall art, in your home. (Specific artists are suggested in the next section.)

Air

____ Skies, clouds, birds

____ Transportation

____ Planes (pictures or models)

____ Kites, balloons

____ Mechanical drawings, plans

____ Machines, technology

____ Architecture, towers[3]

____ Framed or hung documents, sayings, calligraphy

____ Traditional Japanese brushwork

  Subtotal for Air ____

Fire

____ Masks

____ Butterflies in close-up[4]

___ Sunrises, sunsets

___ Cubism

___ Pictures of movie stars or rock stars

___ Sports pictures

___ Erotica

   Subtotal for Fire ___

Water

___ Impressionism

___ Bodies of water (oceans, waterfalls, lakes)

___ Rain, umbrellas, rainy streets

___ Marine life (fish, dolphins, whales)

___ Romance; kisses

   Subtotal for Water ___

Earth

___ Weaving, tapestry on the wall

___ Folk art

___ Illustrations

___ Family photographs

___ Depictions of families, mother and child, etc.

   Subtotal for Earth ___

Artists

This section gives a representative sampling of artists who express elemental themes or ideas, or who create strong elemental impressions. Of course, such a list cannot possibly be comprehensive.

Air

____ M. C. Escher

____ Alphonse Mucha

____ Georges Seurat

____ Maxfield Parish

   Subtotal for Air ____

Fire

____ Mondrian

____ Keith Haring

____ Vincent van Gogh

____ Kandinsky

____ LeRoy Neiman

   Subtotal for Fire ____

Water

____ Monet

____ Robert Doisneau

____ Pre-Raphaelites (John Waterhouse, Edmund Blair Leighton, Dante Gabriel Rossetti)

   Subtotal for Water ____

Earth

___ Frida Kahlo

___ Georgia O'Keefe

___ Norman Rockwell

___ Anne Geddes

___ Rembrandt

___ Vermeer

Subtotal for Earth ___

In the Kitchen

Don't worry about food for now; just focus on decor.

Air

___ Clean, white, or light countertops

___ Lots of reflective surfaces, chrome, metal, high polish

___ Pale tile

___ Very pale, bleached wood

___ Ultramodern gadgets

Subtotal for Air ___

Fire

___ Gas stove

___ Spice rack prominently displayed

___ Hanging garlic, chili peppers

___ Good, sharp knife set

___ Painted tile

___ Exposed brick

Subtotal for Fire ___

Water

___ Water purifier or cooler

___ Fancy teapot

___ Icemaker in the freezer

___ Water dispenser in the refrigerator

___ Double sink

___ No dishwasher

___ Wine rack

Subtotal for Water ___

Earth

___ Canister sets, especially clear ones

___ Open storage—pots, utensils, or dishes stored "out" or visibly

___ Kitchen is the social center; ample seating

Subtotal for Earth ___

In the Bedroom
Bedroom decor is often where we express a private, intimate part of ourselves.

Air

___ Extra room for books at the bedside

___ "Open" furniture with shelves instead of drawers

___ Crisp cotton sheets

___ Few pillows or blankets

___ Decor on the ceiling

Subtotal for Air ___

Fire

___ Erotic art

___ Erotic "toys" in the nightstand

___ Extra mirrors, mirrored ceiling

___ Candles

___ Personal object (i.e., toiletries, jewelry) displayed as decor

Subtotal for Fire ___

Water

___ Waterbed

___ Canopy or curtained bed

___ Dust ruffle

___ Pillow shams

___ Satin bedcover

___ Silky or very soft sheets

___ Nighttime scenes

___ Opaque "privacy" curtains

Subtotal for Water ___

Earth

___ Many pillows

___ Many blankets

___ Stuffed animals

___ Blanket chest

___ Rocker or cozy chair

___ Footstool

___ Homemade blankets

___ Afghans or quilts

   Subtotal for Earth ___

Household Elements Quiz: Totals

	Air	Fire	Water	Earth
Overall Style				
Colors				
Objects				
Fabrics				
Art				
Artists				
In the Kitchen				
In the Bedroom				
Total:				

What About Everything Else?

You may have noticed that not *everything* in your home has been covered in this section. That's because not everything can be clearly assigned to one element.

Take clutter, for example. If you have a cluttered home, you may wonder what element is to blame. Unfortunately, this is a case where any of the four elements could be the cause. An Air home may be cluttered with books. An Air person may have lots of "inspiring" things lying about, or may be too impractical to clean up. A Water person may surround herself with an excess of sentimental keepsakes. She may obsessively cling to everything that reminds her of the past, and may develop deep affection for various household objects. An Earth person's possessive nature may cause him to own more than he has room for. A Fire home is the least likely of the four to be cluttered, but it may be stuffed with eclectic collections and art.

So, this section has covered those parts of your home that can be clearly attributed to one element. As you learn more about your own elemental makeup and that of your family, you'll undoubtedly find more elemental influences in your home than the ones listed here.

BRINGING ELEMENTS INTO YOUR HOME ON AIR

Everything around us has magical associations. Occultists love to create and study lists of associations; all of us have our own *777*[5] in our head or a notebook somewhere. Every plant, animal, and mineral has an elemental, planetary, and Zodiacal association (not to mention Kabbalistic, Tarot, magical, etc.).

But there are associations within associations. For example, the home itself is Earth, but within the home, as we've seen, there are four elements, so that Earth (the home) can be Earthy, Airy, Fiery, or Watery.

Why do I bring this up? Because now we're going to talk about scent—aroma— and aroma is Air. In healing or magical systems, aromatherapy is an Air system because it delivers its magic via the air (just as massage is an Earth system because it delivers its magic via touch). It is important to understand the distinction between the system and its magic. Obviously, aromatherapy can be used for aromas that are associated with any of the four elements. For example, jasmine is associated with Water, the Moon, and love, so jasmine aromatherapy would impart a Watery magic through the air.

Whenever you use scent, regardless of the particular scent used, you are using the element of Air. Depending upon how you choose to scent your home, you can use one or more elements in combination with Air, as the following examples demonstrate.

Aromatherapy in the Home

Air Alone

To scent your home using only Air, spray a perfume directly into the air of the room being scented. You can also add scents to light bulbs, and there are mixtures prepared especially for that purpose. Although the scent is being *heated*, one could argue that Fire itself is not being used. I leave it to your discretion whether to categorize scented light bulbs here or in the next category.

Air and Fire

Use scented candles to mix Air and Fire into the atmosphere of any room of your home. The scent is carried on air, and the burning candle brings fire.

Air and Earth

Use a sachet in a bundle or a dish to scent a room with Earth. A sachet is simply an assortment of dried aromatic herbs, flower petals, or buds. A traditional use is to wrap a sachet up as a small linen bundle and place it in a drawer to scent clothing. A more modern form is to place the herbal mix loose in a bowl, often with a perforated lid. This bowl is sometimes called a potpourri, which is confusing, as another item also uses that term, as we shall see. Although plants, like aromas, can have any elemental nature, using the *body* of the plant is distinctly Earthy.

Air, Fire, and Water

Nowadays, infusers are a popular gift item. These are candle holders with a little dish on top. They generally take a tealight or votive candle, and the flame heats the dish in which a few drops of essential oil have been added to water. As the water heats, the scent infuses the room.

The Perfect Balance: Four Elements on Air

Similar to the infuser, the potpourri is the perfect elemental balancer. It is so compact and practical that it can be used as a portable "altar" wherever and whenever elemental balance is needed. Besides, it is a lovely addition to any home.

The potpourri has a design similar to a double boiler. It can be constructed just like an infuser, except that the top dish is deeper. Place a candle in the bottom dish, and in the top dish, sprinkle herbs, flower petals, etc. (fresh or dried) on top of water that is about an inch deep. Some potpourris have three dishes: the bottom for the candle, the middle for the water, and the top for the herbal mix.

The potpourri begins in Fire, which heats Water, which rises as steam (Air) through the Earthy mixture of plant items, thereby spreading the scent throughout the room. Preparing a potpourri brings you in touch with all four elements and spreads all four elements throughout your house, balancing and enriching it. For this reason, I highly recommend using an herbal mix that is itself balanced in all four elements to emphasize the effect.[6]

THE ELEMENTS AND YOUR BODY

Now that you've balanced the elements into your home, let's bring them into your earthly home—your own body. In this section, we'll address the outer body (cosmetics, perfumes, clothing), the inner body (food), and their intersection (beauty treatments, which have both cosmetic and health benefits).

Elemental Attire: The Air, Fire, Water, and Earth of Clothing and Accessories

How we dress is a part of how we express ourselves; how we show ourselves to the world. This includes the choice not to care what the world sees, as that, too, is expressive of our nature. As we saw with home decor, even the decision to tolerate hand-me-downs is, in fact, a decision.

We have already seen that both color and fabric have an elemental identity. With clothing, we will also learn that *fit* plays a role. We'll look at style, and how our overall look communicates our elemental nature. (Some men may be tempted to skip to the next chapter at this point, but stick it out—this applies to you, too!)

In addition to what we wear, there's also how we *decide* what to wear. The choices we make about appearance, fashion, trends, comfort, cost, convenience, and practicality are all rooted in our elemental personas.

As with home decor, we can look at elemental attire with two purposes in mind: first, to gain insights into ourselves, and second, to effect change. We can both discover the element(s) we're wearing, and make a conscious decision to "wear an element" as part of bringing ourselves closer to that element. For example, if you found you are weak in Air in the Personal Element Quiz in chapter 3, you could wear Airy clothing in addition to doing the suggested meditations.

The Attire of Air

The problem with the way an Air person dresses is that he often wears an *idea*, without giving attention to how that idea has manifested in reality. This is typical Air behavior, of course, and is practically a caricature of the way the "Ivory Tower Intellectual" (read: Air person) dresses.

I was married for a decade to a very Airy person, and it was a behavior I came to recognize. Clothing was used to communicate the concept of the person (a tweed jacket for intelligence), his lifestyle (loud colors to say "I'm a hippie"), or his affiliations (Druids wear white). Like all Air people, he had a weakness when it came to translating ideas into reality. Such Air people look a little cartoonish as a result. Their clothing is too loud or ill-fitting; the look doesn't work.

Other Air people are unconcerned with the physical. They pay no attention at all to their clothing. These are the people with six identical shirts, a pair of jeans, and a tie they got for their birthday. Clothing is to protect you from the weather and to avoid shocking the neighbors. No need to make a fuss over it!

Some Air people do love to shop, but a certain impracticality will come into play, and these people will have a lot of things in their closets that they never wear. They shop based on Air qualities—they buy something that *inspires* them, whether or not they'll ever wear it. Or they buy it without trying it on, because the body is less important than the mind, and if they *think* they want it, that tends to override issues of fit and comfort—at least until they get it home.

As we learned in chapter 4, Air sometimes has difficulty making decisions, and this can be reflected in a reluctance to shop. When Air people enjoy shopping, it is often because they enjoy observing the variety of nice things one can buy. However, choosing what accompanies them to the register can be challenging.

The Internet is a very Airy concept, not just because it is high-tech (which Air loves), but because the essence of the Internet is *communication.* The sending of signals via communication links is in every way imbued with Air. This opens up a whole world of shopping for Air people, and those who once eschewed the process may now enjoy it.

Despite my criticisms of Air's fashion sense, there's a wonderful fancy to it (fancy, after all, is something that takes *flight*). The great fashion designers have often been uninterested in the wearability of their creations, hanging *ideas* on their models more than *clothing.* Perhaps such innovators as Christian Dior were Airy in their approach to design.

Air people don't care about fashion in terms of following trends, which are meaningless to them. Inspiration can come from any source, whether popular or not, current or not.

Air people are generally careless with money, and this will apply to their clothing as well. They don't associate cost with value; that is, the concrete reality of dollars and cents doesn't seem to connect to how useful, interesting, or delightful it is to own a thing. So, Air people have a tendency to disregard price, and buy exactly what they want and need. Some Air people understand the abstract concept of value well enough to have a great distrust of anything that is too cheap—they prefer to pay full price as an assurance of quality. And, some Air people are very thrifty; they have experienced their own carelessness with money often enough to keep a lock on their wallets. In this case, they will tend to underspend, and such people's clothing has the unfortunate tendency to look shoddy.

Looking Like Air

Air colors for clothing and accessories are the same as Air's household colors:

· Light to bright blue (sky tones)

· White

· Pale yellow

· Light gray

Air clothing is loose-fitting (it *breathes*) and comfortable. It tends to hang in clean, straight lines. It is not seductive. It ignores fashion, being neither conservative nor trendy. Sometimes Air clothing expresses a distinct sense of humor, while other times it is quite serious and professorial.

Air fabrics are natural. Summer fabrics are cotton and linen, and winter clothing is woolen or knitted. Cashmere is an Air favorite.

Air's love of language and ideas can be displayed in clothing and jewelry bearing sayings and symbols. It is typical of Air to own many T-shirts bearing clever sayings, although Air doesn't necessarily have the kind of ego that favors monograms or nameplates. More likely is meaningful jewelry depicting pentagrams, the Eye of Horus, a birthstone, or a claddagh.[7] An Air person may have an engraved wedding band or engagement ring.

Air jewelry is simple, often but not always symbolic, and favors a clear, direct design. Simple pendants, small post earrings, and a wristwatch are typical. Even when not so conservative, Air jewelry will be neither heavy nor binding.

Few gemstones are associated with Air.[8] However, several stones are associated with Air colors. Although none of the following are Airy, they will look good with an Air palette: citrine, diamond, aquamarine, mother of pearl, and moonstone. It's important to remember that magical colors and other magical associations won't necessarily overlap. It's okay to use one association even when it contradicts another. So go ahead and wear that Watery pearl necklace that coordinates nicely with your Airy cashmere sweater.

The Attire of Fire

Fire dresses with distinction. The confidence, pride, and even vanity of Fire is apparent in his wardrobe. For Fire, clothing is part of how he makes an entrance, one that is unmistakable and, often, sexy as well.

Fire people enjoy having a signature piece, one that identifies them. This may be a nameplate necklace, a brightly colored Pashmina shawl, or a singular article of jewelry. Sally Jesse Raphael's red glasses are typical of this kind of Fiery trademark.

Some Fire people are interested in fashion, and, as with many Fire interests, they don't go halfway. If they care about fashion, then they are obsessed with the difference between Versace and Prada, and what should be worn when. The drama and artistry of fashion naturally appeals to Fire, although for some Fire people, they'd rather make their own statement, and reject fashion as mere crowd-following.

Most Fire people enjoy shopping because they enjoy the stimulation of color, texture, and style. Fire is generally comfortable in public places (like malls and shopping centers). It's also true that Fire people enjoy spending money. I think that shopping is a kind of transformation—instead of spinning straw into gold, it's spinning money into merchandise—and transformation is Fire's native soil. There is an undeniable magic to walking into a store empty-handed, and leaving it with a bag full of beautiful, exciting new things. Fire understands and appreciates this magic, and will not balk at parking, prices, and the other things that other elements may find inconvenient or annoying.

Fire never forgets sexuality, and clothing will reflect that. Attire will be body-conscious. Clothing that is *too* sexy—too tight, too low cut—has an excess of Fire and should be tempered.

But that's just a critical Earth voice talking. In fact, everyone, even me, can enjoy dressing in a way designed to garner appreciative attention. A sexy Fire outfit displays exactly the right amount of cleavage, is just tight enough in the right places, and is discreetly understated elsewhere. One of Fire's gifts is self-knowledge, and this is helpful when choosing a wardrobe. Fire tends to know its own strengths and weaknesses, so the Fire woman with gorgeous hips and a flat chest will dress in a way that emphasizes her assets while distracting attention from her bust. The beauty magazines are full of exactly that sort of advice, and a Fiery woman reading this book already knows all about it.

A Fire person is perfectly willing to wear an uncomfortable article of clothing if it looks great. Presentation matters to dramatic Fire, who likes to live life to the fullest. "I'll be mellow when I'm dead" is a very fiery statement, and "I'll be comfortable when I'm dead" is an apt corollary.

Looking Like Fire

Fire clothing colors are the following:

- Red
- Orange
- Bright yellow
- Black
- "Autumn" colors (rusts, browns)

You'll notice that black wasn't listed as a Fire color previously (under decor or anywhere else). It isn't. In magical correspondences, black is associated with Earth, with the deep, black soil, darkness, and mystery. However, a man or woman *dressed* in black is dramatic and distinctive—in other words, Fiery. Dressing in black can be high-fashion, body conscious, and ideal for displaying the distinctive accessories that function as Fire trademarks.

Notice also that browns are not normally on a Fire palette. Magically, brown is Earth; it is the color of soil and bark. As the color of many wild and domestic animals, it is associated with hunting and husbandry, and hence with food, which is again Earth. But as with black, brown is different as a fashion color than elsewhere.

When looking at our homes earlier in this chapter, we saw that the Southwestern style of decorating was suitable to Fire decor. Thus we associated pale colors, like sand, with Fire, which is normally bold. A similar logic is possible here. An autumn palette is often worn to express warmth and to emulate the Fiery display of autumn leaves. Clothing created with oranges and reds often comes from this color scheme, and will mix in browns and rusts. So, here is a situation where brown is expressive of Fire. When we get to Earth, we'll see that brown, when worn by an Earthy person, looks rather different.

Fire dresses in fashionably fitted clothing with a distinctive silhouette, or in snugly sexy clothing, or in long lines that sweep into a room. Fabrics are also often special or distinct, such as silk. Fire doesn't require natural fabric, when spandex does the job; there's no resistance to wearing a synthetic! Fire loves gloss and glitter, and every Fiery woman really should have something of gold lamé. Sequins are not out of the question and beaded details are likely.

The glitter and gleam of Fire can be found on collars, fringes, accessories, and jewelry. It's the little extras that add Fire to an outfit—sequins on the collar of a cardigan, a large fake gem on the clasp of a purse, a gold tie clip, beaded fringes on a jacket, etc.

Fire people can sometimes layer themselves in jewelry, wearing, for example, five or six necklaces at once, or bangle bracelets halfway up their arms. This is the same tendency toward excess that can make a Fire person dress like J.Lo. Some people can pull it off—I'm thinking of a priestess I used to know who made me want to wear all *my* jewelry at once. But when I imitated her, all the necklaces got tangled up and I felt like a parody of a priestess, not the real thing. So I left her look to her; on her it didn't seem excessive, it looked glamorous. No doubt if nearly anyone else did it, it *would* look excessive. That's the personal flair of Fire coming out—she made the look her own.

Another Fiery way to wear jewelry is to wear one or two singular, striking pieces. Paloma Picasso's jewelry—chunky, bright, and as bold as a splash of paint—is an example of this style.

Fire jewelry will tend toward gold. To me, the stones that are the most Fiery are amber and tiger's-eye, although any red-colored stone, like ruby or garnet, is also Fire. It goes without saying that diamonds are a Fire girl's best friend.

The Attire of Water

In many ways, Water is the most complicated element. We have seen that Water has the widest range of symbolic associations, manifestations in nature, and personality types. Water's connection to emotions, the subconscious, and passage into other worlds (particularly death) give it permutations in myriad aspects of self. To put it simply, there are different *kinds* of Water people, and this manifests in, among other things, how they might dress.

One type of Water attire is the kind that *flows*. You know the type: they enter a room like water coming over the falls, or like Laurence Fishburne presenting an Academy Award. Long, sweeping lines and layers of fabric create a distinctive, almost magical impression. A Water woman of this type almost always wears skirts or dresses rather than pants. Clothing swirls and eddies about such a person. One immediately imagines that this is an artist, and the sense of deep feeling is conveyed. Picture, for example, a woman wearing a two-layered dress—an opaque underdress with a gauze or mesh overlayer. There is a scarf draped about her neck, tied loosely, if it all. Jewelry is long and flowing too, and the earrings may reach all the way to the shoulders. If the weather is cool, a shawl may be added. A man can achieve this look as well, such as the aforementioned Mr. Fishburne, although it isn't often seen. Because it requires a bit more unaccustomed vanity from a man than from a woman, there's often a strong Fire component in the former.

Another Water look is the romantic or poet. This one is definitely a unisex style. Watery men often affect the flowing sleeves, ornate vests, and leather boots of the Renaissance poet. Barring that, they may go for the Beat poet look: dark turtleneck, dark hat, and Brad Pitt near-beard. Except for the beard and the addition of opaque tights, the Beat poet look is pretty much the same for women. A more traditional romantic look for a woman involves high collars, lace, and frills. Here we have a sort of Merchant-Ivory Victoriana.

You may notice how all of this sounds more like a costume than like an ordinary outfit. This is typical of Water's romantic flair. Fire's dynamic nature may create a signature look that becomes *his* costume, but Water is likely to acquire a costume out of a romantic image of who the wearer might be. Because Water identity is *fluid*, it can be changed, or at least modified, with a change of wardrobe. It is the Water people who intuitively understood what this section would be about, knowing that one can put on character traits when one puts on clothing.

With such fluidity of approach, Water people may well understand fashion and be comfortable changing with the fashions. They may choose to dress how they feel, regardless of trends, or they may view this season's "in" thing as just one more form of self-expression through attire.

Since Water people are moody, they don't necessarily have fixed attitudes about shopping, convenience, and the other issues surrounding the acquisition of clothes. They tend to be careless about money, preferring to spend based on feeling or rule of thumb rather than staying within a budget. The Water person will place comfort secondary to style, but she doesn't like to be bound, and will never wear anything too tight or confining.

Looking Like Water

The colors of a Water wardrobe are as follows:

- Watery tones of blue, from pale to deep
- Watery tones of green, from seafoam to the dark green of the ocean on a cloudy day
- Purples and mauves
- Silvers
- Coral shades (peaches and pinks)

To the Water household palette discussed earlier in this chapter, the Water wardrobe adds the lunar colors and some floral tones. Flowers are very romantic and sensual, and floral perfumes, as we'll learn, are most likely to be Watery. The sensual tones of a tropical flower garden are often found in a Watery wardrobe. Water can also wear black, especially black velvet, as part of a fluid, theatrical outfit.

Water fabrics have a flowing quality to them, and are sometimes translucent as well. Soft cotton blends, gauze, light mesh, and satin are all Watery choices. Water loves paint, and Water people might wear painted fabrics such as batik, tie-dye, or watered silk, or fabrics that create a painterly impression, such as appliqués, brocades, or embroidery. Of course, there is the possibility of lace as well.

Water jewelry is romantic and consistent with the overall costume. For the "flowing" look, pendants and earrings are very long; there are numerous beads, often exotic ones, and in general, jewelry is elaborate. For a Victorian look, brooches and cameos will certainly be seen. Jewelry in the shape of flowers or sea creatures is a definite possibility. Most Watery men will have at least one pierced ear.

In addition to gemstones associated with the element of Water (sapphire, lapis, moonstone), there are jewelry items that come from the sea—coral, pearls, abalone, mother of pearl, and other shells.

The Attire of Earth

I can speak from direct experience here, because I'm pretty Earthy in my clothing style, although with some Fire mixed in.

Earth doesn't have a natural affinity for fashion, for a number of reasons. Earth is practical, so to an Earth person, clothing should be comfortable, useful, and long-lasting. For most Earth people, throw something between "reasonably priced" and "cheap" on to that list as well. These are the concerns of Earth: pragmatism, economy, real-world application, and physical comfort. It is entirely unthinkable, to an Earth person, to wear an uncomfortable article of clothing just because it looks good. Earth doesn't lie on her back to zip up her jeans—if they don't zip standing up, they obviously don't fit! In fact, if jeans are so difficult to fit, isn't it easier and simpler to just wear sweatpants? (Ease and simplicity are important to Earth.)

Earth people *can* turn these very practical concerns into a personal style that looks great, and satisfies Earthy needs, without becoming slobs. They can wear classic styles that never look outdated—simple shirts or blouses, sweaters, blazers, and slacks and/or skirts. A lot of men dress like this—suits, dress shirts, khakis, and crewneck sweaters. It's a straightforward Land's End, Talbot's, or Eddie Bauer style. It never gets old, nor does it look "too young." It's very earthy and smart-looking. It's not creative, but dressing in Earthy attire isn't a creative endeavor.

There are two serious fashion mistakes that Earth tends to make (this is the part I know from experience). The first is to hold on to old clothes that are out of style, inappropriate, or in bad condition. This has to do with possessiveness, stubbornness, and a misguided sense of thrift. The second is to wait until a new fashion is a sure thing. Earth really doesn't like to be avant-garde or to look different from everyone else; Earth likes to look "normal." When a trend has been around for a while, it starts to look normal, and only then will Earth be interested in wearing it. The problem with that, from a fashion point of view, is that any trend that looks *that* normal is on the way out. In which case, Earth will start making the *first* mistake with the item (wearing clothes that are out of style), or will end up never wearing it.

Some Earth people really like shopping, which can be a very tactile experience. Earth isn't really sure about an article of clothing until she tries it on, and while some Earth folks simply don't care about clothing, most relish certainty. Earth really likes convenience, so things like proximity, ease of parking, and quality of service will make a difference. The out-of-the-way shop is not for Earth; she wants something that's on her way home from work!

Earth shoppers love the Internet, because they can shop from their favorite place—home.

As we already know, economy matters a great deal to Earth, the element most connected to money. Paradoxically, this can make Earth an avid shopper, as she feels proud and satisfied when finding a bargain.

Looking Like Earth

Earth colors are natural above all. Bright hues aren't going to be found in Earth's closet. Instead, we'll see the following:

- Brown
- Beige shades, including the undyed shade called "natural"
- Rust
- Khaki
- Deep forest green

Fabrics, too, will tend to be natural—cotton, linen, wool—and pleasing to the touch. Earth's love of the tactile is satisfied by soft, cuddly clothing, nicely textured and cabled sweaters, velvets, and corduroy. Tweed has an appealing naturalness, and traditional fabrics, such as tartan plaids, appeal to Earth's sense of stability. Earth, too, sometimes wears black (a difficult color to nail down!). Black can go well with the natural, conservative tones of an Earth outfit.

In keeping with the cuddly factor, Earth clothing has a roomy fit. Even in nicely tailored clothes, there's an attraction toward items that seem roomy, like cowl-neck sweaters, pleated pants, carpenter pants, and parkas. There's a sense of being enveloped or cocooned in an Earth outfit.

Earth jewelry is natural and chunky. In addition to the gemstones of Earth (emerald, jet, malachite), Earth favors wood, seeds, and found objects, often in odd shapes. Earth, however, will avoid any jewelry that is impractical, such as bracelets that tend to snag, or rings too large to allow one to use one's hands freely. Jewelry can be beautiful, but it must be sensible as well.

Who Is Wearing What? Quiz

Understanding the relationship between clothing and the elements can be informative and fun. When you meet people, you can tell something about their elemental nature by the colors, styles, and jewelry they have on. Imagine you're at a party and you meet each of the following people. Guess their primary elemental nature based on what they're wearing.

1. Kate is in a mid-calf-length sheer dress with an attached underslip; the underlayer is a dark plum color, and the overdress is a pattern of large blossoms in blue, purple, and green. She has two rope-length necklaces on, knotted together flapper-style. One is dark blue with lapis and cobalt-colored crystals. The other is mostly silver tones. Her long beaded earrings match her necklaces.

   Kate is: ____ *Air*   ____ *Fire*   ____ *Water*   ____ *Earth*

2. John is wearing an unironed pale-blue dress shirt and no tie. He is wearing nondescript gray dress slacks. He wears no jewelry except for a Timex watch.

   John is: ____ *Air*   ____ *Fire*   ____ *Water*   ____ *Earth*

3. Marge is wearing an Irish cable-knit wool sweater and black leggings. She has large round earring (about the size of a silver dollar) of onyx and gold. She is wearing sneakers.

   Marge is: ____ *Air*   ____ *Fire*   ____ *Water*   ____ *Earth*

4. Frank is wearing a pair of gray sweatpants with a hole in the knee, a T-shirt with his company logo on it, and a fleece sweater. His only jewelry is a wedding ring.

   Frank is: ____ *Air*   ____ *Fire*   ____ *Water*   ____ *Earth*

5. Lisa is wearing hot-pink spandex pants and a midriff-baring white top. Her crystal pendant is on a long chain so that it lands just at the center of her cleavage. Her nails are blood red. She is wearing an anklet and gold hoop earrings.

   Lisa is: ____ *Air*   ____ *Fire*   ____ *Water*   ____ *Earth*

6. Donna has on a cream-colored lace blouse with elastic wrists and full, ruffled cuffs. Her broomstick-style gauze skirt is long and green. She has a triple strand of pearls at her throat and matching earrings.

   Donna is: ____ *Air*   ____ *Fire*   ____ *Water*   ____ *Earth*

7. Bob is wearing a purple turtleneck and button-fly jeans. He has several silver rings; one in the shape of a dragon with a jewel in its mouth. His ear is pierced, and in it he wears a diamond stud.

   Bob is: ____ *Air*   ____ *Fire*   ____ *Water*   ____ *Earth*

8. Betty is wearing a white blouse, a tweed jacket with leather elbow patches, and beige corduroy pants. She is wearing a watch, a claddagh ring, and a small labrys (the double-headed axe that symbolizes lesbianism) on a silver chain.

   Betty is: ____ *Air*   ____ *Fire*   ____ *Water*   ____ *Earth*

Answers

1. Kate is Water. Were you fooled by the Earthy flowers on her dress? The colors, cut, and shape of everything that Kate wears is suggestive of Water.

2. John is Air. Note the carelessness of his appearance and the lack of jewelry. Note, too, that Air people almost always wear a watch. John's pale-blue and gray color scheme is also Airy.

3. Marge is Earth. The comfort and natural colors of her clothing, combined with the chunky earrings, are your clues.

4. Frank is Earth. You might have thought Air because of the carelessness and the slogan-bearing T-shirt, but Frank's priority is comfort, as seen in the sweatpants and the fleece.

5. Lisa is Fire. There's no question that she wants to be sexy and noticed.

6. Donna is Water. She dresses in romantic lace, while showing Water's flow in the cut of her sleeves and skirt. Green can be associated with Earth or Water, so here we combine the color with other clues.

7. Bob is Fire. His purple shirt is attention-getting, and those button-fly jeans suggest that he cares about creating a "look." His jewelry, too, is Fiery, right down to that fire-breathing dragon.

8. Betty is Air. Her clothing and jewelry are symbolic, suggesting ideas—the idea of "tweedy professor" (the elbow patches) and the ideas of lesbianism and commitment. Note that she is wearing a watch, and that her shirt is white.

Elemental Attire

	Air	*Fire*	*Water*	*Earth*
Keywords	Ideas, symbolic, whimsical, inattentive	Sexy, dramatic, distinctive	Flowing, romantic	Comfortable, practical
Overall look	Simple, clean or haphazard, cartoony	Fashionable, attention-getting	Artistic, costume-like	Cuddly and warm or dowdy

	Air	*Fire*	*Water*	*Earth*
Colors	Light to bright blue, white, pale yellow, light gray	Red, orange, bright yellow, black, "autumn" colors (rusts, browns), anything bright	Pale to deep blue, pale to deep green, deep purples and mauves, silvers, corals	Brown, beige, natural, rust, khaki, forest green
Fit and cut	Loose, open, straight lines	form-fitting, revealing	flowing, layered	Roomy, wearable
Fabrics	Cotton, linen, knits, cashmere	Silk, spandex, glossy nylons, lamé, sequins	Cotton blends, gauze, light mesh, satin, batik, tie-dye, watered silk, appliqués, brocades, lace	Knits, fleece, cotton, corduroy, velvet
Favorite articles of clothing	T-shirts with sayings	Signature piece	Long scarf, "poet's shirt"	Big sweater, parka, sweats
Jewelry	Simple, symbolic, wristwatch	Layers of glittering strands or one bold piece	Long pendants and earrings, exotic beads, cameos, brooches	Chunky, natural, nothing that snags

Elemental Perfumes

Among Pagans and magical people, it is popular, even fashionable, to use essential oils to scent oneself; it is something of a cliché to say that Pagan women smell like patchouli. The magical properties, including the elemental associations, of essential oils and individual herbal or floral ingredients are easy to look up and take advantage of. It is a simple matter to scent yourself with rose (Water) to draw love, or ginger (Fire) to bring courage.

On the other hand, many modern urban/suburban Witches buy more herbs at the supermarket than they grow, and buy more beauty products at department stores than they make themselves. Although growing, making, and creating your own magical tools and implements is important and powerful, no one particular lifestyle is more Pagan than another, and your Paganism can coexist with living in the 'burbs and shopping at the mall. Yet, few books address the magical qualities of packaged products.

Perfumery can be fascinating: its scent, its variety, its often exquisite packaging, and its vague promise of transformation. There is a mystique and a beauty to perfume that cannot be denied. Perfume blends are so complex, so intricate, that they have been thought to be related to alchemy.[9] They create a whole greater than the sum of their parts.

Indeed, there is no way of knowing that a modern perfume contains this ingredient or that by smelling it. Even something as distinctive as rose or as intense as jasmine can be blended into something new and unique. Magically, this makes perfume hard to quantify and therefore hard to use. You can wear perfume to smell good, and most of us will agree that smelling good is a worthy goal; but if you don't know the ingredients, you don't know the elemental (or any other) attributions of those ingredients, and therefore cannot take advantage of a perfume's elemental properties.

Perfumes don't come with ingredient labels like food, but it is possible to find out much of what's in them. Manufacturers, distributers, and books on perfumery are all informative. Of course, that's only the beginning. Certain important perfume ingredients are not found in standard herbals or magical texts. They include resins, gums, and animal products, as well as unusual plants that are rarely used outside of perfumery. Their qualities must be studied before attributions can be assigned. Then there's the naming! In perfume, unusual names for common ingredients are often used, such as *muguet* (which turns out to be a type of lily of the valley), so a certain amount of linguistic research is needed as well. Finally, there are *aldehydes*, artificial ingredients invented especially for perfumery. In attempting to understand these magically, there is no occult tradition to fall back on.

For all the complications, I was determined to discover the magical significance of brand-name perfumes. With study and research, I was able to analyze a number of such perfumes and look at their elemental composition.

It should be noted that major-label perfumes are generally synthetic, not just in their use of aldehydes, but in their use of synthesized aromas that imitate those found in nature. As such, they have no "life," no aura, and this greatly decreases their magical potency. Ideally, in aromatherapy, only true aromas are used. However, synthetics do share the magical association of the product they imitate, so that synthetic rose, while less potent and far less powerful than the real thing, is associated with Water, just as a real rose is.

The book *Essence and Alchemy* lists a number of ingredients that cannot be extracted naturally.[10] If you find a perfume claiming to contain freesia, honeysuckle, violet, tulip, lily, gardenia, heliotrope, orchid, lilac, or lily of the valley, you are dealing with a synthetic version of that scent. No one has yet discovered how to capture these aromas naturally. In addition, of the animal ingredients—musk, civet, ambergris, and castoreum—only civet is still extracted naturally; the rest are imitations.

What the Perfume Information Means

Information that you or I can find about perfume ingredients is always incomplete. The exact composition and proportion of perfumes is considered a great secret. However, manufacturers do readily share the dominant notes of a perfume, and other resources will often go into great detail. Two, four, ten, or more ingredients (natural or the synthetic "equivalent") may be given or figured out.

One day early in my perfume research, I was discussing how to analyze the data I'd gathered with my friend Mickey. In a blaze of generosity, Mickey volunteered to program a perfume database. Using Mickey's database, I was able to enter over 100 ingredients and assign them each an elemental and planetary attribute. Then I entered over sixty women's perfumes and men's colognes (and one unisex scent) and added to each all of its known ingredients.

Now I really had something! The database allows me to look at perfumes by their elemental composition (either parts or percentages) and at elements by their presence in perfumes. I can also cross-reference elements to perfume types.

I selected the perfumes listed under each element in the following pages by choosing only perfumes with a minimum percentage of that element. The percentage varies by element. For example, few perfumes are strong in Air, so for Air I list perfumes with at least 20 percent of that element. Water, on the other hand, is almost always present in perfumes, and is often dominant. For that list, my minimum was 50 percent. Sometimes only a few ingredients are available, so that a perfume with only four known ingredients might be 75 percent Water; I can only assume that the percentage is relatively accurate and would remain so even if more ingredients were known.

In each elemental perfume list, the ingredients associated with that element are named. Some perfumes are listed more than once; for example, *Jean Paul Gaultier for Men* is equally balanced under Air, Fire, and Water (one third each). In such cases, only the pertinent ingredients are listed—the Air ingredients under Air and the Fire ingredients under Fire.

Use the element sections to experiment with perfumes based on element. After the four "perfumes of element" sections (which include men's colognes) are alphabetic lists of women's and men's scents, with the primary and secondary (if applicable) element of each. Here's where you can look up your favorites. People seem to be happiest with scents that match their existing elemental personal nature or elemental love nature. I looked up every perfume I have ever loved and worn, and discovered that they are all spicy florals or floral orientals—that is, Fire/Water. You, too, may find that you want to *match* your own nature aromatically, rather than use scent to correct or balance it.

Perfumes of Air

Modern perfumes are often classified by type, although some, especially newer ones, defy traditional classification. A perfume's type describes its dominant notes—those that are most closely linked with how it actually smells. It will also have other ingredients, other notes, but they will have a blending or stabilizing quality; they will add to and alter the scent, but not change its essential character.

Perfumes categorized as *Green, Green Floral,* or *Fougere* are often Airy. Air *greens* are characterized by the scent of pine or sage, and Air *green florals* have strong notes of lavender, galbanum, or grass. *Aldehydic* perfumes I consider to be of the Air, and some florals—those with muguet or clary sage especially—can be Airy as well.

The women's perfumes with the strongest Air components (from 40–20 percent Air, descending) are as follows:

- **Charlie** from *Revlon*: An aldehydic floral with the scent of grass.
- **Miss Dior** from *Christian Dior*: A green floral with clary sage and muguet.
- **Chanel No. 5** by *Chanel*: The first aldehydic perfume. Also contains muguet.
- **Green Tea** by *Elizabeth Arden*: A green aromatic. Aromatics, including this one, are Fiery, but the green tea itself, and caraway, give strong Air content as well.
- **Arpège** by *Lanvin*: This is a classic floral perfume, primarily Water, but given Air by aldehydes, benzoin, and lily of the valley.

Among men's colognes, the Airiest (43–20 percent, descending) are these:

- **Tommy** by *Tommy Hilfiger*: This popular green scent has bluegrass, spearmint, and lavender.
- **Brut** from *Faberge*: A green with lavender and anise.
- **Chaps** by *Ralph Lauren*: This one has anise and honey.
- **Jean Paul Gaultier for Men** from *Gaultier*: The famous Gaultier perfumes come in matching bottles, one shaped as a man and one as a woman. The men's cologne has equal strength in Air, Fire, and Water. Its Air comes primarily from grass and lavender.
- **Romance for Men** by *Ralph Lauren*: This scent is considered a *wood* type and also has grass and lavender.
- **Cool Water** from *Davidoff*: A green aromatic, primarily Fiery, with lavender and sage adding a strong secondary Air component.
- **Tuscany** from *Aramis*: Almost perfectly balanced in the elements, its Air is derived from lavender and anise.
- **Perceive for Men** from *Avon*: A Fiery cologne with Air from sage.

As you see, Air is not usually the strongest element in a scent, and is often subsidiary to Fire or Water. Men's scents are more likely to be Airy than women's scents.

Perfumes of Fire

Numerous perfume types can be Fiery. Both men's colognes and ultrafeminine florals can have strong Fire components. The most likely types to try are *oriental*, *spice*, *aromatic*, *citrus*, and some *greens* (sometimes called *chypres*).

Oriental and *spicy* perfumes may have such Fiery ingredients as orange, tangerine, clove, ginger, coriander, pepper, and bergamot. A spice perfume might also have cinnamon or pimento.

Chypres often contain a strong bergamot component as well.

Fiery *greens* might have juniper, basil, and/or rosemary.

Aromatics can have strong qualities of spice and green combined. Pepper is typical.

Most *florals* are Watery, often intensely so. A Fire floral will have carnation, marigold, tagetes, or neroli, all of which are Fiery flowers, and might be blended with spicy ingredients such as bergamot or pepper.

Her are some very Fiery women's perfumes (83–33 percent, descending):

- **Dolce & Gabbana** from *Dolce & Gabbana:* An intensely Fiery floral, containing neroli, carnation, tagetes, basil, and orange.

- **Dolce Aura** by *Avon:* A floral with neroli and bergamot.

- **Obsession** by *Calvin Klein:* An oriental with neroli, bergamot, marigold, civet, basil, orange, and coriander.

- **Poison** from *Christian Dior:* A floral spice that includes pimento, neroli, citrus, cinnamon, cedar, carnation, and numerous other ingredients.

- **Green Tea** by *Elizabeth Arden:* A green aromatic. In addition to its Air ingredients, *Green Tea* has bergamot, celery, orange, and peppermint.

- **Coco** from *Chanel:* A spicy perfume with cascarida, neroli, clove, coriander, and angelica.

- **Aliage** from *Estée Lauder:* A green citrus with cedar and nutmeg.

- **Opium** by *Yves Saint Laurent:* An oriental. Its Fire comes from numerous sources, including bay, cinnamon, clove, coriander, and pepper.

- **Perceive** from *Avon:* A floral that is primarily Water, though carnation, cedar, citrus, and pepper give it Fire as well.

- **Romance** by *Ralph Lauren:* A green floral. Like *Perceive,* it is primarily Water, with Fire (from ginger and tangerine) as a strong secondary element.

Here are some Fiery men's colognes (50–33 percent, descending):

- **Curve** from *Liz Claiborne:* A green aromatic with a high concentration of Fire from bergamot, cedar, clove, and lime.
- **Pleasures for Men** from *Estée Lauder:* Another green aromatic, containing coriander, ginger, orange, and pimento.
- **Cardin** from *Pierre Cardin:* Includes bergamot, cedar, clove, and cumin.
- **Polo** from *Ralph Lauren:* Contains basil, carnation, cumin, and juniper.
- **Pour Monsieur** from *Chanel:* Includes bergamot, cedar, and neroli.
- **Perceive for Men** from *Avon:* Orange and cedar provide its strongest Fire.
- **Cool Water** from *Davidoff:* Despite the name, this is a green aromatic with coriander, rosemary, and tobacco.
- **Grey Flannel** by *Geoffrey Beene:* An *oriental wood,* with roughly equal parts of Fire, Water, and Earth. Bergamot and orange are the Fiery ingredients.
- **Chaps** from *Ralph Lauren:* Has roughly equal parts of Fire, Air, and Earth. Bergamot and lime provide the Fire.
- **Aramis** from *Aramis:* Has roughly equal parts of Fire, Water, and Earth. Bergamot and cumin are the Fiery ingredients.
- **Jean Paul Gaultier for Men** from *Gaultier:* Has equal strength in Air, Fire, and Water. Its Fire comes primarily from neroli and peppermint.

Perfumes of Water

The most Watery perfumes tend to be *orientals, woods* (woody perfumes have sandalwood and other wood-based ingredients in strong measure), and *florals.* Most perfumes have at least some Water, since very sweet-smelling things, including most sweet flowers and many sweet resins, are of Water. Most of a perfumer's favorite flowers are Water, including rose, jasmine, gardenia, iris, violet, and ylang-ylang. Vanilla, an important base note, is also Water.

Most perfumes are built on a pyramid of scent, with top notes forming the first impression, which dissipates quickly, middle notes forming the perfume's "heart," and base notes providing a long-lasting foundation. The rich, romantic, Watery florals are common heart notes, even in spicy or green perfumes.

Floral perfumes are dominated by rose and jasmine and are backed by ylang-ylang and tuberose.

Orientals, when Watery, will show the presence of vanilla, labdanum, and cardamom.

Woods usually have sandalwood as a dominant note.

Here are some Watery women's perfumes. Water is so prevalent in perfumes that I am listing here only those with 100–50 percent Water (descending):

- **Donna Karan** by *Donna Karan:* An oriental wood. Fully 100 percent of the stated ingredients are Watery: amber, apricot, jasmine, lily, rose, and sandalwood.

- **Cashmere Mist** by *Donna Karan:* This wood perfume is also 100 percent Water. It is composed of jasmine, vanilla, and sandalwood.

- **Trésor** from *Lancome:* A floral that contains the scents of fruits, rose, vanilla, iris, amber, lilac, and lily of the valley.

- **Gio** by *Armani:* A floral with amber, gardenia, hyacinth, jasmine, rose, sandalwood, and vanilla.

- **Far Away** from *Avon:* This oriental features the scents of freesia, jasmine, and peach.

- **Giorgio** from *Giorgio Beverly Hills:* A floral with notes of chamomile, gardenia, jasmine, rose, and sandalwood.

- **Dolce Vita** from *Christian Dior:* An oriental wood with apricot, peach, rose, sandalwood, and vanilla.

- **Samsara** from *Guerlain:* A classic floral oriental. It is a complex scent with amber, fruits, narcissus, ylang-ylang, jasmine, iris, sandalwood, and vanilla.

- **America** by *Perry Ellis:* A floral with the scents of lilac and lily.

- **White Diamonds** by *Elizabeth Taylor:* A floral with amber, jasmine, lily, iris, tuberose, rose, and sandalwood.

- **Angel** from *Thierry Mugler:* An oriental wood with peach, plum, sandalwood, and vanilla.

- **Beautiful** by *Estée Lauder:* A floral scented with amber, jasmine, lily, rose, sandalwood, tuberose, and ylang-ylang.

- **Pleasures** by *Estée Lauder:* A floral with the scents of lilac, lily, rose, sandalwood, and violet.

- **White Shoulders** from *Parfums International:* This classic perfume is a floral with notes of amber, gardenia, jasmine, lilac, orris, rose, sandalwood, and tuberose.

- **Chanel No. 5** from *Chanel:* An aldehydic floral with amber, iris, jasmine, rose, vanilla, and ylang-ylang.

- **L'air du Temps** from *Nina Ricci:* This classic scent is a floral with gardenia, rose, and sandalwood.

- **Spellbound** by *Estée Lauder:* This one is your author's favorite perfume. It is a floral oriental with amber, apricot, cardamom, narcissus, rose, sandalwood, and vanilla.

- **White Linen** by *Estée Lauder:* A floral with jasmine, orris, rose, and violet.

- **Happy** from *Clinique:* A fruity floral with boysenberry, lemon, freesia, and grapefruit.

- **Jean Paul Gaultier** from *Gaultier:* This scent is the counterpart to *Jean Paul Gaultier for Men*, and comes in a woman-shaped bottle. It is a fruity floral with the scents of amber, iris, orchid, rose, vanilla, and ylang-ylang.

- **Perceive** by *Avon:* A floral that smells of freesia, gardenia, orchid, pear, rose, and sandalwood.

- **Eternity** by *Calvin Klein:* A floral with amber, freesia, jasmine, lily, narcissus, rose, and sandalwood.

- **Chanel No. 19** from *Chanel:* A green floral. This famous perfume is scented with iris, jasmine, rose, sandalwood, and ylang-ylang.

- **Romance** by *Ralph Lauren:* A green floral that has notes of chamomile, freesia, and violet.

- **Bvlgari pour Femme** from *Bvlgari:* A green floral with iris, jasmine, rose, and violet.
- **Chloe** from *Lagerfeld:* This perfume has the strong floral scent of jasmine.
- **Safari** from *Ralph Lauren:* A green floral with amber, hyacinth, jasmine, jonquil, narcissus, orris, rose, and sandalwood.
- **Tommy Girl** from *Tommy Hilfiger:* This floral contains the scents of apple blossom, heather, jasmine, lily, rose, sandalwood, and violet.
- **CK One** by *Calvin Klein:* This scent was promoted as the first unisex perfume. It is a citrus containing cardamom, jasmine, papaya, rose, and violet.

Watery men's colognes are less common, as Water is associated with many scents considered feminine. These have 67–40 percent Water, descending:

- **Eternity for Men** from *Calvin Klein:* This scent has amber, jasmine, rosewood, and sandalwood.
- **Polo Sport** from *Ralph Lauren:* Contains the scents of sandalwood, seaweed, and algae (really!).
- **Égoïste** from *Chanel:* Contains rose, sandalwood, and vanilla.
- **Pleasures for Men** from *Estée Lauder:* This scent features the fragrances of geranium, grapefruit, rose, and sandalwood.
- **Romance for Men** by *Ralph Lauren:* Contains amber, geranium, and rose.
- **Brut** from *Faberge:* This famous cologne features the aromas of geranium and vanilla.

Perfumes of Earth

The ingredients associated with Earth have a distinctly earthy smell, often giving an intensely nature-based impression. They are musky, woody, earthy (literally, with smells reminiscent of soil or moss), or animal-like. Earthy perfumes can be of almost any type, as these ingredients are often too intense to be the dominant aroma of a perfume, and it is the other ingredients that will determine the type.

Earthy *florals* will have honeysuckle, magnolia, or mimosa.

Chypres are Earthy (and Fiery) by definition, containing oakmoss and often patchouli.

Earthy *greens* seem invariably to have vetiver.

If an *oriental* is earthy, it generally has oakmoss, musk, or both.

Here are some women's Earth perfumes (50–25 percent, descending):

- **Chloe** by *Lagerfeld:* A floral; of its two dominant scents, honeysuckle is the Earth one.
- **Tabu** by *Dana:* An oriental containing musk, oakmoss, and vetiver.
- **Bvlgari pour Femme** from *Bvlgari:* A green floral with mimosa, musk, and vetiver.
- **Aliage** from *Estée Lauder:* This green citrus has armoise, oakmoss, and vetiver.
- **Halston** from *Halston:* A wood fragrance scented with moss, musk, and patchouli.
- **America** from *Perry Ellis:* This floral contains magnolia.
- **Chanel No. 19** from *Chanel:* This green floral features the scents of leather, oakmoss, and vetiver.
- **White Linen** from *Estée Lauder:* A floral with moss and vetiver.
- **Shalimar** from *Guerlain:* This classic oriental contains leather, musk, patchouli, and vetiver.
- **Miss Dior** from *Christian Dior:* This green floral features the aromas of leather, oakmoss, patchouli, and vetiver.

Here are some Earthy men's colognes (33–25 percent, descending):

- **Chaps** from *Ralph Lauren:* Contains moss and musk.
- **Grey Flannel** from *Geoffrey Beene:* An oriental wood with oakmoss and patchouli.
- **Aramis** from *Aramis:* Contains musk and patchouli.
- **Tuscany** from *Aramis:* Contains leather, patchouli, and tonka beans.
- **Cardin** by *Pierre Cardin:* Contains moss, oakmoss, and vetiver.
- **Pour Monsieur** from *Chanel:* This one is scented with cypress and vetiver.
- **Curve** from *Liz Claiborne:* Contains musk and vetiver.

Women's Perfumes and Their Elements (Alphabetical)

Perfume	Manufacturer	Dominant Elements	Secondary Elements
Aliage	Estée Lauder	Fire/Earth	Water
America	Perry Ellis	Water	Earth
Angel	Thierry Mugler	Water	Fire/Earth
Arpège	Lanvin	Water	Air/Fire/Earth
Beautiful	Estée Lauder	Water	—
Bvlgari pour Femme	Bvlgari	Water	Earth
Cashmere Mist	Donna Karan	Water	—
Chanel No. 19	Chanel	Water	Earth
Chanel No. 5	Chanel	Water	Air
Charlie	Revlon	Air/Fire	Earth
Chloe	Lagerfeld	Water/Earth	—
CK One (unisex)	Calvin Klein	Water	Fire
Coco	Chanel	Water/Fire	—
Dolce & Gabbana	Dolce & Gabbana	Fire	—
Dolce Aura	Avon	Fire	Water
Dolce Vita	Christian Dior	Fire	—
Donna Karan	Donna Karan	Water	—
Eternity	Calvin Klein	Water	—
Far Away	Avon	Water	Fire
Gio	Armani	Water	Fire
Giorgio	Giorgio Beverly Hills	Water	—
Green Tea	Elizabeth Arden	Fire	Air/Water/Earth
Haiku	Avon	Water	Fire

Perfume	Manufacturer	Dominant Elements	Secondary Elements
Halston	Halston	Water	Earth
Happy	Clinique	Water	—
Jean Paul Gaultier	Jean Paul Gaultier	Water	Fire
L'air du Temps	Nina Ricci	Water	—
Miracle	Lancome	Fire/Water	—
Miss Dior	Christian Dior	Water	Air/Earth
Obsession	Calvin Klein	Fire	Water
Opium	Yves Saint Laurent	Fire/Water	—
Perceive	Avon	Water	Fire
Pleasures	Estée Lauder	Water	—
Poison	Christian Dior	Fire/Water	—
Ralph	Ralph Lauren	Water	Fire/Earth
Red	Giorgio Beverly Hills	Water	Fire
Romance	Ralph Lauren	Water	Fire
Safari	Ralph Lauren	Fire/Water	—
Samsara	Guerlain	Water	—
Shalimar	Guerlain	Water	Fire/Earth
Spellbound	Estée Lauder	Water	Fire
Tabu	Dana	Water/Earth	—
Tommy Girl	Tommy Hilfiger	Fire/Earth	—
Trésor	Lancome	Water	—
White Diamonds	Elizabeth Taylor	Water	Earth
White Linen	Estée Lauder	Water	Earth/Air
White Shoulders	Parfums International	Water	Earth/Air

Men's Colognes and Their Elements (Alphabetical)

Cologne	Manufacturer	Dominant Elements	Secondary Elements
Aramis	Aramis	Fire/Water/Earth	—
Brut	Faberge	Air/Water	Earth
Cardin	Pierre Cardin	Fire	Earth
Chaps	Ralph Lauren	Air/Fire/Earth	—
CK One (unisex)	Calvin Klein	Water	Fire
Cool Water for Men	Davidoff	Fire	Air/Water
Curve	Liz Claiborne	Fire	Earth
Égoïste	Chanel	Water	Fire
Eternity for Men	Calvin Klein	Water	Air/Earth
Grey Flannel	Geoffrey Beene	Fire/Water/Earth	—
Jean Paul Gaultier for Men	Jean Paul Gaultier	Air/Fire/Water	—
Perceive for Men	Avon	Fire	Air/Water/Earth
Pleasures for Men	Estée Lauder	Fire/Water	—
Polo	Ralph Lauren	Fire	Water/Earth
Polo Sport	Ralph Lauren	Water	Fire
Pour Monsieur	Chanel	Fire	Water/Earth
Romance for Men	Ralph Lauren	Water	Air
Tommy Hilfiger	Tommy Hilfiger	Air	Fire/Water
Tuscany	Aramis	Earth	Air/Fire/Water

Elemental Beauty Treatments

A beauty treatment is not a cosmetic; rather, it is a treatment or process that helps the health of the skin and outer body in a way that improves appearance and often well-being, too. Beauty treatments make you look better, to be sure, but they also make you *feel* better. They remove toxins, improve circulation, relieve tension, un-cramp muscles, and are generally pleasurable. Beauty treatments also force us to pay attention to ourselves; they are pampering, nurturing, and indulgent in a healthy way. If you're paying attention to your diet, a facial is a much better treat than a sundae!

I again caution men *not* to avoid this section! The pleasures and health benefits of beauty treatments, as well as their elemental connections, are definitely not for women only.

As in previous sections, we are looking at the elements here in two ways. First, how is the treatment given; that is, does the treatment itself partake of the nature of Air, Fire, Water, or Earth (or some combination)? Second, what are the elemental associations of a treatment's ingredients? Here we will hearken back to the same material as in the perfumes section, the traditional and folkloric qualities of the natural components. Rose petals bring Water to a treatment, rosemary adds Fire, and so on.

Think of a patchouli-scented candle. Candles, obviously, are associated with Fire. Patchouli is associated with Earth. The "delivery system" is Fire, but the item being delivered is Earth. You could burn an incense (Air) made from jasmine (Water), or you could wear an Earthy fleece sweatshirt in red, a Fiery color. The same sort of thing applies to beauty treatments; a treatment has elemental qualities because of what the treatment *is,* and it has elemental qualities based on its ingredients—these qualities may or may not match. This allows you to redouble elemental energies (Fire ingredients added to a Fire treatment), or to combine the elements for a more complex purpose (while helping your skin and enjoying a relaxing experience).

Air Beauty Treatments

Air beauty treatments are those that work because they are inhaled, those that deepen inhalation, and those that reach us on air.

Steam is the most important Air treatment. Steam at first appears to be quite blended in the elements, since it uses heat (Fire) and Water, and is transmitted to your body on Air. But it is the final result—not the creation—that is the *treatment,* so I believe Air is steam's proper attribution.

A steam bath opens the pores and removes toxins. (Purification is also a Fire experience, but almost any cleansing treatment has purifying qualities.) Steam also deepens inhalation and is good for the lungs.

Besides going to a steam room in a spa or health club, you can do steam facials. Steam facial machines are available to buy in any department store or specialty shop, but you can save money by using an old-fashioned "steam tent." Heat a pot of water until it is steaming, and then turn off the heat. Make a tent by draping a towel over your head and around your face. Place your face, in the tent, over the steam so that the pot is enclosed and the steam is trapped (only use steam on clean skin, with no makeup). Come up for fresh air as necessary, but do allow yourself to fully experience the steam, both externally (on your skin) and internally (by breathing it in). In addition to the benefits to your appearance, this technique has been proven to shorten the duration of the common cold.

After a steam treatment, rinse your face or body with lukewarm water, and then with cool water. The warm water washes away any impurities that were drawn out by the steam and remain on the skin's surface, and the cool water closes the pores now that they are clean and purified. Your skin may seem abnormally pink at first, but you'll notice a clear, light quality to your skin within a short time.

You can also use an *inhalation* treatment. People often add herbs to a steam facial, which combines aromatherapy with steam. As mentioned earlier, aromatherapy is an Air-based system, as scent is associated with Air. When using herbs in a steam facial, you combine the magical and healing properties associated with the *scent* with the physical properties associated with applying the herb to the skin. For example, the aroma of chamomile is relaxing, inducing sleep and peace. In skin products, chamomile is used to soothe and revive tired skin, and to reduce puffiness around the eyes. A handful of fresh chamomile in your steam facial combines all these properties.

Certain herbs promote deep inhalation. They open our lungs as we take in their potent scent. Thus, even if they are not associated with Air on a magical level, they can be used in an Air treatment or healing to open breathing passages.

Eucalyptus is magically associated with Air, inspires deep breathing, and is used in cough remedies.

Camphor is magically associated with Water, but has properties similar to eucalyptus. It is often added to steam tents to cure the common cold (or at least hasten its departure) because it opens the lungs. Commercially available *artificial* camphor should not be inhaled; be sure you're using only natural camphor oil or fresh herbs. Even then, use it sparingly. Camphor is sacred to Kali and, on an unrelated note, was inhaled long ago to decrease the sex drive.

Peppermint also deepens the breath and is associated with Air. Magically, it promotes wakefulness and energy. Its best-known cosmetic use is as a foot treatment.

Fire Beauty Treatments

It won't come as a shock to learn that Fire beauty treatments are those delivered to the body via heat. Many such treatments are also therapeutic, since heat is good for muscle and joint pain as well as tension.

The first Fire treatment to consider is the *sauna*. Saunas have many of the advantages of steam rooms, but are more appropriate for people with arthritis or other joint or connective tissue problems, which would preclude them from being in a humid atmosphere. Saunas deliver the heat in a dry environment, which doesn't trigger aches and pains in bad knees, old injuries, and sore muscles the way a moist environment sometimes can. It's important with a sauna to shower thoroughly afterward, so that any toxins that are sweated out are rinsed from the body.

Another Fire treatment is *hot wax*, or *paraffin*. Hot wax is not the same as "waxing." Waxing is a depilatory treatment that uses heated wax. Hot wax is coated onto the skin and then yanked away, after the wax cools, taking the hair with it. If you've never experienced it, I assure you it's not as bad as it sounds, but it's not fun either.

Paraffin treatments are, like the other treatments detailed, a pleasant experience. They are designed to enhance the skin's health by warming and moisturizing. Salons generally offer paraffin treatments only for the hands, although some treat feet as well. Home paraffin kits are designed to accommodate hands and feet, and can be used to treat other rough skin patches, such as the elbows. Spas and some home kits offer full-body paraffin treatments, including paraffin facials.

Paraffin wax is heated in a "bath" to approximately 130 degrees Fahrenheit; this melts it, but keeps it pleasantly warm to the touch. Then the hands or feet, after being washed and (usually) moisturized with lotion, are dipped repeatedly into the wax (drying between dips), so that layers of hot wax are built up. The wax is left in place for fifteen minutes or more and then removed.

Paraffin wax retains heat very well, so that the coated skin stays quite warm throughout the treatment. Sometimes mitts are used (they look like big oven mitts) to retain the heat even longer.

After the treatment, the skin can be massaged, rubbing the lotion deeper into the softened skin.

The paraffin that is sold for these treatments usually has added moisturizers and/or essential oils and/or "aromatherapy" scents. (Nowadays, anything with a scent is referred to as aromatherapy. Artificial scents with weird names like "rain-bath" aren't *really* aromatherapy, but you'll find plenty of advertising that says they are.)

Unlike many beauty treatments, paraffin baths are often recommended for medical purposes. They are soothing for joint and extremity pain, and are helpful with poor circulation to the extremities. They can temporarily increase range of motion in stiff joints, so the treatments are sometimes used prior to exercise or physical therapy. Paraffin baths are highly moisturizing and are used by people with severely dry skin conditions. They are also used prior to massage for relaxation, moisturizing, and softening.

The paraffin treatments I've had were very soothing and felt great. They are certainly Fiery, and have the quality of warming one's hands and feet by a cozy fireplace.

I own a home paraffin bath kit and have tried the hand treatments with and without the mitts. The heat retention is definitely better with the mitts, which also encourage you to hold still—wiggling your fingers breaks the wax seal, and the heat dissipates more quickly. The foot treatments are deeply warming; perhaps because I don't expose my feet to air afterward (I put socks or slippers on right after), my feet feel intensely warm for almost an hour. The only problem with the foot treatments is where to put your feet—especially where to put your right foot while dipping the left, and vice versa. You have to remember to line the floor or a footstool with wax paper or plastic beforehand (advice the kit doesn't provide).

My skin isn't terribly dry. Nonetheless, I'm not that impressed by the quality of moisturizing—my hands and feet feel softened after a paraffin treatment, but not noticeably more than with any number of other moisturizing treatments. This might depend on the brand of paraffin wax you use.

Hot oil treatments are used on the hair for deep conditioning, especially for dry, brittle, or damaged hair, and for split ends. These treatments are good for hair that has been damaged by chemical treatments (including dyes). Because hot oil moisturizes the scalp as well as the hair, some people recommend it for dandruff. The treatments are generally favored by people with very thick hair, and they're great for people of African heritage. Depending on whom you ask, applications are recommended twice weekly, weekly, biweekly, or monthly. Although my own hair is fine and limp—not the recommended type—I found by experimenting that these treatments are great, even for limp hair, if used about every six weeks, and noticeably improve strength, health, and shine.

Oil is heated and applied to the hair, left in for a variable amount of time (usually fifteen minutes), and then shampooed out. Different recipes call for olive, soybean, almond, castor, jojoba, tea tree, and/or other oils, and you can add such extra ingredients as honey, rosemary leaves, ginseng, aloe, comfrey, calendula, nettle, wheat germ, vitamin E, or rose hips.

Generally, the ingredients are mixed in a plastic bag, and the oil is heated by placing the bag in a bowl or mug of hot water. Once hot, the oil is worked into the dry hair. Then the hair is wrapped in a shower cap or towel for fifteen minutes before being shampooed (although some people leave it in as long as overnight). According to the website *The Hair Diva,* keeping the body warm will keep the hair treatment warm, and a half-hour's hot bath or even a workout will raise the body temperature enough to affect the hair.[11] Others sources recommend staying in a hot shower (with the hair covered by a shower cap) for the fifteen-minute conditioning period in order to keep the oil warm,[12] while still other sources recommend using a hair dryer to keep it warm.

After shampooing the oil out, don't use your normal conditioner, as this will overcondition the hair. Return to normal conditioning with the next shampoo, or as you see fit.

Commercial hot oil preparations can be bought in drugstores, supermarkets, or natural food stores. Some of these heat automatically and don't need to be preheated. Others reduce the conditioning period to as little as one minute. Some are applied to wet, rather than dry, hair. Some don't even appear to be oily, and smell and feel much like shampoo.

Your author has, in general, not objected to the research necessary to write about beauty treatments. It has been no great suffering to experiment with facials and paraffin. In the case of hot oil treatments, though, I was concerned about overconditioning my fine hair, which can leave it limp and lifeless.

So I decided to try just two treatments, on opposite ends of the spectrum: first, the commercial preparation of a national brand, and second, a homemade preparation.[13] I avoided the commercial preparations that "heat themselves," since if I wasn't heating anything, it didn't seem very Fiery. I settled on VO5 Hot Oil Treatment.

The first lesson I learned was to make sure to read the ingredients. Although this product has a number of ingredients (such as collagen and amino acids) designed to do the job of a traditional hot oil treatment, it also has a slew of the ordinary chemicals one would expect to find in a commercial shampoo. Thus, while the product certainly *worked*—my hair was ultraconditioned and very soft—it didn't feel like a hot oil treatment; it didn't feel Fiery, although my son insisted that I looked more Fiery the next day. It was quick and convenient, which is excellent if your hair needs this kind of therapy, but disappointing in its lack of pampering focus. How am I to feel I am *treating* myself if the whole thing is over in sixty seconds in the shower?

My hair was definitely superconditioned by the hot oil, and strengthened as well—as evidenced by a noticeable decrease in the amount of hair in my brush and on the bathroom floor. I discovered that I could deal with the overconditioning (my fine curls were definitely less curly) by not using a conditioner after shampooing. In fact, the hot oil conditioned so thoroughly that I didn't need a daily conditioner for a few weeks afterward.

When my hair started to need conditioning again, and started to fall out a little more, I prepared my home treatment. Over the next few weeks, I tried variations on home recipes and ended up liking these two:

Simple Homemade Hot Oil & Honey Treatment

2 tbsps. sweet almond oil
2 tbsps. extra-virgin olive oil
2 tbsps. honey

Simple Homemade Hot Oil & Bergamot Treatment

    3 tbsps. sweet almond oil
    2 tbsps. extra-virgin olive oil
    1 drop bergamot essential oil

Line a coffee mug with a sandwich-sized zip-style plastic bag, so that the mouth of the bag is held open by the mug. Pour all ingredients into the bag and close it. Heat water in the kettle. Remove the bag from the mug, pour the near-boiling water into the mug, and put the bag back into the mug.

Seal the bag and make a small opening in a corner so that you can squeeze the oil mixture out. Apply mixture to your hair and work it in with your hands. This will be somewhat messy, so work over the sink nude or in an old bathrobe. Wrap hair in towel and leave for fifteen minutes.

Shower and shampoo. You may need to shampoo twice even if that isn't your usual routine. Do not use conditioner.

These recipes feel great. The conditioning and strengthening of your hair is every bit as good as with the commercial treatment. With both recipes, the "limpness" is reduced (I didn't lose my curls). With the honey recipe, the hair goes back to being shiny and pretty right away, and the strength of the hair is better (less fallout in the brush). However, honey is a troublesome ingredient. It is difficult to rinse out, and it feels sticky (obviously). It ended up on my skin and I had to spend a lot of shower time scrubbing honey off my shoulders and back. Overall, I found using honey unpleasant even though the results were great, which led to the second recipe.

In my modified recipe, I skipped the honey and added a drop (just one!) of bergamot essential oil, which is quite Fiery. (You could add the bergamot to the honey recipe if you'd like.) This oil-only treatment was easier to apply and more pleasant to rinse. However, my hair was greasy-looking and stiff for about forty-eight hours. Over the long term, I found the oil-only recipe more conditioning and less strengthening. The bergamot gave a very slight burning/tingling sensation, which most people probably would want to avoid, but I liked it; it felt like Fire entering me through my scalp.

So, the exact composition of ingredients is an individual choice. If you choose, skip the honey and its stripping, healing effect, as well as its stickiness. Or add essential oils. Or experiment with different oils. It's up to you—enjoy playing!

Water Beauty Treatments

Not surprisingly, Water beauty treatments use water as a primary ingredient. Most importantly, they are experienced through the medium of water. This is different than steam, for example, which you could say is *made* of water, but experienced through air.

All *soaks* are Water treatments. This includes a foot soak, a bubble bath, or a relaxing hour in a hot tub. Whenever the body, or any part of it, is *immersed,* the treatment is of Water.

As with steam, various herbs, oils, salts, or other items can be added to the soak. For example, *oatmeal,* which is associated with Earth, is magically connected to money and prosperity. For skin treatments, it is added to baths to relieve the itching of sunburn or poison ivy.

Many scents commonly used in bubble baths, such as *rose* or *peach,* are associated with Water and with love. When you soak yourself in a tub scented with such a flower, you are soaking yourself in love. As you absorb the Watery essence of emotion, increasing, psychically, your ability to be emotional and to flow with feeling, you will also magically draw love to yourself with the power of scent.

Another Water beauty treatment is *seaweed.* Seaweed is found in facial and body conditioners, soaks, soaps, masks, and scrubs. It is a cleanser that dries skin oils, leaving oily skin clear and refreshed. Because of its toning qualities, it is often combined with a moisturizer so that less oily skin types aren't overdried by it.

You could do a multilevel Water treatment by putting on a seaweed facial mask—the sort that must be left on for twenty minutes—and soaking your feet and/or hands while waiting for it to dry. If the soaks were scented with Watery floral essences, then you would be working on still more levels to add Water into your life physically, psychically, and magically.

Earth Beauty Treatments

The first and best Earth treatment is *massage.* Massage is a purely Earth experience—it involves touch and the physical body. Perhaps you don't think of massage as a "beauty" treatment, but rather as a health treatment. However, health and beauty are interrelated—we have already seen that beauty treatments condition skin, improve circulation, and remove toxins from the system. Massage not only heals muscle aches, bad backs, and stress, but it also brings blood to the skin surface and improves posture (by releasing knots that hold the limbs or the spine in an awkward position).

Massage is an Earth treatment that achieves the same results as more magical or meditative Earth ventures. It puts you in touch with your physical body, connects you to your tactile self, and grounds you. This, by the way, is true both for the masseur and the person receiving the massage—touch is touch, whether received on the neck and shoulders, or delivered through the hands.

Any beauty treatment based in *mud* is an Earth treatment. This includes mud masks on the face or body, mud soaks, and henna, which is muddy. Most muds draw excess oil out of the skin and soften the skin surface, but there are a great variety of treatments. It all depends on the composition of the mud and the other ingredients used—some are more oily, some drier. A *clay* mask generally dries oily skin and is good for acne. A mud mask, by contrast, may have more emollients and is good for any skin type. Clay and most mud masks are excellent for men's skin, which tends to be more oily and less delicate than women's.

Henna, of course, is used both to dye the hair and to decorate the skin. Because of the bright orange color of the resulting dye, it is sometimes thought of as Fiery, but its smell, texture, and appearance are all quite Earthy.

Exfoliants are another Earth treatment. While masks and soaks deep-clean the skin, exfoliants work by scrubbing the skin's surface, removing dead skin cells and loose particles to reveal a cleaner epidermal layer underneath. While exfoliating, you are also vigorously rubbing the target area. Exfoliation is an Earth activity because it is like massage—it works by rubbing.

Exfoliants are great for rough skin spots, like the elbows or the heels. They remove little impurities that might form acne if left on the skin. They also brighten the color of tattoos, which can appear clouded because of the layer of dead cells that naturally accumulates on the skin. However, exfoliants can also cause tans to fade, as the pigmentation of a tan is only in the skin's outermost layers. Once your tan begins to peel, exfoliants can help rub away the itchy layer.

Exfoliants are made from various ingredients and are of varying textures. Some are quite rough, almost like sandpaper. These are meant for thick, tough skin and calloses. Others are very mild, with lots of added moisturizers. These are meant for delicate skin, including the face. Some people prefer to use a milder product on the body, and rub it onto rough skin with an exfoliating glove or bath scrubby to increase the effect. That way, one product can be used to target different skin areas with different needs.

Basically, exfoliants are made from the following:

· Solid, grainy ingredients, which do the actual work of massaging and are generally Earthy.

· Oils, fats, and/or other emollients, which serve as a carrier for the solid ingredients, soften their impact, and moisturize the skin.

· Astringents, which are (occasionally) added to make the product less greasy, for use on oily skin.

· Soap (occasionally), so that washing and exfoliating can be done in a single step.

· Ingredients added for scent or color.

As already noted, it is the solid ingredients that bring the Earth quality, as well as the exfoliation, to any exfoliant. Each exfoliant is named after its main solid ingredient; there are salt scrubs, sugar scrubs, oatmeal scrubs, apricot scrubs (really apricot seed), and so on.

My favorite body scrub is a sugar scrub. The commercially made ones are becoming increasingly popular. They are gentler than salt scrubs, and appeal to me because my skin is rather delicate.

My initial research into, and experimentation with, salt scrubs left me feeling that they were too harsh. My friend Jennifer Monzón came to the rescue. Jennifer is a Wiccan and an aesthetician, and is passionate about the spiritual value of pampering yourself. A simple salt scrub recipe from Jennifer is included later in this section.

Salt scrubs are available with a wide variety of ingredients, which can add other elements to your beauty treatment. Commercial beauty-supply companies such as the Body Shop and Bath and Body Works, as well as cosmetic companies such as Estée Lauder, make salt scrubs with scents or other ingredients that will add Fire, Water, and Air. I have seen salt scrubs that contain lavender (Air), hemp (Water), and olive (Fire), among many other ingredients.

A homemade salt scrub is relatively easy to devise and to customize to your individual needs. Add more oils and emollients to make dry skin softer, or add an astringent like witch hazel to dry oily skin. Some recipes call for liquid soap, generally glycerin soap, to be used as an additive or even a base. Personally, I prefer to wash first, and then use a scrub. That way, I keep the scrub away from my underarms and even more delicate areas while I'm washing, and I let the oils and scents stay on my skin instead of washing them off. The scrub can remove soap residue from my body while it's removing dead skin cells.

Warning: Don't use salt or essential oils on an open cut, and don't use a salt scrub on a sunburn—ouch! Be very careful with essential oils. Some cause skin irritation and a few are toxic.[14] They are very strong and should only be used in tiny amounts. Make a relatively large amount of scrub so that the essential oils will be sufficiently diluted. You'll probably prefer to use salt scrubs as body scrubs or foot scrubs, since they are too harsh for most people's facial skin, especially women's.

A basic salt scrub can be made with equal parts of salt and olive oil. If you use kosher salt, this recipe is pretty rough. It is excellent for men, and for people who work outdoors, have calloused skin, or just like a very rough massage.

To soften salt, use a blender to powder it. You may find this works best when starting with sea salt, which comes in the form of small rocks. "Pulse" it in the blender until you have a fine powder.

Salts can also be softened and varied by combining them with other solid ingredients. My homemade recipe uses oatmeal and crushed almonds to this end.

In devising salt scrubs, I experimented with a number of mixtures; some too abrasive, some too greasy. For this reason, in addition to providing two salt scrub recipes, I also offer information on creating your own recipes:

· *Oils:* You can simply use olive oil; it is light, pure, and an excellent carrier. An even lighter choice, and one that is wonderful on the skin, is almond oil, which is also fairly expensive. The heaviest choice is soy oil.

· *Salts:* Sea salt is usually purchased in crystal form and should be powdered, as described. Kosher salt is purchased as rough grains, and can also be powdered.

· *Other solids:* You can use pulverized oatmeal, nuts, or seeds, as well as herbs.

Most people love salt scrubs. They leave rough spots like elbows soft, and skin tingly and refreshed. The experience of using them is pleasant, fun, visceral, and sometimes very sensual.

Scrubs tend to come off the body and out of the hands in clumps while you're using them. This sounds icky, and at first it is *icky*—that is, until you realize that part of the Earth experience is physical, messy, and playful. Wallowing in the mud is an Earth pleasure, and so is finding lumpy oatmeal on the floor of your shower. If you can't handle that, then it's possible that you need more Earth in your life anyway.

Wash thoroughly in the shower, and then turn the water off and apply the scrub. Rinse immediately, or leave the scrub on your skin for up to fifteen minutes to let the detoxification have its full effect. Rinse off. You don't need to wash again.

The commercial salt scrubs are less lumpy and messy than homemade ones. I soften my salt with oatmeal (which is also an Earth item), whereas big companies soften their products with laboratory-devised carriers that I can't spell, but that wash nicely down the drain. You pay for the privilege, of course, and you miss out on the fun of creating your own mix. However, I have nothing against buying a scrub in a store, and have tried more than one while researching this section. I can't deny that they feel great, but their acquisition isn't as interesting.

Jennifer's Easy Delicious Salt Scrub

Put ¼ cup of powdered sea salt in a container. Add enough olive oil to cover the salt, stirring the mixture and adding oil until the consistency is smooth. Add three to five drops of any nontoxic essential oil.[15] Stir and enjoy.

Deborah's Yummy Messy Earthy Scrub

Mix equal parts of the following ingredients; ⅛ cup each is enough for a single use:
  Kosher salt
  Oatmeal
  Almond pieces
  Sweet almond oil
  Soy oil
  Honey

Combine in a food processor until oatmeal and almond pieces are fairly fine. Add:
  1 drop essential oil of patchouli[16]
  2 drops essential oil of magnolia

Blend a little more. Add a handful of oatmeal (about a tablespoon) to soak up the excess liquid and continue to blend.

· With this recipe, you end up with more liquid than solid. You may wish to change the proportions to compensate. However, if you're storing the recipe for even a short while, the oil will separate, and you'll have to mix it up again just before you use it. I find it easier to mix it up at the last minute with extra liquid.

· You can experiment with different types of honey for different aromas and thickness. You can also use crystallized honey—the stuff that forms on the bottom of the jar. It adds a sugary graininess to the mixture, and decreases the liquid.

· I am very sensitive to essential oils, so I only use three drops in my recipe. Use no more than five drops per ¾ cup of mixture.

Beauty Treatments that Combine the Elements

You may want to focus on balanced treatments that combine four elements, or you may be working on two or three elements in your life at this time. Perhaps you are a very Earthy person, and your work is to add Air, Fire, and Water. You may be too rational and wish to emphasize the irrational pair (Fire and Earth—see chapter 3). Whatever the case, the ways of combining elements, in beauty as in life, are limited only by your imagination.

The first method of combining elements has already been mentioned—a treatment and its ingredients. A salt scrub with a drop of neroli essential oil combines the Earth of salt with the Fire of neroli.

Here are some additional ideas:

· **Water and Earth:** A bath or soak containing salts combines Water and Earth in their primal forms. Air and Fire can be added by burning candles and/or incense while bathing. You can wash in a shower, turn the shower off, and apply a salt scrub; then, instead of rinsing in the shower, get into the tub. The salt on your body becomes a lovely bath salt for your soak.

· **Earth and Air:** A massage that uses an oil containing an inhalation-inspiring ingredient, such as eucalyptus, deepens breathing during the massage, thus combining Earth and Air. To add Fire and Water, burn candles and pour the oil onto the skin from a seashell container.

- **Fire and Earth:** A paraffin treatment can be followed by a manicure (if you get this done in a salon, this is typical). A salon manicure includes a hand massage, which is not only Earthy, it's delightful! Some nail salons also offer five-minute neck massages. If the manicure includes a soak, Water is added as well. Women can top the whole thing off with a Fiery red nail polish.

- **Fire and Air:** Do a hot oil treatment on your hair. While you're waiting the fifteen or so minutes for the oil to condition your hair, do a steam treatment on your face, using the "tent" method. This has the added advantage of keeping the oil warm.

- **Fire and Water:** Soak in a hot bath while your hair is under wraps with hot oil, or put on a seaweed mask while doing a home paraffin treatment. Massaging the mask into the skin will add a touch of Earth. To add Air, burn incense while you soak or wax.

- **Water and Air:** Try a peppermint foot soak. Not only is peppermint associated with Air in folklore, it deepens inhalation. To add Earth, finish with a callous-removing pumice stone.

Beautifying Your Coven or Group

A number of the elemental beauty treatments discussed in this chapter can be done with a group of people. Because they also have a magical significance, they can be an ideal coven or Pagan group activity. If your group is exploring the elements together, then you might do many Way of Four activities jointly, including the nature exercises, eating elemental foods together (see the next section), and beauty treatments. There are a lot of good reasons to do this; groups need more than just magical things to do together, they need to bond socially as well as spiritually. These beauty treatments can serve both functions. They can provide fun, "safe" intimacy, and the group can walk through its exploration of the elements together.

Sweat Lodges

If you look at a list of the treatments suggested in this section, you'll notice that a *sauna* lends itself to group participation, and indeed, this is a fine way for a group to experience Fire. Once they hear the word "sauna," most modern Pagans immediately think "sweat lodge." Sweats are common at Pagan festivals and New Age events.

However, a lot of Native Americans have objections to the way non-Natives do sweats. Many of the people running them are relatively inexperienced, or have never experienced a traditional Native sweat. Some Native leaders say that New Agers are subjecting themselves to far too much emotional and physical intensity, and that the experience is meant to be gentle. Some people have complained that they had breathing problems during a sweat, but were left unassisted.

My personal preference is to honor experience and teaching. I learned Wicca from an experienced Wiccan Priestess. I wouldn't wish to learn Native ways except from an experienced Native teacher. If your group has the opportunity to participate in a sweat lodge under the auspices of such a teacher, go for it. Otherwise, save your experimentation for less risky ventures.

Saunas, Steam Rooms, and Hot Tubs

Health clubs, spas, and gyms have facilities that can be used by a group to share the experience of Fire, Air, or Water. If the facility is open to the public, you might be inhibited from holding hands and chanting, and you'll just have to focus discreetly on absorbing elemental energies through your skin. On the other hand, it may be possible to rent exclusive use of a section of a facility, and with a large enough group, that can be a great solution, and a great afternoon or evening!

Group Massage

Group massage is the sort of thing that was done in the 1970s by encounter groups, and for good reason—it is an excellent way for a group of people to break down barriers and deepen intimacy. Needless to say, these are important goals for a group that works magic together. Massage in a group is playful, tactile, direct, sensual, and tends to be uninhibited—all Earthy qualities.

It is necessary that you discuss clear boundaries in detail before you begin. There are all sorts of physical boundaries, and they must be explored and respected before touch can begin. Everyone has his or her own feelings about what kind of touch is okay, and where, and in front of whom. If someone doesn't want her feet or hands touched, just because you don't understand or share that limit doesn't mean it can be ignored. There may also be health limits. Assuming that your group doesn't include a licensed massage therapist, you should avoid working muscles or tissue too deeply, and should know in advance the sensitive spots of the person you're massaging.

Beyond the limitations of respectful touch, there are also the limitations of clothing. Will you be skyclad, partially dressed, or "draped"?[17] These are things that must be agreed upon by all. It is not appropriate for one person to strip down when others have agreed to a no-nudity rule, even if that one person is comfortable in the nude.

Knowing and agreeing to all these boundaries fosters communication. When boundaries are honored, it builds trust. Before you begin, you should also decide if everyone will be both recipient and masseur in one session, or if you will schedule multiple massage times.

Once you're ready to begin, lay out plenty of washable sheets. Have a variety of oils and lotions available. Soy oil is a common massage oil; it is thick and smooth. Some people prefer a lighter, less greasy oil, like almond. Some prefer hand lotion. This, too, is an area for communication.

Your massage event can be more or less magical. Perhaps you'll accompany the massage with chanting or music. Probably you'll burn incense. Don't forget to enjoy yourselves, and don't forget to laugh. It feels great, but it's all a bit playful—the greasy hands and bodies, the messy sheets, the touching. Give yourself permission to have fun.

Group Body Scrubs

Doing salt, sugar, oatmeal, and other body scrubs as a group is fun as well as practical. People often have troublesome skin areas on the back, which are hard to reach alone. Most of the rules of group massage apply here. As with massage, doing the scrubs nude is ideal—the buttocks tends to be another problem area—but it's not required and everyone needs to be comfortable.

Like massage, scrubbing one another's skin is earthy, playful, and sensual. You'll also find it's rather messy. The easiest indoor method is to have the person being scrubbed stand in the bath or shower. If you have a massage-type shower head—the kind that can be moved around—you can use it to rinse each other off right there, and this adds Water to the Earth experience.

Group Skin Treatments

If a full body massage or scrub is not your group's cup of salt, how about giving each other facials, foot scrubs, or hand treatments? This is obviously a lower level of intimacy than a full body scrub or massage, but is still a way of bonding and playing together while exploring the elements. Facials can be Earthy if mud- or meal-based, or Watery if seaweed-based. Hand and foot treatments can be Earthy scrubs or Fiery paraffin.

Henna Treatments

Another Earthy group activity that has become quite popular is henna, or mehndi.[18] This can be used as a hair dye or as a temporary tattoo, following traditional or modern design. Because mehndi tattooing is a ritual activity in India, it lends itself to ritual work for modern Pagans.

Group Aromatherapy

This Air activity can be shared by a group. You can pass scents around and explore their nature together. You can choose to share a specific experience together. For example, you could use essential oils of calendula and jasmine to stimulate psychic dreaming, or use essences of apple, freesia, and gardenia to promote peace in the group. Or, try the opposite approach: choose a small number of scents, pass them around, and have people guess what the magical effect of that scent is. It's not really a guessing game, of course, but a psychic attunement—people will be reaching into their present and psychic experience to discover the effect the scent is having. Aromatherapy can also be used as part of a spell (spells will be covered in chapter 7).

Elemental Eating

Eating elemental foods is a way of literally taking an element into yourself. When you eat Air foods, there is that much more Air within you.

Elemental eating can be a part of an elemental attunement—you can follow an elemental meditation with a meal of that element, and then go out wearing clothing of that element. Or you can use an elemental meal to help you focus on one specific goal of the day or evening to follow. For example, you can eat an Air meal before writing, a Fire meal before competing, or an Earth meal to prepare for a long wait (which requires Earth's patience).

You can increase the elemental influence of a meal by bringing the element into its preparation. This can be as simple as opening a window while making Air food. You can also do an invocation of the element during preparation. (For that matter, you can perform an invocation before any elemental process, be it cooking, meditation, or a beauty treatment.) There are many different ways of writing invocations.

(Generic invocations and some writing guides appear in appendix B; the ones provided here are specific to food preparation.) The style you choose for an invocation reflects your personality, your beliefs, and your aesthetic sensibilities. To give you a range of choices, each of the four invocations provided here are in a different style. Choose the one that suits you best. Once you have selected your favorite invocation, you may choose to write three more to match it. (See appendix B for writing matching invocations.)

Air Foods

Air foods are light and fluffy. They are full of air, like a souffle or cream puff. Anything wrapped in filo dough has an Airy exterior. Minty foods are also Airy, for the same reason that minty beauty treatments are Airy—they cause us to breathe deeply. White rice is Airy, both because of its color and because it is fluffed before serving—it needs air between the grains to taste right (sushi notwithstanding). Puffed foods are Airy, including puffed rice, rice and corn cakes, and popcorn. Of course, carbonated beverages are Airy. Other Air beverages are sake (rice wine) and mint-flavored drinks.

While preparing Air food, open the windows or turn on the fan. Listen to flute music or wind chimes. Recite the following invocation:

O Air, blow into this _____.[19]
Make it food of wisdom.
Breathe intelligence into this _____, O Air.
As I (we) partake of it, let me (us) partake of you.
As I eat,[20] *give me inspiration.*
As I eat, give me concentration.
As I eat, give me thought.
So be it.

Fire Foods

Fire foods are hot and spicy. Chilis, curries, and hot sauces of all kinds are Fiery, but if you can't tolerate spice, you can still ingest Fire. Pungent, tangy red sauces, like cocktail sauce and barbecue sauce, might not burn the tongue, but still retain Fiery qualities. Of course, a flambée is Fiery, and so is hard liquor.

Red meat is a Fiery food because of its fierceness. Cooking your meat over charcoals or an open flame is especially Fiery. In fact, *any* food can have Fire added to its nature by cooking it over an open flame.

Keep the kitchen very warm while preparing Fire foods. Use an iron skillet and your sharpest knife. Listen to loud, lively music while cooking.

The Air invocation addressed the element directly—you spoke *to* the element. But some people don't care for this approach. You can also speak *about* the element. This has more the quality of a spell—you are doing the work yourself rather than enlisting the aid of the element. Let's try that now. Note how *repetition* imprints the magical effect of the invocation:

This is the food of Fire.
This food is filled with passion and energy.
This food imparts Fire.
When I (we) eat this _____, I become more alive.[21]
Fire burns through this _____.
Fire comes into those who eat it.
When I (we) eat this _____, I become more alive.
This is the food of Fire.

Water Foods

Most beverages are Watery, unless there is a specific reason to assign them to another element (which is noted under that element). Although all alcohol is traditionally associated with Fire, wine can often be more appropriately assigned to Water, especially sweet wines and dessert wines.

As for solids, in general they are Watery if they are syrupy, gooey, or sweet. An ice cream sundae is a Water food, complete with the cherry on top. A sweet and sour sauce is usually Watery—they're rarely spicy enough to be truly Fiery.

While cooking a Water dish, create a sensual kitchen atmosphere. Don't work under bright lights, and allow the room to get steamy. Listen to love songs.

Another very traditional form of invocation is rhyme. The simplest doggerel—provided it has a good rhythm, is easy to remember, and gets the point across—is very effective. Rhyming was the illiterate Pagan's method of memorizing a spell or set of instructions in ancient times. Here's a rhyming invocation for preparing Water food:

> *Water flow by day and night.*
> *Flow into my every bite.*
> *This food shall deepen all I feel.*
> *with every turning of the wheel.*
> *In this the flowing of the sea.*
> *As I will, so mote it be!*

Earth Foods

The foods of Earth are starchy, heavy, and solid. Grains (except rice) tend to be very Earthy, which makes bread and pasta Earth dishes. Stews, casseroles, and hearty sandwiches are Earthy. Basically, any foods that are primarily filling—comfort foods, the kind you want on a cold, damp day—and whatever you'd describe as a staple, are Earthy. Earth beverages are grainy—beer[22]—or heavy and thick. Milk is Earthy because of its heaviness and because of its association with fertility.

Earth preparations should be tactile; if you can mix with your hands instead of a utensil, all the better. Kneading bread is one of the most satisfying Earth kitchen experiences. The Earth cook samples while she prepares, knowing that direct experience is the truest judge.

A fourth kind of invocation is one done with few or no words, focused mostly on rhythm, visualization, and energy. You chant such an invocation in a steady, rhythmic manner. Words matter less than meter and intention:

> *Earth! In the meal.*
> *Earth!*
> *Earth!*
> *Strength! In the meal.*
> *Earth!*
> *Earth!*
> *Earth! As we eat.*
> *Earth!*
> *Earth!*
> *Strength! As we eat.*
> *Earth!*
> *Earth![23]*

Balanced Meals

- Pasta (Earth) with a spicy (Fire) shrimp (Water) sauce. For a beverage, drink seltzer (club soda—Air).

- Chili rellenos (Fire) with rice (Air). Wash down with a beer (Earth) and have ice cream (Water) for dessert.

- Beef teriyaki (Fire) with a California roll (Air) on the side. Miso soup (Earth—miso is made from soy, which is an Earth grain). Accompany with plum wine or fruit juice (Water).

- Lamb (Fire) with mint jelly (Air). Accompany with potatoes or bread and butter (Earth) and have fruit salad (Water) for dessert.

- Tofu (Earth—soy) and stir-fried vegetables with rice (Air). Use a little chili oil (Fire) when stir-frying. Serve with fresh melon (Water).

- Rice and bean (Air) casserole with chopped dates (Water) and peanuts (Earth). Add onions and pimento for Fire.

Elemental Food Chart

	Keywords	*Examples*	*Possible Purposes*
Air	Light, fluffy, minty, carbonated	*Foods:* Souffle, flaky pastries, rice, puffed corn or popcorn, mint *Drinks:* Club soda, sake, mint julep	To aid concentration, before working on a writing project, to eat/drink while studying
Fire	Hot, spicy, tangy, red	*Foods:* Curries, chilis, barbecue, flambée, red meat *Drinks:* Hard liquor, tomato juice	As an aphrodisiac, to energize, to impassion, to heal
Water	Syrupy, gooey, sweet, liquid	*Foods:* Broth, ice cream, melon, fruit *Drinks:* Water, juice, sweet dessert wines	To soothe, to deepen feeling, to inspire dreams or divination

| **Earth** | Starchy, heavy, simple | *Foods:* Bread, pasta, stews, casseroles, oatmeal, peanut butter *Drinks:* Milk, beer | To ground, for safety, for fertility |

---

1. I believe this will be my only real groaner of a pun in this entire book, so you may set your heart at ease.

2. Vases without flowers, that is. Keeping lots of flowers in the house would be Earthy. This refers to decorative vases around the house that don't necessarily have anything in them.

3. Do not count pictures you may have of the World Trade Center; the complex emotions surrounding September 11, 2001, may connect to any or all elements.

4. Butterflies in flight are Air.

5. Aleister Crowley's classic text of magical associations: *777 Revised: A Reprint of 777 with Much Additional Matter* (New York: Samuel Weiser, 1970).

6. See appendix E for an elemental list of herbs and plants.

7. A claddagh ring is the Irish ring you often see showing a heart between two hands. Originally, if the heart had a crown, it symbolized marriage, and if the heart had no crown, it symbolized romance. Nowadays, one often finds a crowned claddagh worn as a romantic rather than marital token.

8. See appendix E for an elemental list of gemstones.

9. Mandy Aftel, *Essence and Alchemy: A Book of Perfume* (New York: North Point Press, 2001).

10. Ibid., p. 100.

11. See www.thehairdiva.com.

12. See "Robbie's Recipe Collection" at www.robbiehaf.com.

13. Full disclosure: I used quite a number of treatments before getting the recipe right, despite my intentions.

14. My favorite resource for looking up essential oils is *Magical Aromatherapy* by Scott Cunningham (Saint Paul, MN: Llewellyn Publications, 1989). The section on hazardous oils is on pp. 175–177.

15. Jennifer is very open-minded about what oil to use. For an Earth scrub, I recommend patchouli and/or magnolia.

16. The measurements given are for the ¾ cup recipe; that is, for ⅛ cup of each ingredient.

17 As when a professional massage is received: a towel is placed over the private parts, and discreetly moved as needed and when turning over.

18. It's the same thing; it's called *henna* in the Middle East and *mehndi* in India.

19. Name the item being cooked.

20. Or drink, if you are preparing a beverage.

21. Or "I am healed" or "I am energized."

22. In *The Magic of Food: Legends, Lore & Spellwork,* author Scott Cunningham assigns beer to Fire (Saint Paul, MN: Llewellyn Publications, 1996, pp. 204–206, 340). However, there are good reasons to disagree with this attribution. Beer is made from wheat, barley, and hops, which are all of Earth. Beer is a heavy drink, associated with weight gain, and quickly creates the feeling of fullness, unlike more Fiery drinks.

23. And so on. Come up with the specific Earth qualities you wish to add to this meal, and work them into this simple chant.

CHAPTER SIX

The Elements at Work and in Love

Many people have heard that Sigmund Freud summed up mental health as the ability "to work and to love." Like many "well-known facts," this one may (or may not) be apocryphal; since it was said to a reporter rather than written in one of Freud's books, there is some disagreement over whether it was ever said at all.[1] Whether it was said or not, and in whatever context, it is an excellent rule of thumb. Much of our sanity, and much of our unhappiness, is found in our ability or inability to find satisfaction in work and love. So it is fitting to devote a chapter to the elemental qualities of these twin essentials in life.

THE ELEMENTS AT WORK

In chapter 3, we charted possible jobs that suited each element. Some of these are more definitive than others. Nurses, for example, need a strong component of Earth in their makeup, while traveling salespeople need a good deal of Air. No successful politician is weak in Fire, and no psychotherapist lacks Water.

Most of us, though, have jobs that are less distinctly elemental than these. The modern proliferation of office work leaves many of us in somewhat neutral careers that could suit most anyone. Others work in family businesses, or live in areas with few employment choices. What we do does not necessarily match our elemental style.

Nonetheless, work, like everything else, always has an elemental character. The elements are found in how we approach work, what we find satisfying about it, what we need from it, and what we take away from it. Learning our elemental work nature helps us be better employees and employers. We can also modify our work, or our work environment, to balance its elemental qualities.

Try this quiz to see how the elements contribute to your work personality.

Your Work Element Quiz

For the first question, pick up to three answers:

1. My favorite kind of work . . .

   a. Matters to people.

   b. Provides a good income.

   c. Is analytical.

   d. Is creative.

   e. Puts me in the public eye.

   f. Is intellectually stimulating.

   g. Provides opportunity for advancement.

For question 2, choose as many answers as apply:

2. I am better than most people at work when it comes to the following:

   a. Keeping confidential information safe.

   b. Doing routine work without becoming bored or frustrated.

   c. When needed, going without a break or downtime.

   d.   Analyzing a complex problem and finding a solution.

For questions 3–12, choose the one answer that is most important to you:

3. I could never work in a situation where . . .

   a. My work was mindless (i.e., assembly line, data entry, farm hand).

   b. There was no job security and my income fluctuated (i.e., contract work, commission-only sales).

   c. My work was anonymous (typing pool, unseen by superiors, etc.).

   d. Deadlines were constant and inflexible.

4. In work, I feel most satisfied when . . .

   a. I know exactly what I'm doing.

   b. I am meeting challenges and taking risks.

   c. I have genuinely helped someone.

   d. I have solved a tricky problem.

5. The thing I most need to hear from my boss is . . .

   a. That my job is secure.

   b. That I am liked.

   c. That I have done well.

   d. That my input is valued.

6. On the job, I can't stand . . .

   a. Boredom.

   b. Uncertainty.

   c. Stupidity.

   d. Isolation.

7. I would dislike a job intensely if (choose one) . . .

   a. It required a lot of travel.

   b. It was dead-end (no growth).

   c. It was focused on paperwork.

   d. It was mindlessly repetitive.

8. My preference is that my job . . .

   a. Involves working with people.

   b. Is visible and will gain recognition.

   c. Includes travel.

   d. Is stable.

9. I do my best work when . . .

   a. I can concentrate without interruption.

   b. I am under pressure.

   c. I am working with my hands.

   d. I am working on a team.

10. On the job, others see me as . . .

   a. The workplace "Ann Landers"; the one from whom they seek advice.

   b. Almost like family.

   c. A natural leader.

   d. A resource; a repository of workplace knowledge.

11. One of the pleasures of working is . . .

   a. Making my job look good; creating a great impression.

   b. Expressing myself creatively through what I do.

   c. Creating a "home away from home"; personalizing my workplace.

   d. Nailing down the details; dotting the i's and crossing the t's.

12. I approach problems best . . .

  a. When I have several projects going at once.

  b. If I don't have to worry about deadlines and can just let the work flow.

  c. Without supervision—I need to make my own decisions.

  d. In a structured manner, following rules and systems designed to solve those problems.

"Boss" Questions

Either you're a boss, manager, or business owner, or you've thought about it. Answer these questions about management, either from experience or from what you imagine your experience would be.

13. The most attractive aspect of being the boss is . . .

  a. Leadership comes naturally to me, and being the boss is/would be the best use of my talents.

  b. Sometimes work is dehumanizing. By being my own boss, I can/would do productive work and still retain the "human touch."

  c. I prefer to manage my own budget, create the rules I believe are most appropriate, and build a business much as I would build a home.

  d. I like/would like being in charge because I can implement my ideas. I know the job better than others and being part of management is how to make sure it is done the right way.

14. The least attractive aspect of being the boss is . . .

  a. It is difficult to tell others what to do. I care too much about hurting their feelings or about how they'll feel about me.

  b. Being the boss is/would be distracting. I much prefer focusing on what is important to me rather than getting bogged down in the details and needs of management.

c. Sometimes being the boss seems too conventional and at odds with my essentially rebellious nature.

d. Being the boss is too demanding of my time. I prefer to spend more time with my home and family.

True or False

___ 15. Rules are confining; I can do a great job without toeing the line.

___ 16. Listening is an important part of what I do at work.

___ 17. I like to bring food to the office to share with my co-workers.

___ 18. I enjoy opportunities for public speaking.

Answers

Multiple Choice

1. a = Water
    b = Earth
    c = Air
    d = Water
    e = Fire
    f = Air
    g = Fire
    h = Earth

2. a = Water
    b = Earth
    c = Fire
    d = Air

3. a = Air
    b = Earth
    c = Fire
    d = Water

4. a = Earth
    b = Fire
    c = Water
    d = Air

5. a = Earth
    b = Water

c = Fire
d = Air

6. a = Fire
    b = Earth
    c = Air
    d = Water

7. a = Earth
    b = Fire
    c = Water
    d = Air

8. a = Water
    b = Fire
    c = Air
    d = Earth

9. a = Air
    b = Fire
    c = Earth
    d = Water

10. a = Water
    b = Earth
    c = Fire
    d = Air

11. a = Fire
    b = Water
    c = Earth
    d = Air

12. a = Air
    b = Water
    c = Fire
    d = Earth

13. a = Fire
    b = Water
    c = Earth
    d = Air

14. a = Water
    b = Air
    c = Fire
    d = Earth

True or False (Score Trues only)

15. Fire
16. Water
17. Earth
18. Air

How did you do? Did one element stand out? Or two? As you read the following section, keep in mind not only your dominant element, but your second-most dominant one. How you use your elements in the workplace depends a lot on how they combine.

As you read, you'll learn not only about how the elements manifest in your work style, but also in work styles of your co-workers. Later, we'll look at ways to add elemental influences to the work space, which can be used to help modify energies and behaviors.

Just as we saw in the home, not every aspect of work can be "quizzed" for its element. This is because qualities can have more than one elemental component. A "people person" at work may be expressing Water's need for emotional connectedness, Earth's need for a homey environment, or Fire's need to be the center of attention. A loner at work may be expressing Air's need for contemplation or Fire's need for independence. (Yes, it's true: Fire can be contradictory. Whether Fire is a loner or a social animal depends in large part on how Fire perceives attention. If it is recognition, Fire wants it, but if it is supervision, he detests it.) So, while everything is ultimately connected to the elements, not everything can be broken down into a quick-and-easy one of four. Instead, use the more obvious traits, the ones that *can* be broken down readily, to get a snapshot of the elemental character of a person, and from there, you can explore more deeply.

As you read about elemental traits at work on the following pages, be aware that it is not just *people* being described. Although each element is referred to as "he" or "she," and the examples primarily refer to individuals, elements can show up in situations and environments as well. You might find yourself working for an Earth company, or in an Air laboratory. A client or project might be very Watery, or a department may be Fiery. It is pretty common for a sales department to be Fiery and a personnel department to be Earthy, and this can be a recipe for success. On the other hand, an Airy sales staff might never close a deal. As you read, remember that the people being described might also be situations, or even entire companies.

Air at Work

Air is characterized in the workplace by a few keywords: communication, intellect, and movement. Air professions ideally involve teaching, research, speech, travel, or some combination of these ingredients. They maximize flexibility and create a feeling of freedom.

The purest Air people are often solitary. They want to think, write, research, experiment, and conceive. But a dose of Fire's charisma will make Air great in sales and presentation, and a touch of Water's people skills will make Air a superb teacher. Air has the information you need, but, if Water and Fire are very weak, may not have the inclination to teach it.

Air's Assets

When work is not concrete, when it's hard to define, bring Air in. Air is a superb brainstormer, creating important new concepts from wisps of thought. Air solves problems by understanding them, by seeing the big picture. Air is the one to turn to when a problem is abstract, or when the pieces don't seem to fit together.

Air is the "breath of fresh air" in a project or situation that is stuck or stagnant. Connections to both movement and inspiration make Air the ideal person at such a point. Consulting and temporary work are flexible and independent, and consultants—in computers, advertising, marketing, graphics, or any number of other fields—are usually called in when the client is stuck in some way.

Air is always willing, and probably eager, to travel. Hop an inconvenient flight to an unattractive city? No problem, Air's your man. The nature of Air is to travel, and Mercury, one of Air's Zodiacal rulers, is the god of travel. Mercury is also the god of sales: glib, swift, talkative, and interested in commerce.

If Air is the solitary type, he gets his lift not in an airplane, but in that ivory tower. Many Air people are happiest when their work involves quiet, contemplative tasks, such as writing, computer programming, data analysis, and research. Air people can also be gifted at linguistics. This allows them to be solitary scientific types while still engaged with language.

Air's Needs

Air needs as much information as possible to work effectively. Giving Air piecework will be counterproductive. I've worked in computer environments where programmers were assigned specific tasks to program without being told how it would eventually fit in with the overall system. This is exactly the sort of work that undermines Air's abilities—he needs to *know*.

Air is happiest in environments that provide intellectual stimulation, where work is not rote. However, that stimulation can be gradual, as in scientific research, with results that aren't apparent for a long time. Air can adapt readily to the life of thoughtful patience, provided he doesn't have a strong Fire influence. A touch of Earth can help improve his patience.

While the classic Air type is introspective and thoughtful, a touch of Fire's energy turns Air into the wind. He blows in and out. This is the Air person who needs to be free, both physically and mentally. While not as rebellious as Fire, no Air person likes to be fettered by conventional thinking, which can hamper the free flow of ideas. If you allow both physical and metaphorical movement—both work-related travel and the free movement of ideas—your Air employees or co-workers will be happier. Air's need for freedom of movement can also be satisfied in *flexibility*, in allowing the job to adapt and change as Air's ideas adapt and change.

Air's Problems

Air can be "above it all"—distant and remote. This can make him difficult whenever teamwork is required. Although Air is a natural communicator, without a Water influence, Air can forget the *human* aspect of communication; he might, for example, write down detailed instructions but fail to distribute them.

There are other difficulties in working with Air that are associated with this distant quality. He can be distant from all manner of social structures, including politeness and regard for people's feelings. He can disregard office protocol, especially in regard to time. He can be patronizing, expecting others to be as intelligent as he is, and disdainful (perhaps unintentionally) when they are not. Air can be easily bored and prone to restlessness if his work doesn't captivate his attention.

Air as the Boss

Some of Air's problems can be even worse when he is in charge, especially his distance and his disdain. On the other hand, he can be generous about forgiving the little things, because little things don't matter to him. He has less commitment to rules than to ideas, and he'll rarely get on your case about being late. Your Air boss is incredibly knowledgeable and has a lot of resources if you can get him to share them.

Fire at Work

Fire at work is characterized by energy, passion, and ego, qualities of Will that follow Fire throughout all aspects of life. Fire is a dynamo on the job, and ideally has the kind of job that uses this to best advantage. No "slow and steady" for Fire—give him plenty to do and not too much time in which to do it!

Fire is attracted to high-demand, high-profile work. You might find him in politics, or on the floor of the New York Stock Exchange, or working with celebrities in fashion, photography, or decorating. These fields require high adrenaline, an aggressive attitude, and a love of the limelight.

Fire works best when he truly loves his work. One of Fire's greatest assets is his passion, and a job that's just a paycheck will never bring that to the surface.

Fire's Assets

Fire is full of energy; he can go, go, go. When he is excited about a project, he doesn't need rest, and he never feels the need to confine himself to a forty-hour work week. In fact, Fire is ill-suited to a job that *doesn't* require an extra effort, at least occasionally.

Fire also excels at presentation and appearance. He recognizes the importance of looking good in any number of areas, such as advertising, public relations, fashion, marketing, and media. Although aesthetics and beauty are associated with Water, it is Fire who knows what looks good. No difference, you say? You're obviously not a Fire person; looking good is about the impact you make on an audience. A beautiful painting or melody that remains in the background might appeal to Water, but never to Fire. It is Fire who knows how to give the public what they want, how to attract, captivate, and entice.

If you need adaptability, someone who can switch horses midstream and who doesn't need to know what the job is in order to get to work, then you need Fire. He'll blaze in and get moving without needing structure or definition.

Fire's Needs

Fire's needs are part and parcel of his skills. Just as Fire is skilled at being flexible, so he *needs* flexibility, even spontaneity. Fire "goes out" without some variety. It's better to throw too much at Fire than too little.

Fire also thrives on recognition. He wants his work not just to be excellent, but to be noticed. The spotlight, in the form of praise or a bonus, is something Fire needs in order to feel satisfied with work.

Advancement is also a Fire keyword. Just as a fire must continually consume fuel, so must a Fire person continually move forward. A dead-end job will suffocate Fire. Without future possibilities, without potential growth and expansion, work will soon seem meaningless.

Fire's Problems

Rebelliousness is part of Fire's nature, and this can be a problem if not held in check. Fire chafes at rules, resents supervision, and doesn't see insubordination as a problem. He can be a difficult person to have in your employ, and frustrating to communicate with when he "knows" he's right. He might think that rules don't apply to him, which is doubly aggravating, as he may well expect others to follow the very rules he ignores.

Fire can be equally problematic about deadlines. He works very hard, but he works to the task, not to the clock. He may put in many hours of overtime to get the job done, but being on time isn't his priority.

Fire finds routine stifling. He may resist doing the normal but tedious tasks necessary to any job.

Fire as Boss

Like a real fire, a Fire boss can both warm and burn. He can be explosive, demanding, and difficult. He can also be committed to his work in a way that inflames his staff with the zeal to perform. He both inspires and reciprocates loyalty. A typical Fire boss is the eccentric entrepreneur who works tirelessly for his business. He is hard working and driven. Although he isn't easy to work for, working for him *counts*—you're not just a corporate drone.

Water at Work

We've already discussed the complexity of Water. Just as a river can flow into many streams, Water can flow along many paths, including career paths. In the workplace, there are several different kinds of Water people. Water can be the healer or the counselor, soothing and listening. She may be a doctor, chiropractor, or nurse. Or she may be in any kind of job, and do her healing as a co-worker. She can be the office Dear Abby, listening to everyone's problems and to all the gossip, and straightening out the myriad conflicts of office life.

Water's people skills might make her the cheerleader, the team player, the go-between. Or she might use her clear awareness of privacy to work in confidential areas, maintaining secrets as simple as personnel files or as potent as government clearances.

Another Water work style might be creative. She might be in the arts, or she might function in any field by using her creative and intuitive skills. She might not even be able to explain what she does, even though she does it well. She can be very much in her own world—she is probably disorganized and even messy, and often late. Her work is excellent, and she handles change smoothly; she is undoubtedly tolerant and slow to anger. Such a person has frustrating lacks, but rewarding talents that make up for them. She won't adapt well to a buttoned-down environment, no matter how talented she is.

Water's Assets

As we have seen, Water has a range of skills that can be broken down into several broad areas: healing, people, secrecy, and creativity/intuition. Any or all of these might be present in a Water person at work. In an artistic or healing environment, it is likely that Water personalities dominate. In an office, too much Water can be a problem, although it is important to have *some* Water around. Healing is something that needs to happen all the time, no matter what the environment. Whenever people work together, they need a sense of teamwork and camaraderie. Water people can flow between departments in a company, keeping the lines of communication open. They bring compassion to the workplace so that work is not destructive to the spirit.

Water is needed to maintain both company and personal secrets. Confidential files are handled appropriately by Water, and Water is skilled at nipping office gossip in the bud. Although warm and team-spirited, Water is not loquacious and can work happily in silence. She is an excellent counselor and adviser, and can provide sage advice in a private atmosphere.

Like Air, Water is able to think outside the box. Water's ideas move in intuitive, surprising, and original ways. Because Water *flows,* her solutions seem natural and obvious once presented, and are rarely difficult to implement.

Water's Needs

Water's creativity is not just a skill, it is also a need. Stick Water in an environment where everything is already planned out and no personal touch is needed, and watch her wither. She works best with people around, and, as an employee, she responds to warmth. Fire's boss should praise his skill and provide recognition, but Water's boss needs to say "Thank you" and provide appreciation. In other words, although Water needs to make a living like everyone else, she needs *emotional* rewards most of all.

Water should not be isolated; she needs human connections. Nor should she be confined. A dammed river can overflow, and a dammed-up Water employee can become distraught. She needs nonstructured time built into her schedule. In fact, free time is so meaningful to her that she is likely to prefer a generous vacation package in lieu of a salary increase.

Water's Problems

Water's emotions can get her in trouble on the job. She can be moody and is easily hurt. She can be the type who takes everything said to heart, and doesn't account for the heat of the moment.

While Water flows through her emotions, it also flows through her behavior, and flows right past details, rules, time, and paperwork. She can be messy and disorganized.

Water is best teamed with Earth, both because she handles Earth's stability better than Fire's explosiveness, and because Earth can manage the structural things that Water neglects, while Water can nurture the parts of Earth that become too solid. Water teamed with Fire is too easily wounded, and Water teamed with Air is too impractical.

Water as Boss

Water is a nurturing team leader, supportive and helpful. The lines of communication are kept open, and people's creativity is encouraged. She is a superb listener and will be attentive to the undercurrents of a situation, reading far below the surface. On the other hand, Water's compassion can prevent her from giving clear directions and needed criticism. She may let problems go on far too long rather than hurt people's feelings. Her hands-off style can be very welcome by some people, but others really need management. She will rely on her employees to provide the details and organization that she lacks.

Earth at Work

Earth's keywords at work are stability, structure, and results. Earth creates a stable working environment for herself; she knows her routines and rules. She is the type who will do the same tasks at the same time: Monday for filing, Thursday afternoon for follow-up phone calls, and so on. She can be very well organized, or she can be content with a certain sloppiness—Earth likes the job to feel like home, and, unlike some people, her workplace is likely to reflect her home life.

Earth brings home wherever she goes. She perceives work as a home-away-from-home, and this is evident in her sense of relaxation and comfort on the job, in her cozy work area, and in her propensity to feed herself and, probably, her co-workers. She is a great nester—there will certainly be family pictures and other personal touches around, if they are permitted. Like Water, Earth is a welcome team player. While Water is emotionally nurturing, Earth is physically nurturing; she is less a counselor and more a mom (or dad).

Earth is concerned with the stabilizing factors of work, such as money, medical benefits, and job security. She is unlikely to work as a consultant or a temp, or in fields requiring a lot of travel or that are commission-based. None of these things will provide the certainty and predictability that Earth needs.

Earth's Assets

Earth excels at implementing systems. Although Air is more likely to create new systems and structures—since such structures are born of new ideas—it is Earth who can put the system to work, and maintain it in an efficient and helpful way. It is Earth who will determine which parts of the system work better in theory than in practice; Earth is the right one for the shakedown period. Earth is equally efficient at managing time and budgets, as both of these are, essentially, structural systems. She follows instructions well and doesn't tend to resent guidance; in fact, she appreciates it.

Earth takes the idea of a system and creates a tangible, working *result*. In many ways, creating results is the essence of the Earth worker. Recall from chapter 1 that Earth is the result in the cycle of human endeavors: Air imagines, Fire intends, Water creates, and Earth produces. Every endeavor needs all four elements. At work, Earth produces results as diverse as making sure there is a product to sell to making sure there are chairs to sit in. In addition, Earth is skilled at the physical side of a project, and many Earth people prefer to work with their hands.

Earth is patient and is comfortable with the tedium that is part of any job. Whether adding a column of figures, processing routine correspondence, or sewing stitches, Earth understands that repetition is necessary, and she often finds it soothing.

Earth's Needs

In order for Earth to be happy at work, she needs a sense of job security. She probably wants a reliable employer, good benefits, a pension or 401k, and a clear understanding of her responsibilities. She'll also be happiest in a "family friendly" environment, one that is supportive of parents and friendly toward children—she may value this even if she isn't a parent herself.

Earth needs work to function as a home base. She needs to be able to relax and have her own space. She also needs a routine and structure, and is never at her best unless she knows what is expected of her.

Earth's Problems

Earth can be *too* attached to structure. She can become plodding and can be too dependent on direction. She can be rigid about rules, even when it's unnecessary. Earth doesn't think outside the box; she sticks to routine sometimes even when it makes no sense to do so. She is attached to the way things have always been done, and sometimes refuses to allow her job to change and grow. She resists new technologies and directions.

Earth as Boss

Earth can be a rigid boss, too strict, too rule-driven, and too unyielding. She can be a bean counter, looking more to the bottom line than to intangibles.

On the other hand, Earth can be an extremely helpful boss. She provides all the information you need to do your job, and she makes sure you have the means to do it. She's not the kind to leave you out on a limb, requiring you to do something without the resources you need.

She remembers her family-oriented attitude from when she *wasn't* the boss, and is tolerant of your away-from-the-job special needs.

Working Elements in Combination

A fun way to look at the elements is to see what kind of mixes you can come up with. This is like mixing paints on a palette. As most of us learned in grade school, all it takes is red, yellow, blue, black, and white paint, and you can create every color there is. Every nuance of variation creates a different shade. You can see this on your computer, by mixing values of RGB—red, green, and blue—or CMYK—cyan (blue), magenta (red), yellow, and black.

Here are some examples of mixing the elements to come up with different jobs:

	Air	*Fire*	*Water*	*Earth*
Earth	Bureaucrat	Stockbroker	Medical practitioner	Accountant
Water	Teacher	Fashion designer	Painter	
Fire	Salesperson	Politician		
Air	Scientist			

Obviously, there are many ways in which the elements can combine. On a paint palette, two parts of red and three parts of yellow will make a different shade of orange than two parts of red and six parts of yellow. The combination of elements, their strong and weak points and how they express themselves, is endless. You'll also recall from the Elemental Personal Traits chart in chapter 3 that each element, by itself, has several options for jobs or roles. When you combine just two elements, you're multiplying many by many, and you can also combine three or four. The chart above can give you hints about what to look at. Your own observations and imagination can expand it as much as you like.

Communication and information come naturally to Air, and connecting to people is Water's domain. Together, they might choose to teach—to connect to people by communicating knowledge. Or Water's concerns with people and with art might combine with Fire's sense of flair, drama, and presentation to enter into the field of fashion design. If Water's care for people has Earth's physical influence, a healing profession—one that involves touch—is a likely result.

These combinations are intuitive; they're based both on knowing the elements and observing people. You can decide for yourself why the rest of the jobs were assigned as they were, and you can have fun assigning plenty of your own. You can even make a game of it. Have a member of your magical or Pagan group assign jobs to elemental combinations, and then the others can guess which elements go with which job. Or see who can come up with the best jobs for each combination. This game will exercise your imagination and your knowledge of the elements.

BRINGING THE ELEMENTS TO WORK

There are many occasions when you might become aware of an elemental deficit in your workplace. Here are some reasons why you might want to increase one or more elements at work:

Bring Air when . . .

- · People at work are not thinking clearly.
- · The atmosphere is stuffy.
- · Nothing seems to change.

Bring Fire when . . .

- · People at work are moving too slowly or methodically.
- · No one seems to really care what happens.
- · Energy is low.

Bring Water when . . .

- · There are problems with gossip.
- · Creativity is needed.
- · Work is dehumanized; caring is needed.

Bring Earth when . . .

- · Discipline is too lax.
- · Money is low.
- · Projects go on and on without tangible results.

You'll notice that the methods of bringing an element into the workplace are fairly similar to those used to bring that element into your home. It is important to note, though, that when you're in your own home, your effect is more controlled.

Your home is your own domain or your shared domain with family, partners, or friends. The changes you brought to your home by balancing the elements were intentional and focused. Perhaps you performed ritual as well, perhaps not. Perhaps you performed invocations as you were bringing the elemental objects into the house,[2] or perhaps you just had the idea firmly in your mind that this fish bowl was Water, or this kite string was Air. Others at home may have shared these firm intentions.

But at work, there are probably lots of other people, with all sorts of different intentions. You are less likely to be surrounded by like-minded or sympathetic people when it comes to magic, and you may not want to display your Pagan inclinations openly. To balance this lack of conjoined intention, it's a good idea to bring a more structured magic to your work elements; to do this, you'll use a specific invocation. You might do this in advance. For example, if you bring small objects representing an element to work, you might do the invocation over those objects before leaving home.

You may worry that this constitutes "casting a spell on" your co-workers. Not at all! What you're doing is bringing energies to your place of work, presumably for the benefit of all. These energies can *influence* your co-workers, but cannot control them. If you wore a silly hat to cheer people up, or put on a suit to convey sobriety and professionalism, you wouldn't worry about controlling others, even though you'd be influencing them. I can't see how rocks, feathers, and seashells are any different.

Bringing Air to Work

- Make a conscious effort to use Air language; say, "Let's clear the air," "We need a breath of fresh air," or "Let's float some ideas."[3]
- Bring a bunch of small feathers to work and scatter them about. These could be from a down pillow. You might put them on people's chairs or under their desks, or you might put them in public areas, like the elevator or cafeteria. Consecrate these feathers prior to bringing them to work using a simple invocation such as in appendix B.

· Open a window or use a fan, adding Air language such as "Let's bring some air in here!" as a simple, discreet invocation. You might use one of those cute hand-held electric fans to "blow on" problems.

· Incense isn't appropriate in most workplaces. Besides, scents aren't a good idea when there are a lot of people around who may be allergic, or just might not appreciate it. However, you can symbolically bring incense by bringing an empty incense holder. A pretty one will look like a simple knickknack meant to personalize your space. Again, this could be consecrated before bringing it to work, or when placed in your workspace.

· Decorate your work area with a small Japanese fan.

Bringing Fire to Work

· Add something red to the office. Try using red binders or folders for filing. Use simple invoking language like "These will brighten/heat things up around here."

· Use Fire language once or twice a day, every day, at work, for at least a week (a month is better). Say, "Let's light a fire under this project," "Let's get some sparks going on this," or "I feel hot today!"

· Consecrate a handful of matchbooks and leave them around. They can go in drawers, in file cabinets, behind a copy machine, or on the floor of a vehicle. Obviously, this is only appropriate in environments where no children can find them.

· For women, you can create a vanity area. A former co-worker of mine brought in a bunch of toiletries—hand lotion, hair spray, body spray, and so on—and put it in the ladies' room by the mirror for everyone to share. By creating a primping area, Fire energy is heightened.

· Put a piece of consecrated amber or tiger's-eye in a drawer.

Bringing Water to Work

· Bring a few consecrated seashells to your place of business. These will be more decorative than discreet, but they are also a fairly ordinary sort of item for people to have.

· Wash your face (or dab your forehead if you're wearing eye makeup) at least once a day at work. Drink plenty of water during working hours. You can use invocatory language while doing so, like "I'm taking Water in." You might even get a mister for office use.

· Use feeling language often. Replace "What do you think?" with "How do you feel about that?" Other Watery phrases are "go with the flow" and "dive down deep."

· If possible, dim the lights. Water is a dark element, and bright lights, especially florescent ones, can drive away Watery energies.

· Give a consecrated rose, in a vase, to a co-worker. If the co-worker returns the vase to you after the rose has withered, keep it on or in your desk, where it will continue to evoke Water.

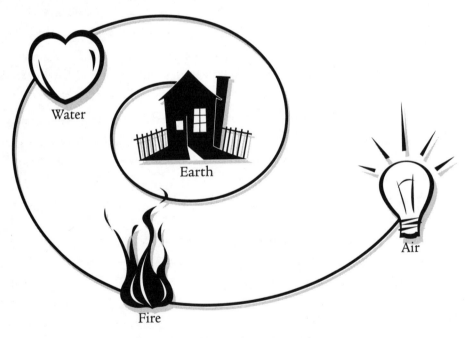

Figure 6: The Elemental Love Progression

Bringing Earth to Work

· Get a plant. If possible, get something large, like a ficus, so that your co-workers can share the Earth experience of having something alive, growing in soil, in the office. Invoke Earth into the plant before or after you bring it to work.

· Bring doughnuts or bagels. Establish a regular day—be it every Friday morning, or the third Tuesday of each month—to share food together in this way. I once worked in an office where we had bagels every Friday morning. The task of picking up the food rotated among administrative staff (secretaries, administrative assistants, and clerks), and the task of paying for the food rotated among the architects, engineers, and executives. This handled the disparity in incomes between the two groups while still allowing everyone to feel that they'd pitched in, making it a real sharing. Earth is invoked whenever bread is broken.

· Sprinkle a small amount of consecrated salt in a public area; a hallway or reception room is ideal.

· Put a nice stone, into which Earth has been invoked, on your desk.

· Find some small repair that needs to be done in your workplace, and do it. Nail a loose board, clean the microwave, or get the cabinet to close properly. Managing physical space is an Earth activity.

In addition to all of these methods of bringing the elements into work, you can also hang artwork, following the home decor descriptions from chapter 5.

THE ELEMENTS IN LOVE

It is possible to work happily with an elemental imbalance. If you are weak in Air and strong in Earth, you can find all manner of employment, both satisfying and productive, that emphasizes the physical and ignores the mental. But it is less likely that you will have a full, healthy love relationship without all four elements present.

In love, the elements influence behavior and attitudes, just as they do at work. However, the elements also define the stages through which love progresses, as mentioned briefly in chapter 3.

Air is the beginning of love, before anything has even happened. It is the idea, the hope, the crush. Air is the idealized partner, before you even know who your beloved really is; it is the pedestal upon which you place him or her.

Fire is lust and desire. Whether in the imagination or the physical (that is, whether or not the relationship has been sexually consummated), Fire is the overriding passion that inflames the senses. Many people confuse Fire with Water, and think that burning desire is love. However, these are different states, different stages. While, in love, Water doesn't put out Fire, the opposite can be true. Fire can, for a time, obliterate more tender feelings; it simply doesn't leave room for them.

Water is romance. Water is the first time you say "the L word." It is stars in your eyes, tenderness and intimacy. Water is "true love conquers all," and it is the sense of timelessness and eternity; the notion that it is romance that gives meaning to life. When swimming in the Water part of a relationship, one tends to believe that this is *it*; it is all you need, and all obstacles can be overcome.

Earth is the stabilizing of a relationship into a commitment. It is the building of a life, home, or partnership together. It is attending to the practical part of a relationship, and it is settling down.

This progression can be viewed as a spiral, as each step adds to, and does not abandon, the previous ones. The order can vary, although the order shown in figure 6 is typical of modern Western romance. I see it as a natural order, moving from East to North, as in the Wiccan tradition. In a culture where arranged marriages are common, Air-Earth-Fire-Water may be a more typical order. If for religious or personal reasons one refrains from having sex until after marriage, the order might be Air-Water-Earth-Fire, although the feelings of lust and desire will probably be present early on, even if not acted upon.

ELEMENTS IN RELATIONSHIP

After considering the elemental behaviors and qualities of relationship, you'll see that it's unnecessary to have another quiz at this point. In love, Air, Fire, Water, and Earth appear in basic, obvious, and clearly delineated form. It is simply so easy to know the element of each characteristic, behavior, and goal in your love life that all the fun of guessing how the quiz will turn out would be lost.

Air in Relationship

Characteristics

Air is the beginning of a relationship, and it is the state of mind associated with that beginning. Air is the imagination of love, and its idealization. Air is falling in love, not with a woman, but with Woman. Air is the love affair with the Muse. Air is also the meeting of minds in a relationship, the discovery that you *think* together.

Behavior

Air is building castles in the air with one's beloved, planning out your future together. It is also the endless talking that characterizes the beginning of many relationships, the coming to know one another's stories. It's that long coffee shop date where you discover that you both hate whipped cream and you both love jellybeans, and that you both always, always cry during *Casablanca*.

Goal

The goal of Air is to create new ideas, and to imagine. In love, Air's goal is to imagine together, to fantasize about each other, and to plan a possible future.

Relationships weak in Air will lack goals, and can sometimes feel too ordinary, too mundane. They are stuck in the present tense. Relationships in which a couple cannot understand one another are also weak in Air. If you say, "We never talk," your relationship needs Air.

Air Statements

"We think alike."

"I guess I have her up on a pedestal."

"It's just like I always pictured it would be!"

Fire in Relationship

Characteristics

Fire is the passionate aspect of relationship. It is desire; it is lust specifically, but it is also being on fire, thrilled with this new person, this connection, this joy. Fire rules the sexuality in a relationship, as well as everything that feels exciting in it.

Behavior

The primary Fire behavior is sex, especially spontaneous sex; sex that you *need*. Urgency is a Fire behavior.

Goal

The goal of Fire is to *consume*. You might not think of this when you're having great sex—you might think the goal is great sex. But just as a campfire consumes wood, Fire in a relationship consumes the passions and consummation of the lovers. It is not just burning with lust that is Fire, it is the longing to abandon yourself utterly to it. In those moments of passion and release in which self is obliterated and sensation is all, you have given yourself to Fire.

If your relationship lacks sufficient Fire, it is passionless. Many relationships, especially long-term ones, go through periods where the Fire has gone out. This is when you feel like you're married to a friend, with infrequent or nonexistent sex, and little intensity. Most people are happy to allow the Fire phase of a relationship to pass, and let things calm down a bit. But a relationship in which the Fire has gone completely is not often a healthy one.

Fire Statements

"There's no such thing as a good relationship without good sex."

"Love is like an obsession."

"If the chemistry isn't there from the beginning, there's nothing you can do about it."

Water in Relationship

Characteristics

Water is romantic. No, strike that. Water is *romance*—the two are practically inseparable. Water exists within love; it is fulfilled by love. Thus Water is the element that sees the spiritual dimension of love, that sees love as a blessing, and that sees the true meaning of life in loving and in being loved. Water's love is timeless; it stretches into eternity, and everything feels new.

Behavior

Water is given to the romantic gesture: to the thoughtful gift, to the surprise dinner, and to reading poetry. It is Water that serenades by moonlight (Water, of course, has quite an affinity for moonlight).

Goal

Water's goal is to love utterly, and to be in love. When a relationship has moved into the Water phase, Water's goal is fulfilled. It wants nothing more than the love that knows no limits. If Water wants a promise, it doesn't want "until death do us part," it wants a promise for all eternity and beyond.

Without Water, a relationship can be practical and ordinary, or it can be calculating, with the two people essentially using each other. A Waterless relationship can be the sort that has everything going for it, but feels lacking somehow; the sort about which you might say it "just isn't enough." Some people live with little or no Water in their long-term relationships. If both partners can agree to this, and neither has a strong Water component to their personality, and if they are very good for each other in other ways, it is possible to have a healthy "dry" relationship, just as it is possible to have a healthy "cold" relationship—a sexless, Fireless one. There will be times, though, poignant and probably moonlit ones, when people in such a relationship will long for that ineffable something that they gave up for their happy marriage.

Water Statements

"True love conquers all."
"I've never felt like this before."
"You're all I need."

Earth in Relationship

Characteristics

Earth is the committed, domestic part of a relationship. It is marriage, setting up a household, and having children. It is also the small, homey quality of taking one another for granted, of companionable silence, and of merging your lives in a practical way. If Earth couples don't have joint finances, they have instead a specific financial arrangement that takes into account both incomes and the couple's joint financial needs. Earth is when you don't leave an "out"—there is no need to beat a hasty retreat—and so Earth relationships have the sort of trappings and enmeshments that are not easy to disentangle.

Behavior

In the Earth part of a relationship, a couple delights in the activities of ordinary life. They cook together, shop together, and just hang out. Of course, Earth dominates in food, finance, and fertility, so any behavior connected to these will have a particular appeal to the Earth side of a relationship. The sex in an Earth relationship may have degenerated into ordinary routine, which is always a risk in any Earth activity, but it may also be frank, direct, and uninhibited—"earthy."

Goal

The goal of Earth in a relationship is commitment and permanence.

A relationship that lacks Earth is one that lacks reality, gravity. No matter how long you've been together, without Earth you're still dating and not really a couple. An Earthless relationship lacks the social weight of coupledom, the obligation, and, most obviously, the commitment. Without Earth, a relationship can have ideals, passion, and love, but it has no foundation, and no glue.

Earth Statements

"I want to build a life with you."
"Love builds over time."
"Hugging and cuddling is more important than sex."

Why Do You Give Your Ladylove Flowers?

Air: It's what you're supposed to do.
Fire: I want to impress her.
Water: It's romantic.
Earth: For a specific goal (before I ask for something special, as an apology, etc.).

Elemental Love Songs

Air: "Dream Lover," Bobby Darin

"I Knew I Loved You," Darren Hayes and Daniel Jones (Savage Garden)

"Goodnight My Someone," from *The Music Man,* Meredith Willson

"Happy Together," Bonner/Gordon (The Turtles)

"Someday My Prince Will Come," from *Snow White and the Seven Dwarfs,*
  Churchill/Morey

Fire: "I'm on Fire," Bruce Springsteen

"I Want Your Sex," George Michael

"I Burn for You," Sting

"Love to Love You Baby," Bellotte/M/S

"Love Me Like a Man," Chris Smither

Water: "Here, There, and Everywhere," Lennon and McCartney

"I've Never Been in Love Before," from *Guys and Dolls,* Frank Loesser

"The Waiting," Tom Petty

"More Today Than Yesterday," Upton

"My Girl," Robinson and White (The Temptations)

Earth: "Marriage Chant," Greg Brown

"Come Rain or Come Shine," Johnny Mercer and Harold Arlen

"The Power of Two," Emily Saliers (The Indigo Girls)

"Honey, I'm Home," Robert John Lange

"Wonderful Tonight," Eric Clapton

"Our House," Graham Nash

fOUR DATES

After a relationship has gone through its cycle of elements and has reached a point
where it has experienced all four elements—it has begun (Air), and there is love

(Water), passion (Fire), and commitment (Earth)—it will still benefit from having all four elements present. In fact, the most common complaints about marriage—that it is ordinary, dull, and confining—are about marriages that turn strictly to Earth once Earth is achieved.

Throughout our process of learning about the elements, we've seen that balance is key: relationships, like everything else, should follow the Way of Four. In this section are four dates that each focus on one element. Rather than testing your relationship to see where it's weak (although you likely already know that), make the time to go on all four dates, and allow your relationship to partake of the full gamut of elemental energies.

Prior to each date, you can do an invocation to bring that element's energy into your relationship. Note that the relationship-specific invocations given for each element are different from generic ones. For example, a generic Water invocation would emphasize emotion in general, flow, dreams, etc., whereas a relationship-specific Water invocation would stress romance. As always, you can modify the invocations offered to suit your personal wants and needs.

What if your partner is not Pagan? As with work, it is important to draw the distinction between performing this elemental invocation and casting a spell on your partner. First of all, it is hard to imagine how you could schedule any of the elemental dates on the following pages without a partner who is a willing participant. If you are trying to pull that off, I'll go out on a limb and suggest that there's a lot more wrong with your relationship than a lack of elemental balance. Work on openness and honesty first, and *then* plan your special dates together.

Secondly, remember that you are bringing elemental energies not to one person or the other, but to the couple, which stands as a unit, a whole greater than the sum of its parts. You are not, for example, using an Earth invocation/date to extract a marriage proposal from an unwilling partner; you are bringing Earthy commitment energy into the couple so that both partners can choose how and when to use it.

In short, elemental energy is a breath of fresh air (or a flame, or a . . .) in a relationship; it is not a forceful change in that relationship. Once you have the energies in balance, change is up to you. You can use your newfound balance to enhance your relationship, or you can squander it. You always retain freedom of choice.

An Air Date

Invocation for the Air Date

Begin by censing each other,[4] or by using a feather and/or your breath to blow air on one another. If you're doing the invocation alone, use a picture of the two of you together, or write both names on a piece of paper. Cense or "air" the representation.

> *We (I) call upon you, O Air, to enter into the relationship of*
>
> *_____ and _____!*
>
> *Air, bring us hopes for the future.*
>
> *Air, bring us ideals.*
>
> *Air, come like a wind into our minds, giving understanding of each other.*
>
> *Awaken our intelligence to one another, and quicken our tongues that we may speak freely and joyfully together.*
>
> *We (I) invoke you, O Air, to come into this relationship now!*

Begin your date in the morning. If you enjoy getting up early, watch the sunrise together.

Have Air foods for breakfast.[5] When eggs are fluffy, as in a souffle or frittata, they are Airy.

Take a trip to a museum, a historical society, or a historic re-creation. These stimulate the intellect, and allow the Air side of your personalities to come to the fore. You might also consider going to a lecture, library, or bookstore.

After your trip, sit down over carbonated or minty drinks and discuss your dreams for the future. Allow yourself to fantasize without commitment. For example, give yourself permission to plan your ideal wedding, even if you are not ready to discuss marriage in a serious way. Agree beforehand that you are spinning castles in the air, and nothing said can be considered a promise. Really let yourself go with your imaginings, getting as detailed as possible. For example, for the wedding, there's the ceremony itself, the guest list, music, clothing, location, flowers—a wide range of fantasy objects!

Here are some ideas for discussions:

· Where you'd like to retire.

· What kind of wedding you want.

· Where you'd like to go on your honeymoon.

· Where you'd live if you could live anywhere in the world.

· What kind of party you'd throw if you had an unlimited budget.

You could end an Air date without making love. If you choose to make love, focus on the verbal—talk through your sex. Tell each other sexual fantasies and spin imaginative stories ("You are . . . and I am . . ."), using language you consider arousing. Make love while it is still daylight, or with the lights on.

A Fire Date

Invocation for the Fire Date

Light a candle and bring it near first one person, and then the other, of the couple. Hold hands and bring your joined hands over the flame together. If you're doing the invocation alone, use a picture of the two of you together, or write both names on a piece of paper, and wave this representation over the flame.

We (I) call upon you, O Fire, to enter into the relationship of

_____ and _____!

Fire, ignite our passions.

Fire, awaken our desire.

Fire, burn in our wills, arousing us toward each other.

Inflame, excite, and ignite us, O Fire, that we may be filled with your heat and your awareness. Make us conscious of each other in our most passionate moments.

We (I) invoke you, O Fire, to come into this relationship now!

Of necessity, a Fiery date is a very sexual affair, although ours will involve other activities as well. It will also require some advance planning.

Your Fire date will involve playing with lustfulness. It can be slightly to very exhibitionist (but not in an illegal way!). The basic plan is to choose a costume that is arousing, wear it out in public, and then make love, either at home or in an exotic location (even a cheap motel room can be exotic if it is a break from routine and an unusual experience for you).

What will your costume be? Well, it should be something you find sexy, and something that makes you into a different person. Ideally, it should be a pair of matching costumes: student and teacher, "strangers" in a bar, master and slave, princess and pirate, animals, space aliens. For bizarre costumes, you can choose a venue where you'll blend in, such as a Halloween party or a Renaissance Fair. In a large city, you can take advantage of a fetish or swinger's club, and don an overtly erotic costume in an environment friendly to eroticism. Otherwise, you can choose something more like a disguise—dressing as another person but not necessarily appearing to be costumed; for example, you could wear a wig and the sort of clothing you never wear. Or your date could be in a very secluded area, where only the two of you will see each other. For example, you might enjoy getting dressed up together or separately at home, and then driving (again, together or separately) to a remote spot, where you could have a Fiery picnic.

Be sure to costume yourself all the way through, wearing your best lingerie and perhaps shopping for the occasion—surprising your partner can be erotic and Fiery. If traditional lingerie doesn't excite you, what about body painting under your clothes? You can paint each other before going out. In fact, you can dress each other beforehand regardless of what you wear.

What will you do in your costume? Because so much energy is put into preparation, keep the activity itself simple and allow it to be lingering and slow. You'll let sexual tension build, and you'll allow Fire to burn through you both.

You might choose to play-act in your costumes. One exciting game is the "strangers meeting for the first time." You arrive separately at a prearranged location, and one of you seduces or picks up the other. This is an easy game to play in public, as it doesn't seem weird to bystanders. Other costumes lend themselves to more specific games.

Whatever roles you're playing, stay in character throughout the date. Theatricality, costume, exhibition, display, and disguise are all Fiery; allow yourselves to partake of all of these on your date.

The traditional time of day for Fire is noon, but the nature of Fiery activities will tend to make this a late-night event.

After a light meal of Fiery foods (see the Elemental Food chart in chapter 5),[6] go to a private place to make love—either your home or the exotic location you've chosen. Definitely light candles for lovemaking, and begin by removing the outer layer of costume so that you can enjoy the lingerie, body paint, or other under-costume. Stay in character, and speak very little. Make animal noises rather than using words.

A Water Date

Invocation for the Water Date

Take a bowl of water and sprinkle each other. Place a drop of water onto each other's third eye,[7] lips, throat, and heart. If you're doing the invocation alone, sprinkle a picture of the two of you together, or write both names on a piece of paper and sprinkle that.

> We (I) call upon you, O Water, to enter into the relationship of
>
> _____ and _____!
>
> Water, bring us the fullness of love.
>
> Water, bring us romance.
>
> Water, flow into our hearts that we may truly know the eternity of love's ocean;
>
> Let us find the depth of feeling for each other that transcends the bounds of space and time.
>
> We (I) invoke you, O Water, to come into this relationship now!

It should go without saying that a Water date is romantic, and should have all the trappings of romance. Far be it from me to assume a traditional heterosexual arrangement, but it would be awfully appropriate if one of you began by giving flowers to the other.

The Water time of day is evening; begin your date then.

An ideal activity for a Water date is a wine tasting. These aren't hard to find; many areas outside of wine-growing country have wine societies or fine food clubs. As an alternative, a poetry reading is a fine choice. Music is another Watery activity, so a concert or dancing would work. "Hot" dancing (rock music or salsa) might be more Fiery, while ballroom is the most Watery dance.

After the wine, poetry, music, or dance, dinner in an elegant restaurant is a must. (If you go to a restaurant with live music and dancing, you can combine the two into one.) A French restaurant is where you'll find a traditionally romantic atmosphere, although an Italian or Greek venue is also a good choice. Don't skip dessert; if the eatery you've chosen doesn't have excellent desserts, go to a separate dessert place afterward. Choosing among sweet and sticky foods is very Watery and very sensual. During dinner and dessert, you might enjoy feeding each other (within reason— you're in public, after all). You might also find that the sensual atmosphere is increased by eating finger foods.

At home after eating, you might read each other love poetry or romantic prose selections. (You could have picked out reading material during your library or bookstore visit on your Air date.) Or you could sing to each other; a serenade is a very Watery way of romancing someone.

Make love slowly, in darkness. Emphasize long, lingering foreplay, with much kissing and caressing. Whisper soft words of love to one another.

An Earth Date

Invocation for the Earth Date

Take a small stone and rub it over each other; touch each other's third eye, lips, throat, and heart. If you're doing the invocation alone, place the stone over a picture of the two of you together, or write both names on a piece of paper and weight that down with the stone.

We (I) call upon you, O Earth, to enter into the relationship of

_____ and _____!

Earth, bring us stability.

Earth, bring us a home together.

Earth, fill our bodies with the reality of our love. Let us know that it as a solid thing, a thing of commitment and permanence, upon which we can rely.

We (I) invoke you, O Earth, to come into this relationship now!

Although the traditional time of day for Earth is midnight, a practical date, filled with practical things, is best done in the middle of the day. (For the purposes of dating, Fire and Earth essentially trade times.) In an ordinary 9-to-5 life, the perfect time for an Earth date would be Sunday afternoon.

Plan your date by first sitting down and discussing the practical things you have been meaning to get done. Are you behind on your laundry? Is there a household repair you've been putting off? Is there a picture you've neglected to hang, a section of carpet you've been meaning to re-tack, or a bookcase you'd like to paint?

Agree to two tasks, one that is important to each of you.

If the tasks require supplies you don't have, plan on shopping first, then having lunch, and then accomplishing the tasks. If you have all the needed supplies on hand, work on the household tasks first. Next comes a hearty lunch of Earth foods (see chapter 5), and finally, your shopping trip.

Shopping is an essential part of the Earth date both because it is a shared practical activity and because money and acquisition are, in general, Earth things.

The next part of your day will be an enjoyable, tactile, very Earthy experience: baking homemade bread. Be sure to choose a recipe before going shopping so that you can get all the ingredients. If you don't own a cookbook, you might start by shopping for that (or you can pick one up on your Air trip to the library or bookstore).

I cannot stress enough how spiritual, how Earthy, and how fun this is. If you have a bread making machine, just this once, don't use it. Allow yourselves to become really involved in the kneading and punching down of the bread—things you miss with the machine.

By the time the bread is finished, you might well be ready for dinner, and so you can eat it right away. After dinner, rest and cuddle for a while.

When it comes time to make love, do so in the spirit of frank practicality that has characterized your day. Be open about your wants and needs, about little discomforts, and about favorite activities. Be uninhibited in saying "I like when you do *this*" or "I like *this* better than *that*." Allow for show and tell.

---

1. Quoted in *Identity and the Life Cycle* by Erik H. Erikson (New York: Norton, 1980) 102.

2. Appendix B provides general elemental invocations that you can adapt to this purpose.

3. "Float" sounded like Air to me the first time I wrote this sentence, like a dandelion seed floating on air. When I re-read the sentence later, it sounded like Water—water floating downstream. Use language that sounds like Air to *you*.

4. To "cense" is to wave incense on and around. Cense another person by holding a smoking censer next to him or her and using your hand, your breath, a feather, or a fan to wave the smoke toward the person's body.

5. Elemental foods will be on your to-do list for all four dates. See the Elemental Food chart in chapter 5 for more suggestions.

6. Staying a little bit hungry, or at least under-full, will help maintain the passionate, desirous edge of Fire.

7. The third eye is located between and slightly above the eyebrows.

CHAPTER SEVEN

The Elements in Ritual and Spellcraft

Having taken the grand tour of the elements within ordinary life—in the home, the body, work, and love—it is time to come back to the magical part of life, and look at Air, Fire, Water, and Earth in ritual and spells.

The ELEMENTS IN RITUAL

The elements manifest themselves in ritual in myriad ways: as themselves, as symbols, and as tools.

The Elements as Building Blocks

The four elements are the building blocks of the universe in much Pagan and Wiccan philosophy. They are the basic stuff of life. Everything that is real derives from them.

That being the case, anything that is created in ritual can be seen as requiring the presence of the elements. In magic, we create something from nothing. We bring into being that which does not yet exist. A magic circle itself is something new; by making mundane space sacred, we are partaking in an act of creation.

Some people believe that the Wiccan ritual of casting the circle is a reenactment of Creation itself; that by creating the universe in microcosm (the circle), we create the universe in macrocosm: As above, so below. To do this, we use the components of creation—the elements.

The Elements as Symbols

The elements can be present in a ritual in order to symbolize the various qualities that we have been learning about—the qualities of self (mind, will, heart, body), the Witches' Pyramid, the seasons, and so on. In a broader sense, they can be present to symbolize *balance*. The four elements combine to represent fullness, the squared circle, and wholeness.

The Elements on the Altar and as Tools

One of the things that happens when you decide to do Pagan ritual is that you have to make all sorts of decisions about what symbolizes what, and how. In chapter 1, we discussed what tools and altar objects might be associated with each element. (This is discussed at greater length in my book *The Elements of Ritual*.[1])

The Elements as Themselves

When the elements are used in circle casting, and/or to build a microcosm of the universe, it is generally not enough to symbolize them with a color or tool. You must have something that is directly connected to Air, Fire, Water, and Earth.

If combined, as in a traditional Wiccan rite, Air and Fire together are burning incense; the unlit incense is consecrated as Air, the lit charcoal is consecrated as Fire before the incense is placed on it, and the smoke is their blending. Water and Earth combined are saltwater; first, clear water is consecrated, then salt, and then the two are mixed together.

Some people use incense to represent Air—the smoke is Air and the lit charcoal is unconsecrated, or stick or cone incense is used and there is no charcoal. Fire is represented by a candle or oil lamp, and the incense may be lit from that. Usually, Earth and Water are still combined as saltwater.

Sometimes a feather or fan is used to represent Air—this is an especially good idea if someone allergic to incense is participating in the ritual. In that case, a candle for Fire is the norm.

Pebbles can be used to line an outdoor circle, and this can be Earth instead of salt. Flower petals can also be used—I find this a particularly attractive choice for a handfasting. I have never seen soil used—it is too messy—although theoretically there's nothing wrong with it.

The following chart shows how elements can appear in their "natural state" in Pagan ritual. Perhaps you can think of other choices.

Air	*Fire*	*Water*	*Earth*
Incense/Smudge	Candle	Water in a dish	Salt
Feather	Lit charcoal (for incense)	Water in a shell	Pebbles
Fan			Flower petals

USING THE ELEMENTS IN RITUAL

You already know that there is an enormous variety of Pagan ritual. Even within the narrower subset of Wiccan ritual, there are still plenty of ways that the elements might be used. In general, the ritual area is marked, or touched in some way, with the four elements, which usually have been consecrated first.

By consecrating the elements, you remove impurities. After consecration, your water is just Water; in a magical sense, it no longer has any Air, Fire, or Earth. A consecration is generally a simple act of saying so, with or without the power of the Gods. It is the act of using your words or will to bring consecration into being.

I consecrate thee, O Air, that thou be the force of wind, intelligence, and thought in our rite.

Or:

In the names of the Goddess and the God, be this Water consecrated!

Or:

Great Mother, consecrate this Fire that it bring passion, will, and heat to our ritual.

And so on. Consecrations may be spoken, sung, shouted, intoned, or performed wordlessly.

Marking the ritual space with the consecrated elements might constitute the entire "making sacred space" portion of the ritual, or it might be one part of it. The space might be very specifically marked, with, for example, Water sprinkled in specific spots and along a specific path, or it might be more freeform, with a sort of generalized sprinkling being the order of the day.

Water or saltwater is sprinkled. Flower petals are strewn. Pebbles are generally placed carefully, one by one (tossing pebbles is not a recommended activity). A candle is carried and sometimes raised at specific spots (such as the quarter points). Incense is waved just below and inside the area to be censed, so that the smoke rises to the desired spot. Feathers and fans are waved just inside the desired spot, so that Air is blown onto it.

Participants might be marked with the elements as well. This, again, might be freeform, with feathers waved and water lightly sprinkled over a group, or each person might be more carefully marked, perhaps on the third eye. Care is taken with candles and incense so that only the *symbolic* Fire touches the skin.

Once again, words might accompany these ritual markings of space and people. The specific words depend upon the intention. Consecration is contagious—you can consecrate an element, and then consecrate a person or space with that element—the sacredness passes from thing to thing. A consecrating statement might be as simple as this:

> *I consecrate you with Earth.*

Or, you might imbue the circle or person with the quality of the element:

> *With this Air, I make you wise.*
>
> *With this Fire, I make you passionate.*
>
> *With this Water, I make you kind.*
>
> *With this Earth, I make you strong.*
>
> *With this Air, Fire, Water, and Earth, I make you balanced.*

Simple word changes can impart different impressions. Watch the following sentence change, and think for a minute about how each variation means something different:

> *I consecrate you with Earth.*
>
> *I give you Earth.*
>
> *This Earth gives you strength.*
>
> *You are now as strong as Earth.*

Earth makes you strong.

Let Earth make you strong.

Be you blessed by Earth.

You are one with Earth.

You have the power of Earth.

So, when using the elements in your ritual, think carefully about your purpose and how best to convey that purpose.

In addition to consecrating the sacred space and the people in it, the elements are often used for other consecrations. For example, if you have a new ritual tool, or a new statue of the Goddess, you will probably want to consecrate it. A traditional part of that consecration would be to touch it with the four elements from the altar. This again uses the magical principle of contagion. To touch an object with a consecrated thing spreads the consecration. It also uses the Way of Four—balance. The consecrated object is brought into a state of wholeness, by having it partake of the four quarters of wholeness. In a way, just as a ritual can be seen as re-creating the universe from scratch, so can a consecration. You take the tool and re-create it as a new thing, starting with the elements.

To do this, you'll use similar language as you used above, to consecrate people. With an object, the easiest way to consecrate is to sprinkle the saltwater all over it (being careful to turn the object over and around to reach all parts) and then pass it through the smoke (being equally careful). This works if you're using the combined pairs of saltwater and incense. If you're using another elemental configuration, modify as needed.

Using the Elements as Symbols or Tools

When elements are used symbolically—as part of a quarter, to represent balance, or to represent abstract qualities—there is more leeway in how they will be represented. The elements can be symbolized in tools whose use reflects the power of their respective elements. In Wicca, these tools are usually the Wand, Sword, Cup, and Pentacle, but there are other options. You might have more than four tools, not all of which correspond to the elements; you might have eight tools in two elemental sets; or you might correspond none of your tools to the elements, and symbolize Air, Fire, Water, and Earth through other means. The following is a list of tools used by Wiccans and Pagans in their rituals, and how they might correspond to the elements:

Tool	Element	Other Symbolism	Use
Wand	Usually Air, sometimes Fire	The male principle, "passive male," power of the magus	Summoning, invocation
Sword	Usually Fire, sometimes Air	The male principle, "active male," the collective will of a coven or group	Invocation, exorcism, casting a circle
Cup	Water	The female principle, "active female," receptivity	To hold the wine or other sacramental drink
Pentacle	Earth	The female principle, "passive female," plenty, magic, wholeness	As a plate or paten
Athame	Usually Fire, sometimes Air	The male principle, "active male," the individual will of a Witch or magician	Invocation, exorcism, casting a circle
White-Handled Knife	Sometimes Fire or Air (like a sword), sometimes Earth (a practical tool)	None	Cutting
Censer	Fire (some people consider a censer the element, some people consider it a tool; as a tool, it is Fire)	The Gods (because smoke rises from the censer and reaches the Gods), communication (with the Gods)	To hold the burning incense
Scourge	Fire	Purification, suffering	Ritual flagellation, for purposes of symbolic suffering, purification, or punishment

Tool	Element	Other Symbolism	Use
Aspergillum	Water	Cleansing	Used to sprinkle water about the ritual area
Fan	Air	None	Used to wave air or incense, to help with censing, or to bring Air into ritual where incense cannot be burned
Staff	Usually Air, sometimes Fire	Power, leadership, travel	Summoning, invocation, leading a procession
Ankh	"Spirit"	Life, sexual union, knowledge	None—a purely symbolic item
Wheel	All	The year, the seasons	None—a purely symbolic item
Sickle	Sometimes Fire or Air (like a sword), sometimes Earth (plants)	Druidism	Harvesting herbs
Broom	Air or Earth	Travel, departure, purification, cleansing, fertility, marriage/ handfasting	Sweeping things out, sweeping things clean, riding in a fertility rite, jumping over in a handfasting

The elements can be represented by tools, or they can be seen within tools. That is, you may not be using the aspergillum to represent Water on your altar. You may already have four elemental tools, but also have an aspergillum because you prefer using it to getting your hands all wet. So, the aspergillum isn't the "Water tool" for your ritual, but if asked, "What element is this tool?" then the answer would have to be Water.

Elements can be symbolized in other ways. In addition to the elements themselves, or elemental tools, there are a variety of representations that might be used. Four candles, or some other set of four objects, might each have a different color symbolizing the elements. Incense might be mixed with herbs of each element.[2] Pictures of elemental beings or animals are often hung at the quarter points. Playful Wiccans have even put stuffed animals representing the four elements in each quarter!

For my personal ritual space, I have long enjoyed a sort of mini-altar at each quarter. Each has three or four symbols of its element. The East has an array of feathers from various sources. The South has two tiger's-eyes and a piece of amber. The West has that stone from Lake Ontario, a shell, and a miniature whale. The North has a piece of petrified wood, a geode, and another stone. A group of items seems to build the elemental energy up in layers.

THE ELEMENTS AT THE QUARTERS

After you have cast the circle and created sacred space in a Wiccan ceremony, including, perhaps, consecrating the participants, the next step is generally to "call the quarters." This means, variously, to mark the four directions, to invoke or summon the powers of those directions, and/or to invoke or summon beings to guard those directions.

Each quarter (direction) corresponds to an element. Although there are many different systems, and therefore variations on correspondences, most North American and European Neopagans use Air in the East, Fire in the South, Water in the West, and Earth in the North, if they use an elemental system at all. Some Neopagans don't, such as the Druids, who mostly use the three worlds concept, as discussed in chapter 3.

There are basically three ways in which the elements might be used or invoked at the quarters:

Summoning the Power of the Directions

First, the power of the element might be invoked as part of the powers of its direction. That might go something like this:

> *I invoke the powers of the East!*
> *I invoke Air, the dawn, and spring!*[3]

And so on. A traditional Wiccan ritual begins with all four elements already in the circle. Usually, they are consecrated before the quarters are called. Since consecration brings the pure element into the circle, they do not need to be called at the quarters—they're already present. Instead of calling something that is already there, you're greeting it in its quarter, or acknowledging its presence there, or summoning the direction and naming its qualities, which include the element.

Air is invoked in conjunction with other Eastern qualities, as in the example just given. What is being summoned is the directional powers, and Air is one of those powers. It is the directional placement that is being summoned, as Air is already on the altar. When the invocations are finished, all four elements will be placed in their proper directions, and each direction will be imbued with elemental power.

The following are sample invocations of the four directions:[4]

O Eastern realm, I call you! (Strike bell, draw invoking pentagram)

Place of Air, place of mighty winds and gentle breezes

You are the cool breath of inspiration and relief

You are the whispered voice of logic and lore

Eastern realm, I call you!

Keep safe your quarter of this sacred circle![5]

Blessed be!

O Southern realm, I call you! (Strike bell, draw invoking pentagram)

Place of Fire, place of raging flame and soothing heat

You are burning passion and searing lust

You are heated anger and the will to live

Southern realm, I call you!

Keep safe your quarter of this sacred circle!

Blessed be!

O Western realm, I call you! (Strike bell, draw invoking pentagram)

Place of Water, place of thunderous storms and flowing streams

You are the passage to the Summerland

You are the human heart, the purifier, the initiator

Western realm, I call you!

Keep safe your quarter of this sacred circle!

Blessed be!

O Northern realm, I call you! (Strike bell, draw invoking pentagram)

Place of Earth, place of towering peaks and sloping fields

You are steadfast calm, you are the hearth and home

You are union and contentment and the body of the Mother of us all

Northern realm, I call you!

Keep safe your quarter of this sacred circle!

Blessed be!

Summoning Elementals at the Quarters

A direction, powerful as it is, is impersonal. Some people prefer instead to call the beings associated with the elements in their quarters. Some place deities in the quarters (of the sky, sea, etc.), but most call elementals or Guardians.

Remember that elementals are beings who consist purely of their own element: a sylph is entirely Air, a salamander is entirely Fire, etc. To call an elemental, you would have to be rather forceful; you would *summon* or *command* rather than *invite*. This is not because you're ill-mannered, but because elementals are simple beings who need to be spoken to very clearly; niceties will confuse the issue. You are calling across a considerable psychic distance—from the world of Spirit (four elements in balance) to worlds of only one element—and a call across such an expanse had best be clear and strong.

When calling an elemental, be specific and descriptive. Get its attention with gesture, sound, and aroma (incense).

The following is a sample set of elemental quarter invocations:[6]

Greetings, wise sylphs (Draw invoking pentagram)

I call you in the East! (Strike bell)

O flying ones, O thoughtful ones

Bring your inspiration to our sacred circle!

In the names of the Lady and the Lord, come to us[7]

Guard and balance our holy rite![8]

Blessed be!

Greetings, passionate salamanders (Draw invoking pentagram)

I call you in the South! (Strike bell)

O fiery ones, O brilliant ones

Bring your willpower to our sacred circle!

In the names of the Lady and the Lord, come to us

Guard and balance our holy rite!

Blessed be!

Greetings, lovely undines (Draw invoking pentagram)

I call you in the West! (Strike bell)

O loving ones, O flowing ones

Bring your intuition to our sacred circle!

In the names of the Lady and the Lord, come to us

Guard and balance our holy rite!

Blessed be!

Greetings, mighty gnomes (Draw invoking pentagram)

I call you in the North! (Strike bell)

O supportive ones, O constant ones

Bring your stability to our sacred circle!

In the names of the Lady and the Lord, come to us

Guard and balance our holy rite!

Blessed be!

But do you really want to call the elementals? As the personal embodiments of their respective elements, they are powerful beings, and can certainly be made welcome in your circle. They are very *natural* beings, partaking in a basic nature that we, complicated and confused as we are, can only imagine—and learn from. However, they can also be difficult to handle. If called at the opening of a ritual, they should be thoroughly and specifically dismissed when the ritual is coming to an end. None of them have any regard for humanity, except as we happen to coincide with what they're up to anyway. Many Wiccans choose to call elementals, but many others prefer to call *Guardians* instead.

Summoning Guardians at the Quarters

When the Guardians are called, it is generally with the utmost respect and formality. These beings are servants of the Gods, and are treated as honored equals and guests. They are referred to as "Lord of . . ." or "Ruler of . . ." when addressed.

Summoning the Guardians is something done in the more traditional, structured Wiccan ceremonies, and Guardians are beings who would probably not be comfortable in a more freeform, eclectic circle. Keep that in mind when deciding how to deal with the quarters in your ritual.

Here is a set of sample summonings used when the Guardians are invited at the four directions:

> *Hail, Guardians of the East!*
>
> *I, Deborah,*[9] *call you forth!* (Strike bell)
>
> *Air Lord, you are wise, and we need wisdom*
>
> *Please attend our circle*[10] *for the Lady and Lord*[11]
>
> *Enjoy and protect our rite.*
>
> *Blessed be!*

> *Hail, Guardians of the South!*
>
> *I, Deborah, call you forth!* (Strike bell)
>
> *Fire Lord, you are passionate, and we need passion*
>
> *Please attend our circle for the Lady and Lord*
>
> *Enjoy and protect our rite.*
>
> *Blessed be!*

Hail, Guardians of the West!

I, Deborah, call you forth! (Strike bell)

Water Lord, you are compassionate, and we need compassion

Please attend our circle for the Lady and Lord

Enjoy and protect our rite.

Blessed be!

Hail, Guardians of the North!

I, Deborah, call you forth! (Strike bell)

Earth Lord, you are firm, and we need firmness

Please attend our circle for the Lady and Lord

Enjoy and protect our rite.

Blessed be!

THE FOUR ELEMENTS WORKING

The "Four Elements Working" is a ritual that we developed in my old group. In this rite, four or five people work together to "become" the four elements (if there is a fifth person, s/he acts as a guide or leader). The technique of automatic speaking, described in detail in chapter 4, is used to speak the elements in a group ritual context.

This ritual was first done with a group of four very experienced Witches, and we found it quite valuable and moving. It's important to remember that this *is* work for more experienced people. The trance-state is surprisingly deep, and we found that, late in the process, it was difficult to force ourselves to recall that we *weren't* elements, that we were whole. That is why the balancing/centering at the end is essential, and that is also why a fifth person, acting as a guide, can be helpful.

All in all, it is best to approach this ritual with a sense of wonder, and also with appropriate caution. You are, however briefly, changing yourself into another thing, and it is reasonable to be guarded about such an activity. I am most comfortable doing this ritual as part of a rite where protections (such as Guardians) have been called or placed.

Beginning the Ritual

The room is quite dark, with only quarter candles and perhaps altar candles lit. No exterior light is visible, and small indoor lights, such as electronic clocks on VCRs, are covered.

The quarters have already been called, and Guardians of the elements invoked. A candle marks each quarter. Be aware when setting up the ritual space that people will be dancing about and sitting in the quarters; make sure the candles are positioned in a safe way—you wouldn't want anyone sitting on them!

In most rituals, there is a section set aside for "work." The Four Elements Working belongs in this section.

Raising the Power

The four people who will do the working join hands. The guide, if you have one, stands outside the circle of dancers, and can drum, clap, or use a rattle. Dance clockwise about the circle while singing an elemental chant.[12]

Dance fast enough to get a little dizzy. In the dark, after having circled many times, you are no longer exactly sure where you are in the circle.

If there is a guide, she will "call the drop," shouting "Now!" at the moment that feels right. If there are only four people, determine in advance who will do this. When the drop is called, *drop*. Sit down at once in the nearest quarter.

Speaking the Elements

There is now one person seated in each quarter, and perhaps a fifth person, who can be seated in the center.

From each quarter, despite the darkness, you'll be readily able to orient yourself and determine which quarter you are in. You already know the relative location of the door, any windows, and so on—take a moment to look around, and ascertain the direction in which you're seated.

Now close your eyes and feel the element. Allow yourself to merge with the element. If you are in the North, become Earth, if you are in the South, become Fire, and so on. You are the element's voice, its human agent. If there is a guide in the center, s/he can say words to this effect:

Close your eyes. Feel the element of your quarter. Allow yourself to merge with that element. Become the element of your quarter. You are that element; you are its human voice.

As you allow the element to become a greater part of you, words will emerge. There is no structure as to who will speak, or in what order. If you just speak as you are moved to, it will work out. My experience is that Earth is usually reluctant to speak, because silence is so much its way; but eventually all four elements will have their say, probably twice or more.

If there are four people, you must listen within yourselves for a sense of having gone far enough. My experience is that there is a sense of internal struggle, as if the human being that I am, and the element that I am channeling, are struggling against each other. Your experience may be different. The point is to pay attention so that you know when it is time to finish. If there is a guide, s/he will listen to both the external cues (people's voices fading away and not coming back) and the internal cues (the energy feels different). In any case, after everyone has spoken two or three or four times, they will probably have said everything they have to say verbally, and will begin to fall silent for longer and longer periods. Or, they may begin to argue (especially Fire). These are signs that it is time to move back to the center.

Balancing and Centering

Either the guide, or someone else, begins speaking:

It is time to come back now. Remember your wholeness. Come to the center. Come to the center. Touch the center.

All move to the center of circle and grasp the altar. Alternately, all can hold hands, clasped together over the altar, and say:

We are each Air, and Fire, and Water, and Earth. We are each Spirit. We are each whole. We are each Spirit. We are each whole.

All can now pick up this statement and repeat it:

We are each Spirit. We are each whole. We are each Spirit. We are each whole.

A centering chant or a simple "OM" can follow. Immediately after the working is done, all should eat and drink.

THE ELEMENTS IN SPELLS

When we talk about the relationship between spellcraft and the four elements, we might mean one of the following three things:

- · Is the purpose of the spell connected to the elements? Does the situation being addressed magically connect to one or more elements, or to their lack?

- · How are the elements, elemental objects, or elemental tools being used within a spell?

- · How are various spells specifically elemental in their nature? What is an Air spell, a Fire spell, a Water spell, or an Earth spell?

I should also point out that "spell" itself means more than one thing. Most of the time (magically speaking), "spell" means an act of magic; a series of steps taken to achieve a magical goal. But the original meaning of "spell" refers to the spelled-out part of magic—the phrase, often in rhyme, that is used to achieve a magical goal. By this definition, a nonverbal magical act, such as the making of a poppet or the burning of incense to achieve your goal, is not a spell. Unless I specify otherwise, I use the word "spell" in its broader sense, as an act of magic.

Elemental Purpose and Focus in Spells

Many spells have an obvious elemental association. Money and fertility spells require Earth. Sex and virility spells require Fire. Love spells need Water, and spells to increase understanding need Air. (The lists at the end of this section give more detail.) Some spells touch upon more than one element, and thus appear in more than one list, along with the reason why. For example, to be more creative, you need Air for inspiration, Fire to put the "fire in the head" (that is, to enliven the creative spirit), and Water to allow intuition to flow through your creativity.

Sometimes, finding the elemental factors in a spell is a key to unlocking the true meaning of the spell; it is a way to discover what the work is all about. In the example of creativity, which has three strong elemental components (and also requires Earth to *finish* the project), you will need to ask serious questions about what is blocking your (or the subject's) creativity. What happens when you attempt to do something creative? What isn't working and what still works just fine? What would the ideal outcome be? As you ask these questions, you'll find that your spell becomes more and more specific in its goal, and specificity is a vital (and often overlooked) part of any spell. Plus, the specifics will tell you a lot more about the elements.

Conversely, the elements may tell you more about the specifics. As a magical person, you can use divination, meditation, or other psychic arts to discover the elemental needs of a spell, and this can tell you what's going on with the subject of the spell. For example, you might find yourself saying: "My card reading tells me that this spell needs Water, and the situation already has lots of Fire. I guess that (the person) is applying too much will and is forcing the creative process too much, and needs to learn to flow, maybe to take inspiration from dreams. Let's do a Water spell that will help (the person) flow creatively."

Psychic knowledge can often take the form of imagery. You allow yourself, in a meditative state, to picture the problem. What does it look like? Such images can be metaphorical; for example, an illness may look like a knot, or a cloud, or rotted vegetables. You might not receive pictures, but get vivid feelings, or colors, or sounds instead. Just allow it to come. These pictures and feelings can be a great help in understanding the purpose and direction of your spell. As a clear picture takes shape, you'll often see an elemental relationship. For instance, if an illness looks like a dark cloud, then Air can blow the cloud away. If it looks like rot, then Fire can burn it.

Both psychic skills and mundane fact-finding can help you determine the elemental needs of a spell. The more you know, the better your spell.

The process of discovery can lead you in unexpected directions. Let's say your friend Steve is unemployed. The obvious solution is to do an Earth spell—Steve needs a job and money, which are Earth things. But before you leap into doing the spell, you ask *why* Steve lost his job. You find out he was fired for poor performance; Steve has been depressed, he has little energy, and he can't seem to get things done. Instead of an Earth spell, you decide on a Fire spell, which will give Steve energy, help break his depression, and allow him to take his life into his own hands.

The Elemental Purpose of a Spell

Air Spell

- To increase understanding.
- To gain knowledge or wisdom.
- To do well in school or on a test.

· To be eloquent; to say the right thing.

· To start or complete a writing project.

· To gain inspiration.

· To bring about a new beginning.

· To travel.

Fire Spell

· To increase sexual desire (libido).

· To increase sexual energy (lust, performance).

· To gain energy.

· To increase personal power or autonomy.

· To increase stamina.

· To gain influence over others (charisma).

· To make a decision (strengthen will).

· To increase life force; therefore to heal.

· For courage.

Water Spell

· To bring dreams.

· To soothe and calm.

· To ease pain.

· To bring romance (both to bring new love and to bring romance into an existing relationship).

· To increase psychic powers.

· To improve intuition.

· To increase "flow."[13]

· To improve lactation.

· To make childbirth easier.

Earth Spell

- · For fertility.
- · For wealth.
- · To get a job.
- · To improve appetite.
- · To grow (can combat wasting illnesses).
- · To improve crops.
- · For longer hair and nails.
- · For marriage.
- · To get a home.
- · To finish things; to bring things to fruition.

Some Differences Between People and Spells

Elemental qualities in their pure forms, as used in spells, are not necessarily a perfect match for the elements as they appear in people. For example, when we say "communication," we know that the element is Air. Air is speech, Air is verbal, and Air should be used in any spell oriented toward communication (i.e., you need to hear news about an important event, you need to receive an important phone call, etc.).

However, an Air person is not often a good communicator, because person-to-person communication requires connection and empathy, and these are qualities that Air people lack. An Air person is verbal and can convey information, but when we say "communication," we are generally talking about a form of human intimacy, which isn't the Air person's strength. Water and Earth people are more connected to the world of humans, and Water in particular is a good communicator in terms of relationship.

Another example is healing. Healing is often associated with Fire, but healers are often Water. The healing Fire is the Fire within, the life force of the person being healed; the Fire needed is in the patient. But it takes a Water person to be sufficiently giving and compassionate to perform the act of healing, especially on a day-to-day basis.

USING THE FOUR ELEMENTS IN A SPELL

Every spell can be balanced in the elements by consecrating objects used in the spell, just as other consecrations are performed. For example, suppose you are doing a distant healing for a sick friend, and you are using a photograph of your friend as a magical connection to her. Before you begin the healing, consecrate the photograph with the elements. The purpose of the consecration is twofold: to turn the photograph into a magical object—it will *become* your friend—and to make the spell whole by balancing it in the Way of Four.[14] Here's a sample script:[15]

Hold the photograph in one hand. With your other hand, dip your fingers into the saltwater and run them all over the picture, front and back. Pay special attention to the parts of the body that are being healed (if they appear in the picture). Say:

> *By the power of Water and Earth, I consecrate this picture. By the power of Water and Earth, I make this picture (Name). This picture is (Name). So be it!*

Now pass the picture back and forth through the incense smoke. Before doing so, add extra incense to the censer and stir it up, if necessary, to get it smoky. Say:

> *By the power of Fire and Air, I consecrate this picture. By the power of Fire and Air, I make this picture (Name). This picture is (Name). So be it!*

Now hold the picture in front of you and say:

> *By the power of Water and Earth, by the power of Fire and Air, it is done!*

This balances the four elements in the spell. But suppose you wish to include one element in particular. Suppose you wish to do an Air spell. How would you go about bringing Air into the working?

Using Air in a Spell

Air is used directly in a spell when the spell is carried on Air, such as via smoke or scent. It is also used when the spell involves speech or writing. Visualization and memory can also be connected to Air. Finally, using Air tools—the wand or sword, depending upon your attribution—brings Air into a spell.

Aromatherapy

The term "aromatherapy" first became popular in the 1980s and is now ubiquitous—everything from perfume to bubble bath is said to have aromatherapeutic qualities. Aromatherapy may be defined as "the use of true essential oils for healing purposes."[16] More broadly, it is the use of scent to achieve a healing or magical goal. The use of a physical healing technique for magic is nothing new, and considering that the line between the two (physical and magical) is not always clear, that makes perfect sense. Just as massage can be physically healing or a form of "laying on of hands," so can aroma have both physical and mystical effects.

As discussed in chapter 5, aromatherapy is an Air activity, so when you use aromatherapy in a spell, especially when you use it in combination with other magical techniques, you are doing an Air spell.

The basic technique of aromatherapy is to visualize your goal and then inhale. You can breathe in anything from fresh flowers, to a resin rubbed on the fingers, to a few drops of essential oil on a cotton ball.

Some people perform spells simply. They prepare as for meditation (see appendix A), visualize, and do the spell. Others perform more complex magical workings. Depending upon your preferred method, you might or might not cast a circle, use an invocation, or employ your magical tools (especially the tools of Air).

Scent and Memory

Aromatherapy generally uses essential oils or other flower essences, and usually employs the magical and/or healing powers of those essences.[17] However, there are a lot more scents than floral and herbal essences, and scent has a lot more associations than the traditional magical ones.

Literature and science agree that scent has the strongest connection of any sense to memory. Proust was certainly not alone in having profound memories flood forth when triggered by a scent from the past. The sense of smell has a direct connection to the central nervous system, whereas sight, sound, touch, and taste travel first to the thalamus before reaching the nervous system.[18] It is aroma, then, that reaches us most directly, and at a primitive, often subliminal, level. This visceral, image-laden experience is ideal for magical work. The things we work hard to achieve—visualization, direct connection to a moment in time, vivid memory—are often brought forth naturally by the right scent.

An aroma that triggers a memory or association has myriad magical uses. Here are some ideas:

- Your spouse is going to be traveling a great deal. Inhale his favorite T-shirt or pillow during a working to keep him safe.

- Your dog is very ill. Inhale his blanket, chew toy, or food while visualizing him healed.

- You are about to go home for the holidays, and your family has a history of conflict. Bake your traditional family cookies or cake and inhale that aroma while visualizing serenity.

- For a prosperity spell, buy something really luxurious, something you associate with wealth, and inhale that. Caviar comes to mind. This is an "it takes money to make money" sort of spell, but the investment will be worth it.

Magical Writing and Speaking

Language, whether spoken or written, is the province of Air, and using writing and speech for magic is a very ancient practice. The spoken word is the root of calling magic a "spell," and remains a part of most spells. To declare one's intention is the very essence of magic: *As I say, so mote it be!* "Magic words," be they as commonly known as Abracadabra, or as deeply secret as the Unknowable Name of God, have always carried great power.

Writing for magical purposes is as old as writing itself. The basics of the technique survive in modern form as affirmations. The magician writes his magical goal, often repeatedly. Typically, a special paper or parchment and a special quill or pen are used. These instruments are usually consecrated and are reserved for strictly magical use—you do not do spells with the same pen and paper used for your grocery list! A magical alphabet, such as Runic or Theban, is often employed (see appendix F).

The technique is as follows. In a cast circle, a meditation space, or at your writing desk, prepare your paper and writing instrument. You may consecrate them as a preliminary step during your spell, or they may have been consecrated in advance. It is traditional to write by candlelight, and you may also burn some incense—preferably incense attuned to your goal. You may choose to speak a simple invocation before you begin. Then write your statement over and over, until the paper is filled with writing. Declare the spell complete and fold the paper into a tiny packet, or place it into a consecrated envelope and seal it with sealing wax. The paper may then be kept upon your altar, ritually burned, ritually buried, or made a part of another magical object (like a poppet). The disposition will depend upon your intention and preference.

Your magical statement should be clear, direct, and positive. It should state that the goal is done, or that it is done by a given date. It should leave no "wiggle room," and it should have no qualifiers, such as "I want" or "I hope."

Magical Statements

Right	*Wrong*
"John's cancer is in full remission."	"I want John to be healed."
Clear, specific, positive, and in the present tense.	"I want" is not the goal; you already want John to be healed and don't need to perform a spell to make yourself want it. "Be healed" is vague.
"I have a well-paying job by the Wolf Moon."	"I have a good job."
A deadline is a good idea.	"Good" is really vague—what exactly do you want from the job and when?
"Whiskers will completely recover from feline leukemia in two weeks."	"Whiskers should get well."
You don't have to name the disease if it's very clear in your mind, but it can help you focus.	"Should" is another qualifier. "Get well" is less specific than "completely recover."
"Whiskers is a completely healthy cat."	"Whiskers will be a healthy cat."
This is another way of accomplishing the same goal—it is fully positive, and works by erasing the idea of the illness.	Really? When will Whiskers be healthy? "Is" works better than "will be."

Using Fire in a Spell

There are basically four kinds of spells that use Fire:

- · Candle spells
- · Spells that burn things
- · Sex magic
- · Spells using Fire tools (sword, athame, scourge)

As the use of tools is a topic for its own book,[19] we'll concentrate here on the first three.

Candle Spells

The great thing about candle spells is the lack of leftovers.[20] In our prior discussion of writing spells, we had to figure out what we were going to do with the written-on paper after the writing portion—the actual spellcraft—was done. Not so with candles! The spell burns the evidence! This is not only convenient, but it creates a satisfying sense of completion; it uses Fire's devouring quality to finish off the spell neatly.

Whole books have been written on candle magic,[21] so let's just cover the highlights:

A candle spell is, at the heart, as simple as lighting a candle while visualizing your intention. Of course, it can get more complicated than that. The color of the candle, the oil used to "dress" it, symbols carved on it, and its placement can all be part of the spell.

Because candle spells are relatively simple and convenient, and because candles themselves are readily available, they are used for all sorts of purposes, not just Fire spells. Fire purposes can be emphasized by using a red or orange candle, and by using a dressing oil scented with a Fire herb.

To dress a candle, use olive oil, with or without a drop of an appropriate essential oil, and rub the candle up and down, all over, while stating the purpose of the spell. Stating the purpose should be done following the guidelines in the Magical Statements chart in the previous section. If you wish, you can consecrate the oil before use.

A symbol, letter, rune, or word carved on to a candle can add Air to a Fire spell and impart extra symbolic meaning to the candle. Runes are common, but so are astrological symbols, words, or a date significant to the spell. A candle representing a person can have that person's birth date on it. A lust spell might use the Venus symbol.

By placement, I mean where you put the candle before, during, and after the spell. A common sort of candle spell is one in which two candles are used: one represents the person, and one represents the goal. The candles are lit every night for a week, and each night, they are moved a little closer to one another. On the final night, they are touching and are allowed to burn all the way down.

Burning It Up

Many spells use Fire at its most basic level—to burn stuff. There are three categories into which we can put such spells:

· Sacrifice or offering

· Letting go or releasing

· Destruction or transformation

It is an ancient belief that Fire is of the Gods and a means of communing with Them. In chapter 2, we discussed the "three worlds plus one." Fire is unworldly; it is foreign to our understanding of nature. Fire seems like magic. It arises spontaneously, or from the heavens (lightning). It isn't born, and when it dies, it is gone utterly. A corpse is like a body, and a cut plant is like a living plant, but ash and ember are nothing like Fire. The realm of Fire is not a natural realm, where natural beings can live; hence it is a spirit realm.

Fire has long been thought of as a gift of the Gods. Prometheus stole fire and gave it to humans, a gift that made us more godlike. Fire is the first step toward civilization; its possession transforms us from animals into humans.

So, when we wish to give things to the Gods, in sacrifice or in offering, we often use fire as the medium. This can be seen more as a religious act than a magical one—more worship than spell. However, one kind of spell is a bargain spell—an offering to the Gods in exchange for the fulfillment of a goal. If the goal is a Fiery one, then a burnt offering is appropriate.

"Letting go" can mean different things. You can release a bad habit, an old behavior, or an old wish. This sort of thing is covered in the next paragraph, as "destruction or transformation." To let go can also be to set free; to set off into the universe, to fly, as it will. Spells are often released in this way. This was alluded to in the writing spell, where one suggestion for finishing the spell was to burn the paper. The spell is set off to do its work. It is also sent to the Gods, or at least to Their realms; as the physical writing disappears, its spirit form is set free and travels to other realities.

Finally, we reach destruction/transformation. The two are one and the same—to transform a thing is to destroy its earlier form. When steel is made (in fire), the iron from which it came is gone. Death destroys life, but childbirth destroys pregnancy, and adolescence destroys childhood. When we burned up the parchment on which our spell was written, we transformed it into a spirit spell.

Fire is an excellent means for transforming something magically. It is a powerful means for releasing a strong emotion, such as grief or anger, and transforming it into positive feelings. It is a good place to discard bad attitudes, negative life conditions (poverty, loneliness), and excess baggage. Consecrate your fire to a specific purpose, and then burn up symbolic (flammable) objects, or written words or phrases, or just shout into the fire.

Sex Magic

Here is yet another topic that can fill a hundred pages in the blink of an eye! The principle of sex magic is simple enough, although its layers of complexity can make you forget that. I'll leave the intricate details of sex magic and Tantra for you to discover,[22] and just review the basics here.

As with any spell, sex magic works by focusing your intention, raising power, and then sending the power toward your target. In sex magic, power is raised through arousal and released on orgasm. The vehicle of sex magic is sexual pleasure, and any form of sexual pleasure can be used. Sex magic can be performed with a partner or alone. Meditation beforehand, consecrations, invocations, and stating your specific purpose aloud may all be used as part of the spell.

Concentrate on your target, visualizing it carefully and intently before you begin. This is exceptionally important when sex is your source of power, because sexual arousal tends to be distracting. It is also important that you don't wait until the moment of orgasm to send the power. For most of us, especially those not trained in advanced Tantric or other sexual techniques, "the moment" is gone very quickly, and the peak of the energy will be lost before the spell is sent.[23] A better technique is to send the spell in the moments before you achieve orgasm, and simply *keep sending* through your climax.

Every spell has the flavor of how it is performed; that's why we discuss elemental spells at all. Air spells have an Air character and are best suited to Air purposes. Because sex magic has a strong and particular character, it is not useful for just any goal. A solitary sexual spell can be performed to gain a sex partner, and fertility magic is (obviously) a natural.

General spells of attraction are a good subject for sex magic. These are spells that call for someone or something to be drawn to you—the sexual energy is used like a bright light, a beacon that attracts those who can see it. The spell is tuned so that only the right people see it. Such spells include finding tenants, finding buyers for a home, finding members for a coven or a band, etc.

Using Water in a Spell

Water can be used directly in a spell when an object is soaked, washed, sprinkled, or painted with water. Drinking as part of a spell uses the element of Water, whether you drink water, wine, or any other beverage. The cup is the tool of Water, so using a ritual cup in a spell adds Water to the spell. The subconscious mind, dreams, and visions are all associated with Water, and so magic involving divination or dreaming is Water magic.

Soaking, Washing, Sprinkling, Painting

Magical soaks are generally used for purifications or mild exorcisms. Water or salt-water, sometimes combined with direct sunlight or moonlight, can rid an object of undesirable psychic influences. These may be negative influences, or they may be benign but not consistent with the object's purpose. For example, if you are to be married with an antique wedding ring, prior to blessing it, you may wish to leave it in a dish of purified water under the full Moon to release it from the energies of past relationships. These may have been good relationships or bad, or the ring may have come to you without information about its history; the point is, you are starting your marriage fresh and wish to leave past influences behind.

A soak might have essential oils, herbs, or other items in it to add additional magical influences.

With washing, you are using water in a similar way, but without leaving the object in the water. Again, you are specifically focused on the cleansing and purifying aspects of Water. It is common to bathe or wash, often in consecrated water, prior to a Wiccan ritual. One might wash one's hands, a tool, or another object as a preliminary step in a magical rite. Washing is preferable to soaking when time is a factor, or when cleansing an object that would be damaged by long immersion.

Washing uses less water than soaking, and sprinkling uses less than washing. Sprinkling is most appropriate when a small, symbolic amount of Water is needed as an addendum to a larger working. Sprinkling is most frequently used when a spell is balanced in all four elements, as the route by which Water is introduced.

Painting with water is a sort of invisible writing. You take the consecrated water and dip your finger into it, and write or paint the symbol, letter, word, or image desired on to an object as part of a spell. This has two advantages. First, it *is* invisible, allowing the object to appear to be ordinary, to "hide in plain sight," or to be used for multiple purposes. For instance, a crystal can be written on in water, and worn for a year and a day or until the magical goal is fulfilled. Then it can be purified and used for a different purpose. Second, it adds Water to a spell that might otherwise not use it. Perhaps you've decided to do a distant healing using a photograph as your sympathetic object. You've consecrated the photo with the four elements to balance the spell, but you also want a little extra Water because your subject is extremely anxious and nervous and you wish to calm her. You could use water to paint a calming rune, the word "CALM," or a peace sign directly over her face or heart on the photograph.

Drinking and the Cup

Magical potions that are meant to be drunk figure prominently in the folklore and imagery of the classic witch, but are rarely used by modern Wiccans. This is in part because the purpose of many such potions isn't very nice, and in part because the use of herbal teas and medicinal brews is no longer considered witchcraft. However, a spell in the form of a beverage still has its uses.

Teas and infusions impart the magical as well as the medicinal properties of their ingredients. Brewing magical teas is an excellent way of bringing carefully targeted

Water energy into your body. For example, make mugwort tea to bring dreams. Prepare the tea while visualizing your goal and, perhaps, saying a dream-bringing rhyme. Drink the tea in a ritual setting.

A certain sort of drink spell is kind of the opposite of the Water spells just described. By soaking, washing, sprinkling, or painting, you can add Water to an object. By drinking, you can add an object to Water. The technique is simple: you take any magical or charged object, place it in a ritual cup, fill the cup, and drink. In this way, you can "drink" a crystal, a stone, a hair, or whatever it is you need to take in.

Dream Magic

"Dream magic" usually refers to using *lucid dreaming* to control events that will affect waking life. Instructions for becoming a lucid dreamer are beyond the scope of this book, but are an exciting subject for your own explorations.[24]

Dream magic can also refer to choosing a dream you wish to have. This is different from lucid dreaming, since, once the dream occurs, you are not attempting to control it. Typically, this is used to answer a question that cannot be answered in waking life. If you believe the answer resides in your own subconscious or superconscious, a targeted dream can be a good idea. Many pregnant women use this technique to converse with their unborn child.

You program yourself to have the dream by using a repeated spell, written or spoken, each night before bed; something like: "Tonight I dream the dream I need. Tonight I see the answer to . . ." You can say the spell aloud or write it in a special dream book by your bedside. Do this immediately before sleep; don't read in bed, brush your teeth, or make love afterward. You can use a dream-inducing herb, such as mugwort, in a tea or in a sachet under your pillow, to augment the spell.

Divination Magic

To divine—to read Tarot cards, runestones, astrological charts, or tea leaves, or scry in water, crystals, fire, or mirrors, or to read palms, practice bibliomancy, or a dozen other psychic arts—can be used in a magical context, or it can be manipulated to magical end.

Divination is one of the most powerful tools a magical person has. To discover what is right or wrong, what is possible or impossible, what the root of a problem is, and the path to its solution—the worth of these things cannot be overstated. Still, although magical, divination itself is not a *spell,* which is usually an act of magical *will.*

When we divine, we discover or uncover fate; we do not choose what that fate will be or impose it.

Divination is used as a pre-spell step, to discover the path the spell should take. Suppose you are having financial troubles. Before doing a money spell, you might do a reading to discover the cause of your troubles and the best solution. Then you could fine-tune the spell—working for a better job at a new company, or a promotion at your current company, or the money to go back to school.

Alternately, divination can be used *in* a spell, by stacking the deck. This works best in structured systems, systems where writing or objects are involved, like Tarot, astrology, runestones, or I Ching. Simply stated, you predetermine your outcome, stack the deck (literally in the case of Tarot), perform your invocation and other preliminaries, and then proceed with the reading as if it were spontaneous. When the desired outcome is seen, say, "So mote it be!" and close the spell.

Using Earth in a Spell

Earth is used in a spell when stones, soil, plants, or food are used. Of course, stones, plants, and foods each have individual magical properties, and can be of any element.[25] When using any of them for Earth magic, focus on their Earth properties and, if possible, use those that are specifically associated with Earth.

Earth is also used when you perform a spell that requires burying or planting, or in fertility magic.

Food Spells

Whenever we eat in order to ground, we are using food to perform Earth magic. We did this in chapters 2 and 4, when we ate after performing Air, Fire, and Water meditations in order to bring ourselves back into the world.

Magic can also be cooked into a meal. One technique I have used for a general purification and blessing spell is to make Circle Stew. This is stew cooked with salt that was ritually consecrated in a magic circle. It brings circle energy to a family meal.

More complicated and specific spells can be done by preparing and/or eating food ritually, with ritual ingredients, and with spells spoken at various points— preparation, serving, eating.[26]

Plants, Soil, and Burial

Anything buried in soil, in the earth, partakes of Earth nature. Burial can be used to dispose of or finish a spell. It can also be used to let a spell set, to "cook" it—not unlike Water used for soaking. This can be done to protect your home, with guardian objects buried at property borders. Since the home is Earth, it makes sense to protect it through Earth. Burial can also be a way of giving something to the Earth Mother, a slower and perhaps more intimate sacrifice than that made in Fire.

Planting is an Earth magic in and of itself. The act of planting is transformative: seed becomes sapling becomes plant becomes food (or herb, or whatever that plant becomes). Among our agricultural Pagan ancestors, planting was a time for ritual, prayers, invocations, blessings, and spells. Burial in the soil can be a symbolic planting—a love token buried can be a "seed" planted with the intention that love will grow.

Stones and Minerals

As with so many other topics, this one could fill a whole book; in fact, a whole shelf of books. However, let's set aside the study of the magical properties and attributions of the many types of gems and stones for a moment, and look just at stones themselves. Rocks. What do we know about them?

At the simplest level, we know that rocks are solid. They are hard. They are slow to change; less malleable, less affected by time than organic matter. In every way, the nature of Earth is seen in stone: solid, real, impassive, apparently unchanging, consistent in shape. We also know that minerals are far more retentive of magical energy than organic matter. In my experience, a gem, a piece of jewelry, or a knife is much more likely to retain a psychic impression than a piece of wood or fabric—check out an antique shop and see for yourself. Minerals absorb energy readily and retain it over a long length of time. This makes them ideal for talismans and magical fetishes of all kinds.

Charge stones up with the energy of a spell and carry them with you for a period of time, or use other objects made of minerals. If you recall that coins are mineral (nickel, silver, copper), you'll see a good magical connection: Earth corresponds to money, which is (sometimes) made of minerals, which are Earth. Coins can therefore by used in spellwork to symbolize the idea that Earth equals money. Take advantage of this by charging coins for money spells. I like to put such coins into charity boxes when the period of a spell is complete.

Use stones as magical reminders; links between you and another person or idea. They can ground you, remind you of a promise, or connect you to the past. A wedding ring is one such link, and it is magical indeed, changing the state of the person who wears it!

Place charged stones in special spots in your home, car, or office. They are there to be touched and drawn upon when needed.

ƒOUR SPELLS

The descriptions of elemental spells in the last section were necessarily brief. The topic of spells and spell casting is an intricate one, and no mere section of a book can do it justice. To put a little meat on the bones of our elemental spell discussion, the following are four detailed scripts for specific elemental spells. Each uses techniques that we just discussed.

The topics for these spells were selected for their relatively wide appeal—doing well in school, releasing obsessions, finding love, and attracting money. I hope that the suggestions in the previous section, as well as the detailed spells that follow, will empower you to design your own spells as well.

The spells are presented as "stand-alone" magic; that is, instructions are provided merely for the casting of the spell, not for whatever ritual context you may choose to place it in. Some people do magic by itself, some do it as part of a Pagan or Wiccan ceremony or as part of another traditional rite, and some people use a variety of approaches. My book *The Elements of Ritual* can provide you with a guide for placing spells within a Wiccan ceremony, but this book doesn't assume that is your path. Although the spells are presented without any specific religious trappings, deities whom it might be appropriate to invoke are listed.

The Air Spell: Improving School Performance

Goal

To do better in school. This spell is designed for someone who is really struggling with his or her studies, who is having a hard time understanding concepts, retaining material, or just keeping up. It still requires that you study, attend class, and do your homework (darn it).

Target

This is a self-improvement spell; you are aiming at yourself.

Needed Tools

- Ritual pen (this can be a fountain pen, a quill, or any pen you have set aside for ritual work)
- Parchment or other ritual paper
- Envelope
- Sealing wax
- Appropriate essential oil (see the following section)
- Candle

Air Oils

Air and Mercury (for communication, gathering information, intelligence, speed of thought, language):

- Caraway
- Clary sage
- Lavender
- Spearmint

Air and Jupiter (for good luck and success, the higher mind, philosophy and education, growth):

- Anise/star anise
- Sage

Notes

The spell is meant to be done alone, over a period of time. Before you begin, you should have written the spell proper (the part you're going to write and say), if you're not using the text provided. The sealed envelope will be used daily for a while; decide where you're going to keep it. Also decide how you're going to dispose of it when the spell succeeds.

Appropriate Deities

Sarasvati, Thoth, Apollo, Oghma.

The Spell

1. Consecrate all tools to Air.

   Bring the pen, paper, sealing wax, and essential oil[27] to your altar. Have sage burning. Pass the pen back and forth through the sage smoke, saying:

   By Air is this pen consecrated. May all the words it writes be true. So mote it be!

Pass the paper [28] back and forth through the sage smoke, saying:

   By Air is this paper consecrated. May all written upon it be manifest. So mote it be!

Pass the sealing wax back and forth through the sage smoke, saying:

   By Air is this sealing wax consecrated. May it hold, contain, and seal words of truth. May it do its work rightly! So mote it be!

Pass the essential oil, in its bottle, back and forth through the sage smoke, saying:

   By Air is this oil consecrated. May it open my mind and speed my thoughts.[29] So mote it be!

Now you are ready to begin the spell.

2. Begin by preparing your magic space and grounding and centering.[30] Light the candle. Make sure you have sufficient light by which to write; add additional candles as needed.

   Pick up your pen, and have your paper before you. Say:

   May this work be true, and for the good of all! Blessed be!

Visualize your goal clearly in your mind. Picture passing grades, or excellent test results, or whatever it is you need. With this image firmly in mind, begin writing the spell. Write it over and over, slowly, until you fill the page. Write:

   My mind is open and alert. I understand my course of study.[31] I am a success at school.

Leave enough room at the very end to write "So mote it be!" Sign your name (your magical name, if you have one). Say out loud:

   So mote it be!

Take the oil and, using a cotton ball or swab, scent the paper with the oil. Surround the outside of the writing in oil, as illustrated in figure 7. If you'd like, you can add a rune or astrological symbol by painting it in oil, using the swab, over the body of text. (See figures 8 and 9 for two runes you might choose.)

Fold the paper and place it in the envelope. Seal with sealing wax.[32] Say:

So mote it be!

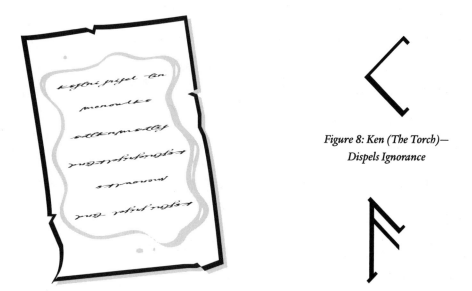

Figure 7: Magical Text

Figure 8: Ken (The Torch)—
Dispels Ignorance

Figure 9: Os (The God)—
Brings Light, Knowledge, and Speech

The spell-casting is complete. Place the envelope on your altar, or wherever you decided to keep it.

3. Many spells have a time period based on nature. The cycle of one full moon, or one moon phase, is often used. Other spells are done for a week, or on the same weekday for a set period of weeks. This spell has a period of time based on your school calendar. If you've been worried about failing, there is a point in time when you'll know you've passed—when report cards are issued, or test results are posted, or what have you. The duration of the spell will be from its beginning—preferably in

a waxing moon, but again, based on your school schedule and need—to the time that you've determined you'll recognize as its end.

Determine the beginning and end in advance, before doing the spell. This will prevent you from playing a mental game of "Is it working yet?" Such thoughts drain a spell of power.

For the period of the spell, every day, pick up the envelope. Inhale the aroma of the essential oil and visualize again your goal. Say:

> *My mind is open and alert. I understand my course of study. I am a success at school. So mote it be!*

4. At the end of the period of the spell, give the envelope to Fire or bury it in the earth.

The Fire Spell: Freedom from Obsession

Goal

To free yourself from an obsession or addiction. I designed this spell with a sexual or romantic obsession in mind—an unhealthy longing for the wrong person, either from the past or present. This combines three Fire qualities: lust, obsession, and freedom. However, any obsession or addiction can be released into the fire. The goal is freedom.

Target

The target is the obsession itself, which will be burned up in the fire.

Needed Tools

- Symbols of obsession (can be notes with significant words written on them, or any token that represents the object of obsession)
- Fire-building materials (wood, matches, kerosene, etc.)
- Fire-safety materials (sand, fire extinguisher)
- Drums and other instruments
- Blankets to sit on

Notes

Normally, this spell is done in an outdoor setting, in the woods, around a campfire. It can be done indoors, with the fire built inside a cauldron. However, keep in mind that the noise level is liable to be pretty high, so don't try this where neighbors are likely to complain.

This spell is designed to be done in a group. It is ideal for a group of people who share a common addiction or obsession, and perhaps are meeting to support one another in recovery. It is less "witchy" than most spells, and, if no circle is cast and no gods are invoked, it is suitable for people who enjoy New Age-style ritual, but are uncomfortable with Paganism or Witchcraft.

You'll probably want some chants related to fire, freedom, and/or empowerment.[33]

Appropriate Deities

Agni, Kali, Thor, Hathor, Dionysus, Zeus.

The Spell

1. Gather in your location and build the fire. It should be going nicely before you begin. Make sure your fire extinguisher and sand are nearby before you start. Make sure everyone is comfortable, with blankets laid out and drums at hand. All participants need their symbol, token, or slip of paper with them by the fire.

If you are going to cast a circle or do invocations, do so after the fire is going.

2. Ground and center as a group. Chant softly and get your drums warmed up. Begin your freedom chant. Let the drumming build slowly. It is important at this point not to really cut loose yet, not to let the drumming go into that wild, ecstatic thing that drumming often reaches toward. A slow, steady climb is what you're after.

3. Whoever is moved to do so goes first. The first person stands up and says something in the following pattern, while throwing his or her token into the fire:

I, (Name), release X. Go to the fire, X! I, (Name), am free!

Here is an example:

I, Mary, release my obsession with John. Go to the fire, obsession![34] I am free of my longing for you. I, Mary, am free!

Everyone now begins to chant:

> *Mary is free! Mary is free! Mary is free!*

The drumming builds to a higher pitch (but still not completely cut loose yet, as the work will continue). While everyone drums and chants for Mary, she can chant along, scream, drum, or whatever moves her.

Gradually this is allowed to subside, the drumming remains at a low tempo, and Mary returns to her place.

4. Each person, one by one, will release his or her obsession, and throw his or her token into the fire. Each person will have his or her name chanted and drummed, and be declared free.

5. When everyone has gone, the chant can change to this:

> *We are free! We are free! We are free!*

Now you can cut loose. Let the drumming build as much as you like. Shout, scream, dance, shake rattles, shake your groove thing, let go! You are free!

6. As the drumming dies down, resume your opening chant. Let it fade slowly. Say:

> *So mote it be!*

(Everyone should echo the first person who says this, so that all say it.)

7. Make sure you have safely doused the fire before you leave.

The Water Spell: Finding Love

Goal

To find a loving relationship. This spell is not to attract a particular person, but to bring a person as yet unknown into your life.

Target

The target is yourself; specifically, your heart—your emotional heart, not your cardiac muscle. This spell places an attractant around the heart. For most people, the best visualization is of a pink-white light surrounding your heart, drawing your beloved inexorably toward you. However, if you prefer, you may imagine a sweet sound or a delightful aroma, irresistible to your beloved but undetectible to others.

Needed Tools

- A piece of rose quartz or a rose-quartz bead
- Your ritual cup
- May wine or other strawberry-flavored wine
- Athame
- Pink or red flowers (optional)
- Representatives of the four elements (a dish of water, a dish of salt, incense, and a candle). You will consecrate the stone by four elements, and use the wine and cup for the additional Water influence.
- A sweet incense. There is a vast array of herbs and flowers associated with love. The following are some that have Water as their element, Venus as their planet, and a folkloric association with love or love magic: apple blossom, freesia, geranium, thyme, and violet.

Notes

- The spell should be done alone, in a waxing Moon.
- You should be skyclad (nude).
- Friday is the traditional day for love spells.
- If you are planning on using a bead rather than a stone, have a string or chain for it. If the string isn't waterproof, put the bead on it after the spell is completed.
- Candles should be pink.
- It is always best if a bottle of wine is uncorked before a ritual begins.

Appropriate Deities

Aphrodite, Freya, Lakshmi, Oshun.

The Spell

1. For love spells, it is important that the altar/spell area be beautiful and pleasant in every way. Arrange the flowers around the goblet, get the incense going nicely, and set up everything so that it is appealing to you.

2. Visualizing your target, consecrate the rose quartz as follows:
    Pass stone through incense smoke, saying:

    By Air may my love begin.

Pass stone through candle flame, saying:

    By Fire may my love be passionate.

Dip stone in water dish, saying:

    By Water may my love be deep.

Roll stone in salt dish, saying:

    By Earth may my love be firm.

Figure 10: Beorc (The Birch)—
Brings Love and Fertility

(You can moisten your finger in the water to wipe off any excess salt from the stone so that your wine won't taste salty.)

3. Continue your visualization. Place the rose quartz in your ritual cup. Fill the cup with wine. Plunge your athame into the cup, saying:

    I consecrate this wine to love!

4. Lay your athame aside (wipe the blade—wine left on the blade will damage it). Still visualizing, as strongly as possible, dip your finger in the wine and make a love rune (figure 10) or the sign of Venus over your heart, while saying:

> *I make my heart a place where love will come.*

5. Say:

> *I bring love into me, love is in me, love will come to me, love belongs to me.*

Drink down the entire cup. Say:

> *So mote it be!*

6. Carry the rose quartz with you at all times (this is why a strung bead comes in handy). Sleep with it as well.

The Earth Spell: Bringing Money

Goal
To bring money into your life.

Target
You are sending "abundance energy" into the plants. Your target is the plants, which are being filled with this energy. Your secondary target is yourself; you are establishing a connection between yourself and the plant, and receiving abundance through that connection.

Needed Tools

- Peas for planting in a bowl or dish—enough for each participant to have one
- Potting soil, enough for all, in a large bowl or cauldron
- A transplant pot for each pea
- A pitcher of water; enough to water each new plant
- A small trowel or large spoon to help with planting
- Athame (optional)

Notes

The spell as written below is for a group, but can easily be done solitary. If done with a group, you can skip the use of an athame and make the spell less witchy and more New Age by just using your hand for consecrating.

Decide in advance where you're going to plant your pea, and if you're not a gardener, it would be a good idea to study up in advance on the ideal conditions, growing season, watering needs, etc. In a group, everyone in the group needs this information.

Figure 11: Altar Setup

Appropriate Deities

Demeter, Lakshmi, Habondia, Amalthea, Freyr.

The Spell

1. Ground and center. Do an opening chant or "OM" while holding hands (touching is very Earthy).

2. Plunge your athame (or hand) into the soil, saying:

   O Earth, be consecrated! O Earth, be a fertile ground where abundance grows. Be the soil where our hopes become reality! So mote it be!

All respond:

   So mote it be!

Plunge your athame (or hand) into the dish of peas, saying:

   O seeds, be consecrated! O seeds, as you grow, bring us wealth. Be the seed of hope that grows into the plant of fulfillment. Nurture us with abundance! So mote it be!

All respond:

   So mote it be!

3. Each person, one by one, comes to the altar and plants a pea into the transplant pot, using the consecrated soil. Use the pitcher of water to immediately water the little seed. As you plant your pea, say the following spell:

   Money in the earth, money rising up, money coming into me. So mote it be!

All respond:

   So mote it be!

Leave each little pot on or near the altar, in the center of the circle. The plants will form an inner circle, as shown in figure 11. Each person will be behind her own plant, but will have enough room for power-raising.

4. When all the peas have been planted, use chant and rhythm to raise power. While drumming, chant:

Money in the earth, money rising up, money coming into me. So mote it be!

When the power reaches a peak, someone calls, *Now!* and all throw power into the plants, concentrating on money growing out of the peas, and coming into yourself.

5. Bring the peas home and transplant them into a permanent spot. Every day, water, weed, or just check up on your plant, and say:

Money in the earth, money rising up, money coming into me. So mote it be!

6. When the first peas are ready for harvest, join together with your group and eat the first ones in a ritual setting. Sit in circle, and one by one, lift your pea pod and say:

This is the fruit of my labor. This is my abundance and my wealth. Wealth flows into me. So mote it be!

All respond:

So mote it be!

When everyone has eaten, celebrate!

---

1. *The Elements of Ritual: The Air, Fire, Water & Earth of the Wiccan Circle* (Saint Paul, MN: Llewellyn Publications, 2003).

2. Herb, gem, and color charts appear in appendix E.

3. The generic invocations from appendix B can also be adapted for quarter-calling.

4. From *The Elements of Ritual.*

5. For "sacred circle," you can substitute the occasion; i.e., "Keep safe your quarter at this sacred full Moon circle."

6. From *The Elements of Ritual* again.

7. Remember that elementals can be mischievous and hard to handle. Invoke by the power of the Gods to bring a bit more strength, credibility, and control.

8. "Holy rite" is the phrase that can be substituted for the specific occasion; i.e., "Guard and balance this handfasting."

9. Using your own name is a traditional way to add power to an invocation.

10. Use the special occasion for "circle" as needed.

11. Guardians serve the Gods, so doing this in Their names is appropriate. You might want to substitute specific god names.

12. There are many good collections of chants and Pagan music available on tape or CD. Two elemental chants that I use are "Air Moves Us," which is on *Chants: Ritual Music* (available from Reclaiming at www.reclaiming.org), and "Air I Am," which is on *All Beings of the Earth* by MotherTongue (available from the EarthSpirit Community at www.earthspirit.org).

13. See *Flow: The Psychology of Optimal Experience* by Mihaly Csikszentmihalyi (New York: Harper & Row, 1990).

14. My first step would be to invoke the Gods and ask Their aid. Then I would use the elements. Since we are focused here on the elements, we'll leave a discussion of invoking the Gods for another time. See *The Elements of Ritual* for more detail.

15. This sample script and others in this chapter are based on the combined pairs of elements: Water/Earth and Fire/Air.

16. *Magical Aromatherapy* by Scott Cunningham (Saint Paul, MN: Llewellyn Publications, 1989) xi.

17. A good guide for looking up herbs is *Cunningham's Encyclopedia of Magical Herbs* by Scott Cunningham (Saint Paul, MN: Llewellyn Publications, 1987).

18. *Essence and Alchemy: A Book of Perfume* by Mandy Aftel (New York: North Point Press, 2001) 13–14.

19. This is also covered in *The Elements of Ritual*.

20. I'm pretty sure it was my friend Constance Godfrey who first pointed this out to me.

21. Including: *The Master Book of Candle Burning: How to Burn Candles for Every Purpose* by Henry Gamache (Highland Falls, NY: Sheldon Publications, Inc., 1942), and *The Magic Candle: Facts and Fundamentals of Ritual Candle-Burning* by Charmaine Dey (Plainview, NY: Original Publications, 1982).

22. One good book is *Ecstacy Through Tantra* by Dr. Jonn Mumford (Saint Paul, MN: Llewellyn Publications, 1988).

23. In which case, darn it, you'll have to try again!

24. Try *Exploring the World of Lucid Dreaming* by Stephen Laberge (New York: Ballantine Books, 1991).

25. Charts in appendix E illustrate this.

26. Detailed food magic can be found in *The Magic of Food: Legends, Lore & Spellwork* by Scott Cunningham (Saint Paul, MN: Llewellyn Publications, 1996). The renamed new edition has an updated bibliographic entry: *Cunningham's Encyclopedia of Wicca in the Kitchen* (Saint Paul, MN: Llewellyn Publications, 2003).

27. Some of these may already have been consecrated as ritual tools. This consecration is meant only for new tools.

28. Consecrate a package or stack of paper all at once. The spell calls for one sheet of paper, but you'll have the rest for future use.

29. Here you can adapt the wording to your specific needs.

30. See appendix A.

31. For "course of study," you can substitute the specific course that is troubling you; i.e., "calculus," "physics," "Russian poetry." This spell doesn't rhyme, so you don't have to worry about the name of the course changing the meter. On the other hand, you can rewrite it so it does rhyme.

32. If you've never used sealing wax before, practice beforehand. It can be tricky and it is easy to burn yourself.

33. The CD *Chants: Ritual Music* (available from Reclaiming at www.reclaiming.org) has an appropriate song called "Rise With the Fire."

34. Do not send people into the fire! Release the obsession, not John.

Preparation for Meditation or Magic

YOUR MAGICAL ROOM

A room in which meditation or magic is performed needs two things: it needs to *allow* an altered state of consciousness, and it needs to *encourage* such a state. In other words, you need to create a space free of the distractions and disturbances that keep you trapped in mundane experience, and you also need atmosphere and props that help you reach a meditative or magical place.

You should meditate and/or do magic in the same place each time, when possible. This is practical, as it allows your tools and other necessities to be kept in a convenient place. It also serves a magical function. Repetition, including repeated location, helps induce trance. Familiar things, associated with the same event, will begin to cause (or at least encourage) that event. Just as Pavlov's bell eventually caused his dogs to salivate, your magic room and the things in it will begin to cause your consciousness to shift.

The first order of business is *privacy*. The distraction of wondering if the door will open, the phone will ring, or you will otherwise be interrupted is virtually guaranteed to disrupt a meditative state. The door to your magic room should have a lock, unless you live alone. But a locked door and an unplugged phone are not enough. You should also make sure that the rest of your household is able to allow you the privacy you need. Are the kids in bed? No, *really?* Do the cats have fresh water in their dish? You don't want anyone chasing you down to meet his or her needs.

You also don't want *you* chasing you down. Are there any nagging tasks that simply must be done? I prefer not to save any chores for after meditation, because then my mind has "after" in it. Your magic is more free when you haven't the thought in the back of your head that you shouldn't take too long.

That's all the negatives; with these handled, you *allow* meditation. Now, how do you encourage it?

The Room

- · Should have a comfortable spot for sitting.

- · Not too bright, or candlelit.

- · A place (drawer, chest) where your tools and paraphernalia can be easily found. It is more than a little irritating to interrupt a spell because you've run out of matches and can't find more!

- · Comfortable temperature. I like to keep a throw blanket handy, as I sometimes get cold in the middle of things.

- · Know your directions! When you move into a new place, use a compass to find north, east, south, and west, and remember which is which.

- · Are you using an altar? An altar is the center of a Wiccan rite, as well as many other Pagan and magical rites. On it are your elemental and magical tools, candles, incense, idols, etc. You may wish to meditate before your altar, even when you aren't doing a ritual.

Meditation Checklist

- · Is the door locked?

- · Is the phone unplugged or the ringer turned off?

- · Have necessary chores been done (pets fed, children in bed, dishes done)?

- · Am I in comfortable clothing (or comfortably skyclad)?

- · Have I a comfortable place to sit?

· Is the temperature comfortable?

· Have I the incense, candles, etc., that I will want?

The final item on this list alludes to a second checklist, one for ritual or magic. It is useful to have your own such list, so that you can review it before starting a rite, but the enormous variety of ritual makes it impossible for me to provide a useful sample. However, remember that you do not want to be interrupted! If you use charcoal for your incense, have a spare; if you use candles, have fresh ones available, and a candle shaver in case they don't fit readily into their holders. In this way, you make sure that your ritual will run as smoothly as possible.

GROUNDING AND CENTERING

The phrase "grounding and centering" is so commonplace that I'm using it to avoid confusion. However, in a group ritual, there is a third part to the process, so it should more correctly be called "grounding, centering, and merging."

Here are the steps:

· *Grounding*—Getting in touch with the Earth.

· *Centering*—Getting in touch with ourselves.

· *Merging*—Getting in touch with each other.

To make it easier to work alone, I have kept the merging portion of the meditation separate. Just stop when you get there if you're working alone. Keep going in a group.

Grounding and Centering Meditation

Close your eyes and take a deep, cleansing breath. Then another. Then another. Allow the cleansing energy to fill you, relaxing and focusing you, from head to toe. It fills your head, and any tension in your head, jaw, or brow becomes relaxed.

Let the energy fill your neck and shoulders, and your neck and shoulders relax. Now let the breath fill your arms, your upper arms, your forearms, and your wrists, and release any tension in your arms. Your wrists, hands, and fingers are relaxed.

As the cleansing energy fills your chest, your torso and upper back become relaxed. As the breath fills your stomach, your tummy and lower back now relax. The energy fills your hips and groin, releasing all the tension in that part of your body.

Now the energy is flowing down through your legs, relaxing your thighs, knees, calves, and ankles, and finally filling your feet and toes.

Now you feel that your body is flowing with energy; that energy is your life force, it is *you*—relaxed, aware, and full of life. Send a cord of that energy down through the soles of your feet, down through the floor, down into the Earth.

You are connected by this tail to the Earth. You reach deep into the soil, rooting yourself in the cool, damp, loving embrace of Mother Earth. The energy that extends from you is like a taproot, and from the Earth you draw planetary power up, into you. The power of Mother Earth, thousands of times greater than your own, reaches up your taproot, into your spine, and fills your body. The Mother's energy nourishes and supports you. It anchors you, keeping you in touch with the stability and safety of Earth; you are grounded and strong.

Now connect to your center. Find the center of yourself, the place within your body that you feel is *you*. Connect to your center and feel the energy throbbing there. Feel the pulse of your center's power. Feel the Earth energy rushing into your center. Know yourself as whole, as centered.

Merging

Now notice the others around you. Notice that they each have a pulsing, powerful root connecting them to the Earth. Picture those roots now, all drawing power from the shared soil beneath you.

Observe how you are all connected, joined through the power below you, and joined, too, by the shared purpose you have in being together now.

Generic Invocations

The following invocations can be used or adapted for any purpose for which the elements are called upon. They can be used in quarter invocations, spells, consecrations, meditations, etc.

To write your own invocation, or to adapt the ones offered here, consider the following:

1. Clear statement of purpose:

I invoke you.

Be thou consecrated.

I summon you.

2. Specific name:

Element of Air.

3. By what power (optional):

By my Will.

In the names of the Gods.

4. Appropriate description. See samples; words that describe the element.

5. Declaration of success:

So mote it be!

It is done!

6. Degree of formality. Compare the following:

I invoke thee, O Earth, O majestic one.

versus

Mighty Earth, I invoke you.

When adapting your invocations, are you a "thee" and "thou" kind of person? Do you enjoy flowery language ("majestic"), or prefer to keep it simple ("mighty" or "strong")?

7. Are you talking *to* the elements, or *about* them? Compare the following:

I invoke you, O Earth.

versus

I invoke Earth.

This has to do with how much you want to connect to elementals, and how connected in general you choose to be to the elements on this particular occasion. Are you viewing them as *beings* or as *things*? If you are asking the help of the Gods (or a particular god) or of Guardians, you'll use the third person for the elements:

Great Goddess, aid me in invoking Earth.

Here you are talking *to* the Goddess, *about* Earth.

INVOCATIONS IN SETS Of fOUR

I've attended many rituals where the four quarters were invoked in four wildly different styles. To me, invocations are more balanced, and more reflective of wholeness, when they match. If you write your own invocation using the guides in the previous section, write them in sets of four.

Matching an invocation is simply a matter of replacing one element's specific words with those of another, as you'll see in the following samples. For instance, if I say "Air, you are intelligence, be here," it would be pretty straightforward to come up with "Water, you are feeling, be here," and so on. Make sure all four have the same level of formality, and that all four are in either the second or third person. Don't invoke a sylph for Air and then a Guardian, rather than a salamander, for Fire.

Four Formal Invocations

I invoke thee, O Air! Come to my aid!

O sweeping wind, O gentle breeze,

O intelligence and inspiration!

Thou who art the mind, thou who art the sky

I invoke thee now!

So mote it be!

I invoke thee, O Fire! Come to my aid!

O raging blaze, O soothing heat,

O intensity and passion!

Thou who art the will, thou who art the flame

I invoke thee now!

So mote it be!

I invoke thee, O Water! Come to my aid!

O mighty wave, O trickling stream,

O emotion and intuition!

Thou who art the heart, thou who art the sea

I invoke thee now!

So mote it be!

I invoke thee, O Earth! Come to my aid!

O towering cliffs, O rolling fields,

O foundation and strength!

Thou who art the body, thou who art the land

I invoke thee now!

So mote it be!

Four Informal Invocations

Air, I invoke you. Come to me!

You are the wind, both harsh and gentle.

You are intelligence and inspiration!

I invoke you, Air, mind and sky!

So mote it be!

Fire, I invoke you. Come to me!

You are heat, both burning and soothing.

You are intensity and passion!

I invoke you, Fire, will and flame!

So mote it be!

Water, I invoke you. Come to me!

You are bodies of water, both wide and narrow.

You are emotion and intuition!

I invoke you, Water, heart and sea!

So mote it be!

Earth, I invoke you. Come to me!

You are the mountains, fields, and plains.

You are foundation and strength!

I invoke you, Earth, body and land!

So mote it be!

Musical Accompaniment for Each Element

Music can be used to help create an elemental atmosphere in a number of situations:

· As background music and/or cues for your elemental meditation tapes

· In ritual, to invoke without words, or to accompany invocations

· As accompaniment for an elemental spell

· As background music while doing elemental beauty treatments or elemental cooking

· As a way of timing something in ritual where a clock would be intrusive

AIR MUSIC

· Flute

· Wind chimes

· Traditional Japanese music, such as *shamisenongaku* or *sokyoku*

· *A capella* music, or music emphasizing harmonic vocals

· Enya and similar New Age vocalists

FIRE MUSIC

· Hard rock and heavy metal

· Martial music

· Marches

· Salsa; latin dance music

· Spanish guitar

· Bluegrass

WATER MUSIC

· Standards with Nelson Riddle arrangements

· Tchaikovsky

· "Smooth" jazz such as David Benoit or Kenny G

· Harp music

· Dreamlike, hypnotic music; for example, "Tubular Bells" by Mike Oldfield

EARTH MUSIC

· Tribal drumming

· Blues or blues rock

· Any slow, percussive instrumentals

The Way of Four Balancing Exercises

The Way of Four balancing can be done as a meditation or as a ritual; that is, entirely in your head, or with actions accompanying it. The instructions for both are written to be done alone. In a group, the meditation can be read aloud, or the ritual can be performed jointly. However, the act of balancing is often private—something done when you feel out of sorts, disoriented, "off." The balancing is done as needed, not necessarily on a schedule, so it may not lend itself to a group that meets on a schedule.

THE WAY OF FOUR MEDITATION

Prepare your meditation room.

Relax your body. Ground and center.

Visualize Air entering you through your head. It rushes into your body as a pale white wind, starting at your forehead and moving through your body. It has a cleansing quality; it blows away the bad, and blows in freshness, invigoration, and clear thought. Your mind is clear. Picture the Air moving throughout your entire being; it is stronger and brighter in the head, but it is everywhere within you. Think, or say aloud:

I am Air.

Take a long, slow, deep breath.

Visualize Fire entering your body through your solar plexus. It is a flame that starts in your center and grows, glowing bright red, increasing in size until it fills you entirely. It has an energizing quality. As it moves through you, it fills you with vigor and aliveness. See this red glow filling you, from your center to your toes and fingertips. It is brighter and hotter at the solar plexus, but is everywhere within you. Think, or say aloud:

I am Fire.

Take a long, slow, deep breath.

Now visualize the Air, still there, still blowing inside you, and the Fire, glowing within. They coexist. Visualize them blending, interacting, strengthening each other. Think, or say aloud:

I am Air and I am Fire.

Take a long, slow, deep breath.

Visualize Water entering your body through your heart. It is a deep blue stream, flowing into your heart, and from there, flowing throughout your entire body. It brings with it deep feeling. As it flows through you, you feel open, loving, and intuitive. This is a stream of depth; depth of knowing and depth of feeling. This deep blue stream flows through you, touching every part of you. It is deeper and bluer at your heart, but is everywhere within you. Think, or say aloud:

I am Water.

Take a long, slow, deep breath.

Now visualize the Air, still there, still blowing inside you, and the Fire, glowing within. Remember how they mingled, and add Water to that mingling. The white of Air, the red of Fire, and the blue of Water are moving in you, all together. Visualize them blending, interacting, strengthening each other. Think, or say aloud:

I am Air, I am Fire, and I am Water.

Take a long, slow, deep breath.

Visualize Earth entering your body through your skin. It touches the outside of you, a rich, green blanket that envelops you. Earth seeps into your body, through every pore, bringing stability and peace. It is a fertile green plain within you, making you real, strong, and sure. As it solidifies all through you, in every part of you, you become deeply connected to the physical within yourself, and in the world. This fertile greenery starts on the outside, on the skin, and reaches deeper and deeper until all parts of you are Earth. Think, or say aloud:

I am Earth.

Take a long, slow, deep breath.

Now visualize the Air, still there, still blowing inside you, the Fire, glowing within, and the deep blue flow of Water. Remember how they mingled, and add Earth to that mingling. The white of Air, the red of Fire, the blue of Water, and the green of Earth are in you, all together. Visualize them blending, interacting, strengthening each other. Think, or say aloud:

I am Air, I am Fire, I am Water, and I am Earth.

Take a long, slow, deep breath.

Think, or say aloud:

I am whole. I am balanced.

THE WAY OF FOUR RITUAL

Prepare your meditation room.

It is preferable to perform this ritual skyclad, so make sure the thermostat is at a comfortable level.

Set up your altar with symbols of the four elements. For this rite, it is best if there are four *separate* symbols, so don't mix Air and Fire in the censer. You can use the following:

· Incense or a feather for Air

· A candle or oil lamp for Fire

· A dish of water for Water

· A dish of salt or a stone for Earth

Relax your body. Ground and center.

Pick up the Air symbol and touch it to your forehead. Say:

Air enters me.

Visualize Air entering you. It rushes into your body as a pale white wind, starting at your forehead and moving through your body.

Move the symbol of Air down your body. Do this by holding it to your forehead, and then moving it straight down to your feet and bringing it back up to chest level. Assuming you are right-handed, move it now down your left arm, to the fingers, then put it in your left hand and reverse the procedure. (Reverse the order if you are left-handed.) Then bring it back to your forehead.

You visualize Air as having a cleansing quality; it blows away the bad, and blows in freshness, invigoration, and clear thought. Your mind is clear. Picture the Air moving throughout your entire being; it is stronger and brighter in the head, but it is everywhere within you. Say:

I am Air.

Place the symbol of Air back on the altar.

Take a long, slow, deep breath.

Pick up the symbol of Fire and hold it near your solar plexus, close enough so you can feel heat from the flame. Say:

Fire enters me.

Visualize Fire entering your body. It is a flame that starts in your center and grows, glowing bright red, increasing in size until it fills you entirely.

Move the symbol of Fire over your body, by first bringing it from the solar plexus up to the head, and then following the same procedure as for Air.

You picture Fire as having an energizing quality. As it moves through you, it fills you with vigor and aliveness. See this red glow filling you, from your center to your toes and fingertips. It is brighter and hotter at the solar plexus, but it is everywhere within you. Say:

I am Fire.

Place the symbol of Fire on the altar in such a way as to have it touch the symbol of Air. (If this is a fire hazard, or if the censer might melt the wax, do this only for a moment and then place them near each other.)

As you do this, visualize the Air, still blowing inside you, and Fire, glowing within. They coexist. Visualize them blending, interacting, strengthening each other. Say:

I am Air and I am Fire.

Take a long, slow, deep breath.

Pick up the dish of water and dip your fingers into it. Touch the water to your heart.

Visualize Water entering your body through your heart. It is a deep blue stream, flowing into your heart, and from there, flowing throughout your entire body.

Using your fingers (and replenishing as necessary), anoint your entire body with water. Do this by touching power points only: forehead, eyes, lips, shoulders, heart, hands, solar plexus, groin, the small of your back, knees, and feet.

Visualize Water as bringing deep feeling. As it flows through you, you feel open, loving, and intuitive. This is a stream of depth; depth of knowing and depth of feeling. This deep blue stream flows through you, touching every part of you. It is deeper and bluer at your heart, but it is everywhere within you. Say:

I am Water.

Place the dish of water on the altar in such a way as to have it touch the symbols of Air and Fire.

Now visualize the Air, still there, still blowing inside you, and the Fire, still glowing within. Remember how they mingled, and add Water to that mingling. The white of Air, the red of Fire, and the blue of Water are moving in you, all together. Visualize them blending, interacting, strengthening each other. Say:

I am Air, I am Fire, and I am Water.

Take a long, slow, deep breath.

Pick up the symbol of Earth. If you are using a stone, pick up the stone. If you are using a dish of salt, dip your finger in the salt just as you did with the water. Touch the symbol of Earth to your pubic bone.

Visualize Earth entering your body through your pubic area. It enters you from your groin, and becomes a rich, green blanket that envelops you.

Move the Earth symbol over your body. If using a stone, do this as you did for Air and Fire. If using salt, use the anointing method you used with Water.

Picture Earth seeping into your body, bringing stability and peace. It is a fertile green plain within you, making you real, strong, and sure. As it solidifies all through you, in every part of you, you become deeply connected to the physical within yourself, and in the world. This fertile greenery starts at the groin, and reaches throughout your body until all parts of you are Earth. Say:

I am Earth.

Place the symbol of Earth on the altar so that all four symbols now touch; they are clustered together.

Now visualize the Air, still there, still blowing inside you, the Fire, glowing within, and the deep blue flow of Water. Remember how they mingled, and add Earth to that mingling. The white of Air, the red of Fire, the blue of Water, and the green of Earth are in you, all together. Visualize them blending, interacting, strengthening each other. Say:

I am Air, I am Fire, I am Water, and I am Earth.

Now arrange the symbols on the altar into a square, each in a corner. The square is a symbol of wholeness. Say:

I am whole. I am balanced. So mote it be!

Charts

COLOR GROUPINGS

When working with the elements ritually, you'll often want a specific color for each element. This applies in many cases where colors are used symbolically, for example, having a different-colored candle for each element.

It can sometimes be confusing to come up with a consistent color system. Consistency and clarity are very important in magic and symbolism. Symbols communicate with us and empower us by reaching the subconscious mind, so it is a mistake to use any symbols that require you to pause and think, even for a moment. Pausing and thinking are *conscious* mind functions! You definitely don't want, for example, sea green for Water and forest green for Earth. Even though they look different, it is your conscious mind that will make the distinction, while your unconscious mind thinks, "Green means . . . ?"

Each suggested group in the following chart has colors that will work together well. In each group, the colors can readily symbolize their element, and the colors stand out clearly from each other.

	Air	*Fire*	*Water*	*Earth*
Bold Primary 1	White	Red	Blue	Black
Bold Primary 2	White	Red	Green	Black
Muted Natural	Blue	Orange	Green	Brown
Bold Natural 1	Blue	Red	Green	Brown
Bold Natural 2	Yellow	Red	Blue	Green

ELEMENTAL HERBS, FLOWERS, AND OTHER PLANTS

Since this is a sampling and not a comprehensive list, I tried to select only those herbs that are readily available in perfumes, teas, tinctures, or in the wild. I also looked for unusual relationships between the elements and the planets, as this can sometimes be very handy when working magic. Certain planet/element relationships are obvious and expected: Air to Mercury, Fire to the Sun or Mars, Water to Venus or the Moon, etc. In cases where something is more properly a food (like grapefruit) or less readily available, I have included it if the unusual relationship makes it worthwhile.

Herbs of Air

Planet	*Herb*
Jupiter	Anise, dandelion, endive, maple, sage, star anise
Mars	Hops, pine
Mercury	Almond, caraway, clary sage, clover, lavender, lemongrass, lemon verbena, lily of the valley, mace, marjoram, mint, spearmint
Sun	Chicory, honey
Venus	Goldenrod

Herbs of Fire

Planet	*Herb*
Jupiter	Clove, nutmeg, sassafras
Mars	Basil, coriander, cumin, garlic, ginger, hawthorn, pepper (black pepper), pimento (red pepper), tobacco, woodruff, yucca

Mercury	Celery, dill, fennel, peppermint, pomegranate
Moon	Camelia
Sun	Angelica, bay, bergamot, carnation, cedar, cinnamon, goldenseal, heliotrope, juniper, lime, marigold, neroli (orange blossom), peony, rosemary, sesame, sunflower

Herbs of Water

Planet	*Herb*
Mars	Cranberry
Moon	Camphor, gardenia, jasmine, lemon, lily, myrrh, rosewood, sandalwood, willow, wintergreen
Sun	Chamomile, grapefruit
Venus	Apple blossom, cardamon, freesia, geranium, heather, hyacinth, iris, jonquil, lilac, narcissus, orchid, orris, plumeria (a.k.a. frangipani), rose, thyme, tuberose, vanilla, violet, yarrow, ylang-ylang

Herbs of Earth

Planet	*Herb*
Jupiter	Honeysuckle, oakmoss, tonka beans
Moon	Honesty
Saturn	Cypress, horsetail, mimosa, oleander, patchouli
Venus	Magnolia, mugwort, primrose, tulip, vervain, vetiver (a.k.a. vetivert), wood sorrel

ELEMENTAL GEMS AND STONES

Most gems are minerals, but such organic items as pearl and coral are included. Highly ambiguous stones have been omitted, as they require more in-depth study than a simple chart can afford. For example, you'll notice that quartz crystal is not included. This may seem strange, given its near ubiquity in magical work. However, quartz crystal has been associated with the Sun and Fire, with the Moon and Water, with Air because of its clarity, with the Goddess, and with the God, and is often used to symbolize Spirit by people using a five-element system. Now *that's* what I call ambiguous!

Stones of Air

Planet	Stone
Jupiter	Flourite
Mercury	Aventurine, jasper (mottled), mica, pumice
Saturn	Sphene (a.k.a. titanate)

Stones of Fire

Planet	Stone
Mars	Bloodstone, flint, garnet, jasper (red), lava, onyx (also Saturn), rhodocrosite, rhodonite, ruby, sard, sardonyx, tourmaline (red), tourmaline (watermelon—also Venus)
Mercury	Agate (banded, black, brown, or red)
Pluto	Spinel
Saturn	Apache tear, obsidian, onyx (also Mars), serpentine
Sun	Amber, carnelian, citrine, diamond, pipestone (also Mars), sulphur, sunstone, tiger's-eye, topaz, zircon
Venus	Watermelon tourmaline (also Mars)

Stones of Water

Planet	Stone
Jupiter	Amethyst (also Neptune), sugilite
Mercury	Agate (blue lace)
Moon	Aquamarine, beryl, chalcedony, moonstone, mother of pearl (also Neptune), pearl, sapphire, selenite
Neptune	Amethyst (also Jupiter), lapidolite (also Jupiter), mother of pearl (also Moon)
Venus	Azurite, calcite (blue or pink), chrysocolla, coral, jade, lapis lazuli, rose quartz, sodalite, tourmaline (blue, green, and pink)

Stones of Earth

Planet	*Stone*
Earth	Granite and ordinary found stones can be assumed to be associated with both the planet and the element of Earth
Mercury	Agate (green and moss)
Neptune	Turquoise (also Venus)
Pluto	Kunzite (also Venus)
Saturn	Alum, coal, hematite, Jasper (brown), jet, salt, tourmaline (black)
Venus	Calcite (green), cat's-eye,[1] chrysoprase, emerald, jasper (green), kunzite (also Pluto), malachite, olivine, peridot, tourmaline (green), turquoise (also Neptune)

---

1. This is the natural stone sometimes known as "hawk's-eye." The iridescent "stone" with the iris-like center stripe that is sold as cat's-eye is a kind of optical glass.

Magical Alphabets

RUNIC AND THEBAN

A	ᚠ	ᛅ	K	ᚲ	ᒻ	U	ᚾ	ᛘ			
B	ᛒ	ᛃ	L	ᚱ	ᛘ	V	ᛞ	ᛘ			
C	ᚲ	ᛖ	M	ᛗ	ᛉ	W	ᛈ	ᛘ			
D	ᛗ	ᛖ	N	ᛏ	ᛘ	X	ᛈ	ᛘ			
E	ᛗ	ᛖ	O	ᛩ	ᛖ	Y	ᛇ	ᛖ			
F	ᚡ	ᛖ	P	ᛢ	ᛖ	Z	ᛉ	ᛘ			
G	ᚷ	ᛖ	Q	ᚲ	ᛪ	.	⠂	ᛘ			
H	ᚺ	ᛖ	R	ᚱ	ᛘ	,	,	⸱			
I	ᛁ	ᛒ	S	ᛋ	ᛦ	?	?	ᛢ			
J	ᛦ	ᛒ	T	ᛏ	ᛖ	!	!	ᛚ			

Figure 12: Magical Alphabets
Based on an illustration courtesy of Isaac Bonewits.

Bibliography

My son often asks me, "Mom, how do you know that?" causing me to throw up my hands in frustration. I don't know how I know what I know! Hence, this bibliography is rather lopsided, filled with resources I needed to check and new books I needed to uncover, but lacking in those about topics I already know.

Aftel, Mandy. *Essence and Alchemy: A Book of Perfume*. New York: North Point Press, 2001.

Campbell, Joseph. *The Hero with a Thousand Faces*. 1949. Reprint, Princeton, NJ: Princeton University Press, 1972.

Crowley, Aleister. *777 Revised: A Reprint of 777 with Much Additional Matter*. New York: Samuel Weiser, 1970.

Csikszentmihalyi, Mihaly. *Flow: The Psychology of Optimal Experience*. New York: Harper & Row, 1990.

Cunningham, Scott. *Cunningham's Encyclopedia of Magical Herbs*. Saint Paul, MN: Llewellyn Publications, 1987.

———. *The Magic of Food: Legends, Lore & Spellwork*. Saint Paul, MN: Llewellyn Publications, 1996. Repackaged as: *Cunningham's Encyclopedia of Wicca in the Kitchen*. Saint Paul, MN: Llewellyn Publications, 2003.

———. *Magical Aromatherapy*. Saint Paul, MN: Llewellyn Publications, 1989.

Dey, Charmaine. *The Magic Candle: Facts and Fundamentals of Ritual Candle-Burning.* Plainview, NY: Original Publications, 1982.

Erikson, Erik H. *Identity and the Life Cycle.* New York: Norton, 1980.

Farrar, Janet and Stewart. *The Witches' Way: Principles, Rituals and Beliefs of Modern Witchcraft.* London: Robert Hale, 1984.

Farrar, Stewart. *What Witches Do: A Modern Coven Revealed.* Custer, WA: Phoenix Publishing Co., 1971 and 1983.

Gamache, Henry. *The Master Book of Candle Burning: How to Burn Candles for Every Purpose.* Highland Falls, NY: Sheldon Publications, Inc., 1942.

Groom, Nigel. *The Perfume Handbook.* London: Chapman & Hall, 1992.

Laberge, Stephen. *Exploring the World of Lucid Dreaming.* New York: Ballantine Books, 1991.

Lipp, Deborah. *The Elements of Ritual: Air, Fire, Water & Earth in the Wiccan Circle.* Saint Paul, MN: Llewellyn Publications, 2003.

Mumford, Dr. Jonn. *Ecstacy Through Tantra.* Saint Paul, MN: Llewellyn Publications, 1988.

Osborne, Marijane, and Stella Longhand. *Rune Games.* London: Routledge & Kegan Paul, 1982.

Tyson, Donald. *Rune Magic.* Saint Paul, MN: Llewellyn Publications, 1988.

Winter, Ruth, M.S. *A Consumer's Dictionary of Cosmetic Ingredients.* Fifth edition. New York: Three Rivers Press, 1999.

WEBSITES

Astrology: Astrodienst: www.astro.com.

Chants and Pagan Music: Reclaiming: www.reclaiming.org. Also, the EarthSpirit Community: www.earthspirit.org.

Hot Oil Treatments: www.thehairdiva.com, and Robbie's Recipe Collection: www.robbiehaf.com.

Perfume: Perfumania: www.perfumania.com. A retail store, what distinguishes this site is that it gives the history and background, as well as the ingredients, of every perfume it sells. Also, the Web-encyclopedia of World Perfumes: www.perfume-world.net.

Personality Tests: Consulting Psychologists Press, Inc.: www.cpp-db.com. Also, Team Technology, Inc.: www.teamtechnology.co.uk/tt/t-articl/mb-simpl.htm.

Index

777, 180

addiction, 52, 87, 101, 256–257

aether, 12, 15–16

Agni, 12–13, 257

agoraphobia, 53

akasha, 12, 15

alchemy, 55, 146–147, 180, 265

alcohol, 77, 177

alphabets, magical, 242

amalthea, 263

amniotic fluid, 7, 41

ankh, 227

Aphrodite, 259

Apollo, 253

Aquarius, 5, 39–40

Archangels, 21

Aries, 6, 39, 42

Aristotle, 14–16

aromatherapy, 130, 147, 160, 162, 175, 180, 241, 265

aspergillum, 227

astrology, 39–40, 55, 250

athame, 5, 22, 90, 226, 244, 259–263
Attention-Deficit/Hyperactivity Disorder (AD/HD), 50
automatic speaking, 99, 233
automatic writing, 79, 98–101

beer, 179–181
betta, 111
boredom, 87, 186
boundaries, 27, 97, 173–174
broom, 227
burial, 251

Cancer, 8, 39, 243
candle spells, 244–245
Capricorn, 9, 39–40
censer, 219, 226, 240, 281, 283
channeling, 99, 235
"Charge, The," 77, 101
clutter, 129
consecration, 223–225, 229, 240, 265
Court Cards, 60–61
Crowley, Aleister, 180

Demeter, 263
Dionysus, 257
divination, 179, 237, 247, 249–250
Doisneau, Robert, 110, 124
dream magic, 249
Druids, 10, 132, 227–228
drum, 234, 258

Empedocles, 13–14, 23, 56
Escher, M. C., 105, 124

exfoliants, 167–168
exorcism, 226

fan, 89, 176, 203, 219, 222–223, 227
fertility, 9, 12, 113, 178, 180, 210, 227, 236, 239, 247, 250, 260
Fishburne, Laurence, 137–138
food spells, 250
freedom, 17, 32, 81, 108, 192–193, 212, 256–257
Freud, Sigmund, 183
Freya, 259
Freyr, 263

Gaia, 9, 16, 31
Geddes, Anne, 113, 125
Gemini, 5, 39
gnome, 9, 17, 19–20, 22, 32, 37, 231
Golden Dawn, 5, 22
gossip, 87, 196, 201
grounding and centering, 92–97, 254, 269
Guardian, 17, 20–22, 230, 232–234, 251, 265, 272–273

Habondia, 263
Haring, Keith, 108, 124
Hartmann, Franz, 18, 22
Hathor, 257
henna, 167, 175, 180
Hippocrates, 14
Holy Grail, 8
homeopathy, 18
hot oil, 163–165, 172
hot tub, 166
hot wax, 161–162

inhalation treatment, 160

invocation, 78, 175–178, 202–203, 212–214, 216–217, 226–227, 241–242, 250, 265, 271, 273

Jung, Carl, 53, 55–57

Jupiter, 253, 286–288

Kabbalah, 1, 5

Kahlo, Frida, 113, 125

Kali, 161, 257

Kama Sutra, 109

Kandinsky, 108, 124

King, 11–12, 60–64, 73–74

Klimt, Gustav, 110

Knight, 60, 62, 68–69, 75

Lakshmi, 259, 263

Leo, 6, 39

libido, 54, 72, 238

Libra, 5, 39–40

love songs, 177, 211

magic words, 242

Mars, 40, 286–288

massage, 71, 130, 162, 166–167, 169, 171–174, 180, 241

memory, 7, 94, 101, 240–242

menstrual cycle, 7

Mercury, 40, 192, 253, 286–289

merging, 209, 269–270

mermaids, 19, 110

Mondrian, 108, 124

Monists, 13

Moon, 7–8, 23, 40, 79, 130, 243, 247, 255–256, 259, 264, 286–288

Mucha, Alphonse, 105, 124
mud, 49, 167, 170
Myers-Briggs, 55–58, 75

Neiman, LeRoy, 108, 124

O'Keefe, Georgia, 113, 125
oatmeal, 166, 168–171, 174, 180
obesity, 53, 87
obsession, 150, 157, 208, 256–258, 266
oghma, 253
Oshun, 259

Page, 60, 62, 66–67, 98, 254
Paracelsus, 17–19, 22
paraffin, 161–164, 172, 175
Parish, Maxfield, 105, 124
pentacle, 9–10, 22, 90, 225–226
pentagram, 9–10, 15–16, 22, 229–231
Picasso, Paloma, 137
Pictorial Key to the Tarot, The, 5
Pisces, 8, 39
Plato, 14
Pluto, 288–289
potpourri, 131
Pre-Raphaelites, 110, 124
privacy, 46, 104, 111, 127, 196, 267
purification, 160, 226–227, 250

quarters, 16, 78, 225, 228–230, 232, 234, 273
Queen, 11, 60–63, 70–72

Rackham, Arthur, 18

Raphael, Sally Jesse, 135

Rembrandt, 113, 125

Rockwell, Norman, 113, 125

Rossetti, Dante Gabriel, 124

rune, 83, 245, 248, 255, 261

runic, 242, 291

sacrifice, 245, 251

Sagittarius, 6, 39

salamander, 5–6, 18–20, 23, 27, 230–231, 273

salt scrub, 168–171

Sarasvati, 253

Saturn, 287–289

sauna, 161, 172

Scorpio, 8, 39–40

scourge, 226, 244

scrying, 31, 83, 249

sealing wax, 243, 253–255, 266

seaweed, 7, 112, 154, 166, 172

selkies, 19

Seurat, Georges, 105, 124

sex magic, 244, 246–247

shopping, 64, 133, 135, 138, 140, 146, 215, 218

sickle, 227

sirens, 19

skyclad, 26, 34, 174, 259, 268, 281

soaks, 166–167, 247

staff, 191, 195, 205, 227

steam bath, 160

steam facial, 160

stubbornness, 85–87, 89–90, 140

Sun, 4, 7, 40, 286–288

sweat lodge, 26, 65, 172–173

sylph, 5, 17–19, 24, 230, 273

sympathetic magic, 3

Tantra, 246, 265

Tarot, 1, 5, 7–9, 44, 55, 60–64, 70, 75, 83, 130, 249–250

Taurus, 9, 39–40

Theban, 242, 291

Thor, 27–28, 79, 161, 164, 170, 232, 257

Thoth, 253

travel, 18, 94, 101, 186–187, 191–193, 198, 227, 238, 241

undine, 8, 17–20, 231

Upanishads, 12, 22

van Gogh, Vincent, 108, 124

Venus, 40, 245, 259, 261, 286–289

Vermeer, 113, 125

Victorian, 18, 22, 110, 117, 139

Virgo, 9, 39–40

Waite, Arthur Edward, 5, 18, 22, 75

Watchtowers, 20–22

Waterhouse, John, 110, 124

Wheel, 37, 178, 227

Witches' Pyramid, 4, 6, 8–9, 22, 41, 222

Zeus, 14, 257

Zodiac, 1, 6, 8–9, 42

 # LLEWELLYN ORDERING INFORMATION

Order Online:
Visit our website at www.llewellyn.com, select your books, and order them on our secure server.

Order by Phone:
- Call toll-free within the U.S. at 1-877-NEW-WRLD (1-877-639-9753). Call toll-free within Canada at 1-866-NEW-WRLD (1-866-639-9753)
- We accept VISA, MasterCard, and American Express

Order by Mail:
Send the full price of your order (MN residents add 7% sales tax) in U.S. funds, plus postage & handling to:

Llewellyn Worldwide
P.O. Box 64383, Dept. 0-7387-0541-1
St. Paul, MN 55164-0383, U.S.A.

Postage & Handling:

Standard (U.S., Mexico, & Canada). If your order is:
$49.99 and under, add $3.00
$50.00 and over, FREE STANDARD SHIPPING

AK, HI, PR: $15.00 for one book plus $1.00 for each additional book.

International Orders (airmail only):
$16.00 for one book plus $3.00 for each additional book

Orders are processed within 2 business days. Please allow for normal shipping time.
Postage and handling rates subject to change.

The Elements of Ritual
Air, Fire, Water & Earth in the Wiccan Circle

DEBORAH LIPP

Many books may tell you how to cast a Wiccan circle, but none really bother to explain why. When you finish reading *The Elements of Ritual*, you'll know what each step of the circle-casting ceremony means, why it's there, and what it accomplishes. You'll learn several alternative approaches to each step, and you'll be empowered to write your own effective ceremonies using sound magical, theological, and pragmatic principles.

0-7387-0301-X, 312 pp., 7½ x 9⅛, illus.   **$16.95**

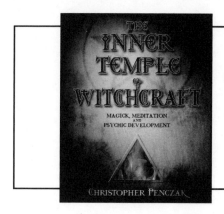

The Inner Temple of Witchcraft

Magick, Meditation and Psychic Development

CHRISTOPHER PENCZAK

Enter the Inner Temple and discover the power of your magick! For the serious seeker, *The Inner Temple of Witchcraft* lays the foundation for deep experience with ritual. Instead of diving right into spellwork, this book sets the student on a course of experience with energy and psychic ability—the cornerstones of magick. You will explore witchcraft's ancient history and modern traditions, discovering the path that suits you best. The thirteen lessons take the student through meditation, instant magic, ancient philosophy, modern science, protection, light, energy anatomy, astral travel, spirit guides, and healing, culminating in a self-initiation ritual.

0-7387-0276-5, 352 pp., 7½ x 9⅛   **$17.95**

CD COMPANION

Explore your Inner Temple—your personal sacred space where there are no boundaries and all things are possible. This four-CD set helps open the door by calming your mind and guiding the visualizations vital to magickal success. It is designed to complement the course material presented in the year-and-a-day study course *The Inner Temple of Witchcraft*.

Each companion CD allows you to experience the book's lessons on a deep and personal level, with an experienced teacher guiding the way. The reinforcement of the techniques, soothing music, and personal guidance form the building blocks needed to create and maintain a spiritual, inner practice of witchcraft that will strengthen your ritual work.

0-7387-0387-7 Four-CD Set in 5¼ x 7½ Amaray DVD Case   **$24.95**

To order, call 1-877-NEW-WRLD

Prices subject to change without notice

The Outer Temple of Witchcraft
Circles, Spells, and Rituals

CHRISTOPHER PENCZAK

As you enter the heart of witchcraft, you find at its core the power of sacred space. In Christopher Penczak's first book, *The Inner Temple of Witchcraft*, you found the sacred space within yourself. Now *The Outer Temple of Witchcraft* helps you manifest the sacred in the outer world through ritual and spellwork. The book's twelve lessons, with exercises, rituals, and homework, follow the traditional Wiccan one-year-and-a-day training period. It culminates in a self-test and self-initiation ritual to the second degree of witchcraft—the arena of the priestess and priest.

0-7387-0531-4, 448 pp., 7½ x 9⅛, illus.   **$17.95**

CD COMPANION

Reading meditations from a book is one thing, but when you can relax to the author's voice and appropriate background music, it is much easier to immerse yourself in the elemental realms and build a personal relationship with the goddess and god. This four-CD set leads you through many of the exercises in the book *The Outer Temple of Witchcraft*. It guides you through the meditations, the journeys to the elemental realms, and the casting of a magick circle. It even includes chants for celebrating the seasons and raising power, along with ritual music (without words) for setting the tone of your ceremonies.

0-7387-0532-2, set includes four CDs, 5¼ x 7½ Amaray DVD case   **$24.95**

Pagan Ways
Finding Your Spirituality in Nature

GWYDION O'HARA

Do you feel the spirituality in nature? Are you full of questions about mainstream religion? Do you long to engage in rituals that have meaning for you? Perhaps you are a Pagan at heart.

Pagan Ways is your first step toward finding your personal spiritual truth. It is designed to offer enough understanding and insight to allow a fully thought out and firm decision as to whether or not Paganism is, indeed, the path for you.

Explore the history of Paganism and the founders of the modern Craft movement. Learn how the Pagan God is found in the cycles of the seasons, how to get in touch with nature spirits, what celebrations are included in the Pagan calendar, the tools used for magick and worship, how to erect an altar, how to conduct a ritual, how the eight Pagan virtues fit into your life, and what the stages are to becoming a Priest or Priestess.

1-56718-341-7, 216 pp., 5³⁄₁₆ x 8   **$7.95**

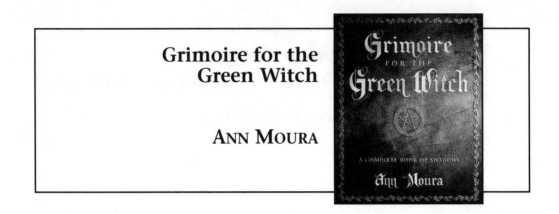

Grimoire for the Green Witch

ANN MOURA

The author of the popular Green Witchcraft series presents her personal book of shadows, designed for you to use just as she uses it—as a working guide to ritual, spells, and divination. It is a book to set on the altar and pass along to the next generation with new notations and entries.

Use *Grimoire for the Green Witch* much like a cookbook. Flip through and select what you need at any given time. It is a reference of circle-casting techniques, traditional rituals for the Esbats and Sabbats, easy-to-make crafts, and a staggering array of correspondences used in creating spells. It is a distillation of Green practice, with room for growth and new inspiration.

0-7387-0287-0, 304 pp., 8 x 10, illus.   **$17.95**

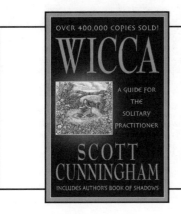

Wicca
A Guide for the Solitary Practitioner
Scott Cunningham

Wicca is a book of life, and how to live magically, spiritually, and wholly attuned with Nature. It is a book of sense and common sense, not only about Magick, but about religion and one of the most critical issues of today: how to achieve the much needed and wholesome relationship with our Earth. Cunningham presents Wicca as it is today: a gentle, Earth-oriented religion dedicated to the Goddess and God. This book fulfills a need for a practical guide to solitary Wicca—a need which no previous book has fulfilled. Here is a positive, practical introduction to the religion of Wicca, designed so that any interested person can learn to practice the religion alone, anywhere in the world. It presents Wicca honestly and clearly, without the pseudo-history that permeates other books. It shows that Wicca is a vital, satisfying part of twentieth- century life.

This book presents the theory and practice of Wicca from an individual's perspective. The section on the Standing Stones Book of Shadows contains solitary rituals for the Esbats and Sabbats. This book, based on the author's nearly two decades of Wiccan practice, presents an eclectic picture of various aspects of this religion. Exercises designed to develop magical proficiency, a self-dedication ritual, herb, crystal and rune magic, as well as recipes for Sabbat feasts, are included in this excellent book.

0-87542-118-0, 240 pp., 6 x 9, illus.   **$9.95**

Earth, Air, Fire & Water
More Techniques of Natural Magic

SCOTT CUNNINGHAM

A water-smoothed stone . . . the wind . . . a candle's flame . . . a pool of water. These are the age-old tools of natural magic. Born of the Earth, possessing inner power, they await only our touch and intention to bring them to life.

The four Elements are the ancient powerhouses of magic. Using their energies, we can transform ourselves, our lives, and our worlds. Tap into the marvelous powers of the natural world with these rites, spells, and simple rituals that you can do easily and with a minimum of equipment. *Earth, Air, Fire & Water* includes more than seventy-five spells, rituals, and ceremonies with detailed instructions for designing your own magical spells.

This book instills a sense of wonder concerning our planet and our lives; and promotes a natural, positive practice that anyone can successfully perform.

0-87542-131-8, 240 pp., 6 x 9, illus.   **$9.95**

The Complete Book of Incense, Oils & Brews

Scott Cunningham

For centuries the composition of incenses, the blending of oils, and the mixing of herbs have been used by people to create positive changes in their lives. With this book, the curtains of secrecy have been drawn back, providing you with practical, easy-to-understand information that will allow you to practice these methods of magical cookery.

Scott Cunningham, world-famous expert on magical herbalism, first published *The Magic of Incense, Oils and Brews* in 1986. *The Complete Book of Incense, Oils & Brews* is a revised and expanded version of that book. Scott took readers' suggestions from the first edition and added more than 100 new formulas. Every page has been clarified and rewritten, and new chapters have been added.

There is no special, costly equipment to buy, and ingredients are usually easy to find. The book includes detailed information on a wide variety of herbs, sources for purchasing ingredients, substitutions for hard-to-find herbs, a glossary, and a chapter on creating your own magical recipes.

0-87542-128-8, 288 pp., 6 x 9, illus.   **$14.95**

Cunningham's Encyclopedia of Wicca in the Kitchen
(Formerly titled The Magic of Food)

SCOTT CUNNINGHAM

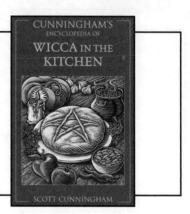

Put the magic back into eating! There's a reason caviar has a reputation as a love food, but a little vanilla or peppermint can work wonders too! You'll savor mushrooms like never before after experiencing their intuitive-raising effects, and a munch of celery will resonate with new meaning as it boosts your sexual desire and psychic awareness.

Change any area of your life when you select food for its magical energy and eat it with a specific goal in mind. This is food magic, and it's served up here in spoonfuls of lore and fact.

0-7387-0226-9, 432 pp., 6 x 9   **$15.95**

Magical Aromatherapy
The Power of Scent

SCOTT CUNNINGHAM

Scent magic has a rich, colorful history. Today, there is much we can learn from the simple plants that grace our planet. Most have been used for countless centuries. The energies still vibrate within their aromas.

Scott Cunningham has now combined the current knowledge of the physiological and psychological effects of natural fragrances with the ancient art of magical perfumery. In writing this book, he drew on extensive experimentation and observation, research into 4,000 years of written records, and the wisdom of respected aromatherapy practitioners. *Magical Aromatherapy* contains a wealth of practical tables of aromas of the seasons, days of the week, the planets, and zodiac; use of essential oils with crystals; synthetic and genuine oils and hazardous essential oils. It also contains a handy appendix of aromatherapy organizations and distributors of essential oils and dried plant products.

0-87542-129-6, 224 pp., illus.   **$5.99**

The Witch's Guide to Life

KALA TROBE

Some days it's not easy being a witch. Life is full of relationship problems, global crises, personal karmic drama . . . not to mention the challenge of practicing your craft in a world of nine-to-five mortals.

This comprehensive guide to magickal living spans the intellectual, physical, magickal, and philosophical aspects of a witch's life. It focuses on the history and development of modern Wicca; its core beliefs and practices; and magickal techniques such as successful spellcasting, aura reading, and Tarot and rune reading.

- A witch's guide to integrating the Wiccan/Magickal philosophy into everyday life
- Delves into the practicalities of living life as a witch, including the issues of marriage, food, drugs, illness, menstruation, and menopause
- Provides a wealth of information on color magick, myths and symbolism, the chakra system, auras, qabalah, Tarot, Enochia, and runes
- Features biographies of significant occultists, a brief history of witchcraft, and a survey of the witch in art and literature
- Allows you to reference any subject with the word index, and consult the Quick Guide to Spells for directions to specific spells, techniques, and visualizations

ISBN 0-7387-0200-5, 7½ x 9⅛, 480 pp.   **$19.95**

To order, call 1-877-NEW-WRLD
Prices subject to change without notice

Llewellyn's 2005 Witches' Spell-A-Day Almanac

This contemporary spell book with an antiquated, Book-of-Days style returns for its third successful year. Witches and pagans will find spells for all occasions, along with recipes, rituals, and meditations. It also includes crucial information for spellcasters: when the spell is appropriate, necessary implements, and where the spell should be performed. Icons categorize each spell under various headings: health, love, money, and purification, and so on. Users who combine spells with astrology will find daily Moon signs and phases.

0-7387-0229-3, 264 pp., 5¼ x 8   **$7.95**